Changing Creative Writing in America

NEW WRITING VIEWPOINTS

Series Editor: Graeme Harper, *Oakland University, Rochester, USA*
Associate Editor: Dianne Donnelly, *University of South Florida, USA*

The overall aim of this series is to publish books which will ultimately inform teaching and research, but whose primary focus is on the analysis of creative writing practice and theory. There will also be books which deal directly with aspects of creative writing knowledge, with issues of genre, form and style, with the nature and experience of creativity, and with the learning of creative writing. They will all have in common a concern with excellence in application and in understanding, with creative writing practitioners and their work, and with informed analysis of creative writing as process as well as completed artefact.

Full details of all the books in this series and of all our other publications can be found on http://www.multilingual-matters.com, or by writing to Multilingual Matters, St Nicholas House, 31–34 High Street, Bristol BS1 2AW, UK.

NEW WRITING VIEWPOINTS: 15

Changing Creative Writing in America

Strengths, Weaknesses, Possibilities

Edited by
Graeme Harper

MULTILINGUAL MATTERS
Bristol • Blue Ridge Summit

DOI 10.21832/HARPER8811
Library of Congress Cataloging in Publication Data
A catalog record for this book is available from the Library of Congress.
Names: Harper, Graeme, author.
Title: Changing Creative Writing in America: Strengths, Weaknesses, Possibilities/
Edited by Graeme Harper.
Description: Blue Ridge Summit, PA; Bristol, UK: Multilingual Matters, [2018] |
Series: New Writing Viewpoints: 15 | Includes bibliographical references and index.
Identifiers: LCCN 2017023814| ISBN 9781783098811 (hbk : alk. paper) |
    ISBN 9781783098804 (pbk : alk. paper) | ISBN 9781783098842 (ebook)
Subjects: LCSH: English language – Rhetoric – Study and teaching (Higher) – United
    States. | Creative writing (Higher education) – United States. | Authorship – Study
    and teaching (Higher) – United States. | Creation (Literary, artistic, etc.)
Classification: LCC PE1405.U6 C47 2018 | DDC 808/.042071173 – dc23 LC record
available at https://lccn.loc.gov/2017023814

British Library Cataloguing in Publication Data
A catalogue entry for this book is available from the British Library.

ISBN-13: 978-1-78309-881-1 (hbk)
ISBN-13: 978-1-78309-880-4 (pbk)

Multilingual Matters
UK: St Nicholas House, 31–34 High Street, Bristol BS1 2AW, UK.
USA: NBN, Blue Ridge Summit, PA, USA.

Website: www.multilingual-matters.com
Twitter: Multi_Ling_Mat
Facebook: https://www.facebook.com/multilingualmatters
Blog: www.channelviewpublications.wordpress.com

Copyright © 2018 Graeme Harper and the authors of individual chapters.

All rights reserved. No part of this work may be reproduced in any form or by any means without permission in writing from the publisher.

The policy of Multilingual Matters/Channel View Publications is to use papers that are natural, renewable and recyclable products, made from wood grown in sustainable forests. In the manufacturing process of our books, and to further support our policy, preference is given to printers that have FSC and PEFC Chain of Custody certification. The FSC and/or PEFC logos will appear on those books where full certification has been granted to the printer concerned.

Typeset by in Sabon and Frutiger by R. J. Footring Ltd, Derby, UK

Contents

Foreword. Reconstruction: On the Road Toward a More Sustainable Future   vii
Joe Moxley

Introduction: The Possibilities for Creative Writing in America   1
Graeme Harper

1. Histories and Historiography in Creative Writing Studies   17
Alexandria Peary

2. Writing as Spiritual Practice   34
Katharine Haake

3. We Serve Writing Here   52
Tim Mayers

4. Theory and Pedagogy in Introductory Writing Textbooks: Creative Writing Leads the Way   69
Stephanie Vanderslice

5. The Print Doctrine   80
Angela Ferraiolo

6. The Convergence of Creative Writing Processes and Their Neurological Mapping   95
Dianne Donnelly

7. Rewriting Creative Writing   112
Bruce Horner

8. Toward an Interdisciplinary Creative Writing   132
Joseph Rein

9. Creative Writing in First-Year Writing: Let's Remember, or Re-teach, the Value of Fiction   144
Kate Kostelnik

10 Against Appropriation: Creative Writing in/and the Making of Knowledge 163
    Patrick Bizzaro and Christine Bailey

Contributors   193
Index   197

Foreword. Reconstruction: On the Road Toward a More Sustainable Future

> And we hear the mockingbirds on the chimneys
> or tops of the trees in the moonlight
> hunting down the center of our lives
> and singing and singing to save the state.
> William E. Stafford, 'Walking away from an undeclared war'

Nearly 30 years ago I compiled a collection of essays titled *Creative Writing in America: Theory and Pedagogy*. I wanted to tear down the walls between disciplines. Composition, Literature and Creative Writing were all firmly siloed, sequestered within their cold little offices. There was then a great call for mapping disciplinary boundaries, for calling dibs on certain topics, for circling the wagons. As I wrote then, 'in our eagerness to pursue intellectual territory germane to our disciplines and interests, we have established mutually exclusive lexicons, subjects, journals, and methods of inquiry' (Moxley, 1989: 25). I declared these boundaries arbitrary, even corrosive (pp. 42, 25). As I argued, regardless of disciplinary allegiance, we are passionate about the study of humanities, housed under the same roof.

Now, three decades later, we find ourselves at a crossroads: that is, the intersection of Graeme Harper and *Changing Creative Writing in America*. In this inspirational work, Harper anchors the concept of change with his memory of entering the old house of Mason Thomas, who was once the community's celebrity author. As Harper enters the old colonial, he comments that '[t]here are ways in which experiences intertwine, one with the other, over time. This is the working of experience and memory, sight and insight, hindsight too of course.' To Harper, and to the authors of this new volume, change does not mean razing the past, but recognition, recirculation, perhaps renovation.

While in my younger, more vigorous years I wanted to tear down walls, that action now strikes me as violent. True, the history of our field presents itself as what Stephen North calls a House of Lore: a 'rambling

'... old manse, wing branching off from wing, addition tacked to addition, in all sorts of materials – brick, wood, canvas, sheet metal, cardboard – with turrets and gables, minarets and spires, spiral staircases, rope ladders, pitons, dungeons, secret passageways – all seemingly random, yet all connected' (North, 1987: 27). Similarly, as Harper wanders the rooms of a fellow writer's dwelling, he ponders the concept of habitat. Inside the house, as in most of our houses, were piles and piles of papers. The house held a world inside – a microcosm of the writer's life. And yet Harper and his team were determining whether demolition of this microcosm would harm the overall ecosystem of the community.

I present Graeme Harper's old colonial alongside Stephen North's metaphor of the House of Lore, from *The Making of Knowledge in Composition*, to illustrate a tension I see in this field today, concerning place. We have difficulty placing Creative Writing, as we have difficulty placing Rhetoric and Composition, as we have difficulty placing Literature. Indeed, I cannot even say that Creative Writing, Rhetoric and Composition, and Literature are the 'only' fields housed by the English department anymore. Since my impassioned cry to tear down the walls of the disciplines in 1989, the landscape of the humanities has expanded. Does our rambling manse now house Professional and Technical Communication? Cultural Studies? Game Studies? New Media? I say 'yes!' because I believe that our field is the humanities, our study is the study of storytelling – that is, the engagement of our collective imagination. Yet there is tension in the house; the National Center for Education Statistics (2010) classifies a general English program as 'focus[ing] on the English language, including its history, structure, and related communications skills; and the literature and culture of English-speaking peoples'. So simple, so seemingly innocuous, and yet I sense every occupant of this rambling old manse bristling, slamming shut their disciplinary doors and certainly not coming down for supper.

Meanwhile, alone in my outmoded kitchen, I adjust my recipe accordingly. A meal for one, *again*. Over and over, we have confronted the boundaries of our disciplines, beat our fists against the graffitied walls and slumped away for another long winter. And as Graeme Harper says in his introduction to this book, as he gazes at this messy rundown colonial, 'I think I had already predicted the end result and I could therefore jump forward here to the demolition and save our generous publisher some paper'. So many years of fighting, of construction and deconstruction, and the end can be predicted: demolition.

As Alexandria Peary writes in her chapter, 'Histories and historiography in creative writing studies', 'If we imagine what is lost without historical studies of creative writing in the United States, we gain a sense of what could be recovered if historical evidence were not treated as ephemeral'. If we continue to shut our doors, to refuse to talk to anyone outside what we think of as 'our' disciplines, then what will be left will be dusty records, obsolete recordings, moldering rooms in a condemned house.

It is clear, then, that we cannot continue to draw lines in the sand, to put our collective feet down (unless we are dancing together). Thirty years later, and I am tired of fighting these fruitless disciplinary battles. My colleagues in Rhetoric and Composition have embraced the words of Bruno Latour, a sociologist, who in 2004 wrote:

> Wars. So many wars. Wars outside and wars inside. Cultural wars, science wars, and wars against terrorism. Wars against poverty and wars against the poor. Wars against ignorance and wars out of ignorance. My question is simple: Should we be at war, too, we, the scholars, the intellectuals? Is it really our duty to add fresh ruins to fields of ruins? Is it really the task of the humanities to add deconstruction to destruction?

And so I have changed in the 30 years since *Creative Writing in America*. I have seen students change. I think we are tired of placing our disciplines, of building and tearing down walls when we could be enriching ecosystems, exploring habitats.

My friend Graeme Harper writes that 'habitats are not merely containers, the holders of life, nor are they fixtures with which life interacts'. When reading this volume, I see author after author considering the idea of place, and of *displacement*. For I think it is clear to us that we cannot keep building turrets, minarets and spires. We will run out of space. And in other areas the carpets will fade, the curtains will sprout moths. And in the end, demolition.

Stephen North mitigates his metaphor of the House of Lore by writing that 'useful as the metaphor might be, though, lore is finally not a house, but a body of knowledge' (North, 1987: 29). Again, I see this concept intersect with what Harper and his fellow authors do in this book.

For we cannot keep tearing down and rebuilding this house. We need to focus on a sustainable ecosystem, a circulatory knowledge for ourselves and our students. Put simply, we need to step outside. This Graeme Harper and his colleagues accomplish in *Changing Creative Writing in America*. Harper breaks the bonds of discipline, asking pertinent questions that cause all of us to come out of our houses of lore, re-examine our complicated pedagogies, ask our students what they care about, what they want to learn. This book traces tangled threads through the field and beyond. *Changing Creative Writing in America* examines the line between work and practice for creative writers and teachers of creative writing. It challenges the liberal arts to advance their purpose in a culture which increasingly favors STEM education (science, technology, engineering and mathematics). It forces creative writers and teachers of creative writing to ask themselves what new technologies they should use, and how new writing practices can help students achieve their writing goals.

These are not easy tasks we face, nor can they be completed (if they can ever be completed) by simply opening the doors of this House of Lore. The writers in this book understand the enormity of the task they have undertaken and know that answers may come slowly, circuitously, yet more simply for the pace at which we proceed. No essay, no volume could answer all these questions at once; *Changing Creative Writing in America* takes the first step forward in this new (and yet incredibly ancient) endeavor to reconstruct our world, to build a vibrant, sustainable community of creative writing of the future.

Joe Moxley

References

Latour, B. (2004) Why has critique run out of steam? From matters of fact to matters of concern. *Critical Inquiry* 30 (2), 225–248.

Moxley, J.M. (1989) Tearing down the walls: Engaging the imagination. In J. Moxley (ed.) *Creative Writing in America: Theory and Pedagogy* (pp. 25–45). Urbana, IL: National Council of Teachers of English.

National Center for Education Statistics (2010) Detail for CIP Code 23.0101. Title: English Language and Literature, General. At https://nces.ed.gov/ipeds/cipcode/cipdetail.aspx?y=55&cipid=88357 (accessed 8 July 2016).

North, S.M. (1987) The practitioners. In *The Making of Knowledge in Composition: Portrait of an Emerging Field* (pp. 21–55). Portsmouth, NH: Heinemann.

Stafford, W.E. (1972) Walking away from an undeclared war. *Poetry Magazine*, September, p. 323.

Introduction: The Possibilities for Creative Writing in America

Graeme Harper

Every act of creative writing is an act of possibility. Creative writers explore possibility through their creative writerly engagement with what they see or what they imagine, or both, and generate it too through the influence of their works. A creative writer's influence might simply be the impact on one person, momentarily, that temporary, singular response to something read or seen or heard that was the result of someone's creative writing. On occasion, the influence of a creative writer might be greater than this, impacting on entire groups, even broadly informing cultural and societal understanding.

Creative writers bring artistic works into the world that did not previously exist. Those who teach creative writing encourage and support creative writing by others and endeavor to equip them with the knowledge, skills and understanding to pursue creative writing. The actions of bringing artistic works into existence and of teaching creative writing involve not only possibility but acts of change. Change is defined as making or becoming different in some way. Change is not necessarily positive. Changes, and their impact, can be located on a spectrum from the extremely good to the extremely bad. Change also impacts in different ways, at different speeds, and to greater or lesser extents. A simple example from creative writing is change connected with the process of drafting a piece of work. Successful drafting can be said to be writing where changes made have improved a piece of creative writing; unsuccessful drafting is, by this measure, changes where a later draft is weaker than an earlier draft. Generally, to make change positive we need knowledge, we need understanding, we need openness and we need a concerted informed analysis of the situation that presently prevails.

America offers the largest example of English-language creative writing teaching and learning in the world. It also offers a large national market for completed works of creative writing originally published, performed or otherwise delivered in English, in all the potential creative writing forms and genres. With a strong and decidedly public history of teaching creative writing, particularly in post-secondary education and especially over the past half a century, what impacts on creative writing in America potentially impacts on the world. Such a notion was the impetus behind the creation of this book.

In 2017 the American Association of Writers and Writing Programs (AWP) celebrated its 50th anniversary, and held its annual conference, in Washington, DC, on 8–11 February, with this anniversary very much in evidence. That conference declared itself on the AWP website (http://www.awpwriter.org) to be 'now the largest literary conference in North America'. It would therefore seem to be a good time to look at creative writing in America, and particularly creative writing teaching and learning in America, with a critical eye on the past, present and future. It might be that the notion of 'changing' any of it would constitute 'unsuccessful drafting', and that nothing should be changed. Or it might be that all change would result in 'successful drafting' and have a positive impact. Most likely, points on the spectrum of change could be identified and explored. One thing is certain, that if every act of creative writing is an act of possibility, then considering changing creative writing in America can only initiate a productive conversation, perhaps highlight some ideas already in evidence, and most likely suggest further discussion to the benefit of all.

In what is admittedly a somewhat idiosyncratic approach, I favor examining the conditions of creative writing in America through three conceptual lenses. These I summarize as *aliveness, echolocation* and *habitat*. These lenses work to focus thoughts and provide a way of examining evidence of what is, as well as of considering what might be.

Aliveness relates to our living sense of self, our more or less informed assessment of things in the world, our feelings and emotions, our beliefs, beyond our mere condition of animation. In other words, to be alive is not merely to walk and talk, but is to have both reason and sentience. Echolocation is all about the relationship between an individual interpretation and a wider environment. Habitat involves both found and fortuitous physical manifestations and the created (and that which is created by us involves aliveness). A habitat can also be considered in its micro condition, that is, related to an individual or a small group, or it can be considered in terms of its macro condition, in which many individuals, a large group, are influenced by and influence an ecosystem. Considering the possibilities for creative writing in America today thus begins for me in the following way:

Aliveness

In the spring of 2001, the Arts and Humanities Coalition of Michigan announced its intention to consider the renovation of the former home of Mason Thomas. Thomas had died three years earlier, during a particularly brutal northern winter, and the house had remained unoccupied ever since. It was a late-Victorian place overlooking what is now the Yoga Trail and Memorial Garden, with something of Henry Hobson Richardson about it. A brown stone cylindrical tower on its right façade, its front-door entrance deeply recessed; just its simple gables and gray shingled gambrel roof giving away its colonial heritage. The thought had been that it would need to be demolished as the upkeep had outgrown the interest of those in town, but a vote at the town council had paused that idea, pending a site inspection. While Thomas had once gained minor recognition on account of the strength of his first novel, *The Pears of Walton* (Thomas, 1964), and had been for a time the town's most well known celebrity – outranking Lane Parry, who had taken Nicklaus to the last hole at Westchester and only lost when his putting gave way to what is colloquially called a 'greens shiver', something he never managed to steady after that day – the Thomas home had by 2001 become little more than a passing curiosity to those who read the work of, or simply read of, its one-time occupant.

Landscapers (Thomas, 1966), Thomas's second novel, about a group of artists living precariously by selling forgeries of works by great landscape painters, had been followed by a fallow period, which didn't do much to help his notoriety. During that time few paid much if any attention to the house or its occupant, other than to notice the arrival and departure of the small green punt in the driveway, the kind that crabbers use on the river, as they're pulling up their traps from the reed beds on the leeward side in the early morning. At night, poling up into the reaches with tender ropes, hauling fishes' heads and strips of mealy beef, already brown and smelling like mouse; and if they were lucky a mud crab would reach out and grasp their rope and they'd pull in maybe a five pounder or a pair of them, fighting to the death, so much so that they barely noticed themselves being pulled from the water, or the jute covering known as the boat sack or the gaff that poked them back into the hold or the kerosene that Michigan crabbers like Thomas used to burn off leeches or scold out the sting of a gopher fish, or the billy floats that with their individual markings, stripes in a certain color and order, spots daubed on their cork peaks and sides, mark a crabber's individual ownership of one sunken crab pot or another.

When in 1981 Thomas returned with *Perpetual* (Thomas, 1981), a masterly study of a long relationship between an astronaut and a dancer, many had forgotten that the overgrown house overlooking the newly resurfaced play park and the somewhat unkempt expanse of riverside meadow was anything more than the home of a river tramper, pulling in his truck in the early hours with the river water dripping from its rusty flatbed, mesh netting left hanging to dry between the ragged crepe myrtle and alder. The year 1983 saw the publication of *Mistaken Fear* (Thomas, 1983), which appeared and disappeared without attention, its thematic concern with somnambulism seeming overwrought and possibly out to step with the times, and a short story collection entitled *Curious Midnight and Morning Stories* (Thomas, 1987) came out in 1987, revealing his considerable abilities with a comic turn and his love of astronomy. The stories 'Caught Running' and 'The Vinyl House' were both reprinted to some acclaim in *10 of 10: Best Stories of the Decade* (Bush, 1990). In 1994, following the submission of a PhD dissertation that mentioned Thomas's work, in the company of two other writers, Alice Orton Munt and Steven Hilderhaus, as the leaders of a movement the dissertation writer described as 'new evidentialism', there was a brief interest in interviewing each author. Thomas's interview appeared sandwiched between that of Orton Munt and Hilderhaus in the July 1996 edition of *New Literary Review*.

Thomas's interview was awkward and unwieldly; the interviewer and former PhD student (whom I'll respectfully leave nameless) pressed questions the size of chapters into the service of the idea he was determined to use to bind the group of three together. While Orton Munt and Hilderhaus seemed at least accepting of that ride on the curling wave of foaming analysis, Thomas appears in his replies to be reluctant, indisposed and uncooperative. When asked about his first novel he answers that he couldn't possibly because he has entirely forgotten it. Pressed to suggest ways in which his works might have a similarity of concern with issues explored by Orton Munt and Hilderhaus, he says that he can't comment because he hasn't read a single one of their works. Finally, when it is suggested that he has been one of the most subtle users of language seen over the last quarter of century of prose fiction writers in America, he is clearly taken aback, answering abruptly: 'You think I've been subtle?'

Greeting Helen appeared in 1997, and *The Broad Tree* in 1999, a year after his death, with a foreword by Allen Park Winter, Thomas's editor, who himself was planning his retirement, in light of what he called 'the dilemma of staying current'.

When I entered the house for the council's site inspection, the third in a group of three, my role was clear enough. Leonore, who represented the council, the new owner of the property following the subsequent probative default on town taxes, went in first. After all, she had the key. Kevin, the librarian, represented the district's heritage and was somewhat of an authority on Thomas, at least as far as the district was concerned and as far as the library stocked copies of Thomas's books. Me, as a public policy intern, carried the camera, with which we would record the condition of the house.

I think I had already predicted the end result and I could therefore jump forward here to the demolition and save our generous publisher some paper. But the moment was one that bears recording and the thoughts it brings about are particularly relevant to a book entitled *Changing Creative Writing in America: Strengths, Weaknesses, Possibilities*. There are ways in which experiences intertwine, one with the other, over time. This is the working of experience and memory, sight and insight, and hindsight too of course. There are things we devolve to the past even when they appear in our immediate vision. A kind of cataloging of importance in operation as we step through each day in life, each thing to its place and its purpose. There are things on which we dwell, even when they are long past. They come back uninvited and mostly uncontrolled, flash into the mind, the inner eye's view as strong as the moment they were seen, heard or felt. These things are part of what I have called 'aliveness'. Elements of aliveness come back so strongly and so often because we cannot let them disappear without losing something of our living selves.

Intertwined in the experience of entering Mason Thomas's home for the first and, as it turned out, last time was my burgeoning sense that I would not continue in the field of public policy, the examining of city-managed economic development programs or considering tax abatement schemes for businesses and residents, that kind of thing. My own aliveness needed something other than that, I'd decided – or, that is, I was just about to decide that day. Change was coming for me, and creative writing was going to be part of it. There was also the house itself, which, even as the door was opened and the musty unopened lather of the place hit us full force, seemed to carry with it some announcement, a meaningful declaration.

The door opened into a vestibule, cluttered with fishing poles and waders, a hefty gaff, and strong old boots. We each had a flashlight, but when Leonore hit the light switch we could see through the frosted glass of the inner door that the lights of the house came on. That created a disconnect between the roving beams of our lights and the dispersed glow from within; it also meant that no one had turned off power to the house, so whatever was known to be owned in taxes was to be added this. The water was probably still on too, I figured.

Leonore pushed on the inner door and it opened, being already unlatched, and we stepped into the stair hall. To the right was a living room, and I took three shots of it, not that it stood out in any way. It was dimly lit, uninviting room of two wooden armed sofas, an old grey TV on a heavy wooden roller cabinet, two windowpane cabinets with little in them but what appeared to be ordinary plates and bowls and cups, and a jumble of boxes, suggesting maybe he'd been planning to put some things into storage or even to move. I took two more shots, inside the room, just because. There was something unused about, as if the words 'living room' were covering up the fact that the last thing anyone did in this house was live in this room. It was a façade, the curtains open so that if you were able to see in from the sidewalk you could make false assumptions. Leonore and Kevin, seeking an answer to the 'Is the water still hooked up?' question, went toward the kitchen at the back of the house. I decided to head upstairs.

Echolocation

I had not at that point read any of Mason Thomas's work, though I had once briefly picked up a copy of *The Pears of Walton* in a library display. 'The East Michigan Lakes in Literature' the display was called. It was mostly a collection of works about certain small lake towns and the families who made them, and about the building of clinker-bottom wooden boats, and about the East Lakes white fish, its prevalence and its ambitious spawning habits, and about a school house that educated four generations of successful river trampers, skilled and crabby crabbers, and about the East Lakes aviation company that for a good 30 years ran a mail plane service in a little amphibious Piper. But then there was one book on display I noticed that was not like any of the other books.

The Pears of Walton is a coming-of-age story that begins with the stealing of a truck from a local farm, a night of drunken stupidity in which three boys on the brink of adulthood scatter the possessions of the old farmhand who owned the truck down the main street of the small lake town of Walton and then, bored and confused as to what to do next, take the old man's truck and drive it up onto the prim front lawn of the Lakeside Funeral Home. Left there on the lawn, the truck subsequently returns to each of them in visions, as they travel through life. *The Pears of Walton* is a moving work about guilt and about heritage – not that I knew it at the time.

Up on the landing, the house divided into four bedrooms and a bathroom. I took a shot of the landing, dust rising in the waxy light. The rooms did nothing to invite anyone in. I figured on taking a few shots in each and going back downstairs. I could hear Leonore and Kevin in the kitchen. The water had indeed been still on, and they'd discovered that in the obvious way – by turning on the kitchen faucet. But the faucet was old and once it was opened it wasn't so inclined to be closed. Leonore was trying to close it. Kevin was suggesting it could be turned off outside. Both had started laughing at the silliness of the situation. Something was going on with the water in the kitchen sink. The faucet was starting to spray water. So it was, downstairs in the house.

A creative writer's habitat is defined as the place in which they dwell. We can include in this simple definition not only the existent physical factors of that dwelling – in the case of Mason Thomas, the rooms in which he wrote, the short overgrown drive in which he pulled up his crabber's punt, the make-believe living room in which he determinedly never really lived – but also those biotic manifestations that impact and reflect choices, attitudes, responses to the world and those who dwell in it. Habitats are not merely containers, the holders of life, nor are they fixtures with which life interacts. Rather, habitats are ecosystems and, as such, they involve both simple physical manifestations, the found or fortuitous and the created, and they involve aliveness.

In the rooms upstairs in Mason Thomas's house there were boxes and piles of papers over almost the entire floor. Some had toppled onto others and the papers had shuffled themselves. There was a trestle desk and a barrel chair, equally submerged, a light-blue portable typewriter, visible in the mess on the desk, a swing-arm desk lamp, a non-descript brown coat over the back of the barrel chair, a few other small tables, on which books were stacked high, a standard lamp hooked up to the lighting, so it had come dimly on, a bright red club chair, two dining chairs, two oil heaters, a tangled fishing pole, a plastic globe, a dead pot plant of some kind (a palm by the look of what was left), a thick rolled collection of charts and maps. I dutifully took pictures of it all.

Creative writing takes place both in a micro and in a macro habitat, that of the space, place, attitudes, feelings, physical and biotic conditions of the creative writer, and in the larger realm of culture, society, the nation, the economy, history. Alone upstairs in that doomed house, while Leonore and Kevin were downstairs apparently encountering something akin to the 'Sorcerer's apprentice' scene in the Disney movie *Fantasia* (1940), I wondered in each shot I took what it was that I was capturing. What was left behind from an ecosystem that was Mason Thomas and yet everything but him. A communication out from him and back in to him. East Lakes crabbers call this kind of thing 'echolocation'.

Crabs echolocate in a similar but different manner to that used by whales. With crabs it is not the series of sighs, groans and high-pitched squeals that the blue whale or the fin whale produces. Nor is it the clicking and buzzing of a bat. Bats use their open mouths and occasionally their noses to create echolocating calls, varying the intensity and the harmonic series modulating tones. Depending on what they are doing – searching for prey, searching for direction into and out of a space, searching for one another – bats send out and vary their rate of pulsing; they cross-correlate, using one signal with another, zeroing in, examining the connectivity, to venture, and investigate and resolve each question there in the dark or dim light. But crabs, mud crabs that live in the upper reaches of the Walton River, Michigan, at some distance from Walton Lake into which it feeds, or blue swimmer crabs that live on a shallow sea reef, or soldier crabs that bury themselves at the water's edge of a beach, echolocate by clacking together their pincers. The sound is intensified by the echoic chamber of the crab's carapace and rhythmically accompanied by the beating of its swimming legs and the tapping of its walking legs. There in Thomas's house I couldn't help but make a connection between the echolocation of a river crab, which he regularly sought to catch, and the typing Thomas had undertaken on that old light-blue portable typewriter.

Indeed, what remained in Mason Thomas's Walton Lake house seemed to me also evidence of a kind of echolocation. Each page in a pile was an addition, a reconsideration, a reworking, a subtraction, a repositioning. Each book, every move to another chair, in one room or another, each stack of miscellaneous readings and notes on a trestle table or on the floor was related to modulation or to cross-correlation.

Echolocation is all about the relationship between a micro or individual interpretation and a macro or wider environment. So is creative writing and its teaching and learning. The creative writer and the creative writing learner are positioned in creating both their own habitat and a habitat that allows them to navigate their place in the wider world, culture, society and community with which they ultimately communicate, and to which their verbal art is ultimately referring. Such echolocation involves the development of verbal arts skills, the honing of the use of writerly tools, varying from the mechanical forms of graphic setting out and textual appearance to the aesthetics of writing forms and structures, to the impact of rhetorical devices. It is the intuitive, bringing together the intellect and the imagination with the specific aim of navigating. Entirely based in the individual and yet by necessity aware of the location of others, creative writing brings an individual's aliveness and their sense of habitat into correlative exchange with the aliveness and habitats of others.

The verbal arts, those arts that primarily use words, have such a commonplace origin. While certainly a creative writer might reach for an exotic noun or a rarely used adjective, the arts themselves are profound because of their chiseled ordinariness in the simple act of inscription, the desire for recording, the practicalities supporting communication. Much like the signals and pulses of echolocation, creative writing takes the otherwise day-to-day practical acoustics of the verbal and applies them to a purpose that appears transcendental. It is as if, without the work of creative writers, we couldn't quite see the view entirely, the reality completely, the possibilities additionally, the direction possibly; and it is through their echolocating that creative writers link the relative ordinariness of the day to day with the extraordinariness of the human condition. If some might describe this as a spiritual practice, it is easy to see why. If others endeavor to suggest ways that creative practice and critical awareness communicate, the reasons for concerning themselves with this have much to do with the sense of mystery that is felt about the methods used.

Approaching creative writing this way leads here to considering how we might explore conditions in the teaching and learning of creative writing.

Creative Writing in Habitat America

What are the possibilities for creative writing in America in the future, informed by the past and considering any changes that might be applied to the present? We can already recognize a range of influences and evolutions that have occurred in the practices and the results of creative writing over the past few decades. One clear example is the impact of contemporary digital technologies on the creation and distribution of works by creative writers. Because of contemporary digitalism, not only the distribution strategies for works of creative writing have changed, but creative writing practices have changed too.

Here in *Changing Creative Writing in America: Strengths, Weaknesses, Possibilities* the discussion is specifically concerned with creative writing teaching and learning in colleges and universities. If creative writing is an act of possibility, how might the present and future of creative writing teaching and learning embrace possibility in the national habitat of the USA? The actions of echolocating come to mind in approaching this question, analyzing the relationship between the micro or individual interpretation of conditions and the macro or wider US environment, and the ways in which we each move around this habitat.

To be candid, with a habitat in mind, and the story of the Mason Thomas and the crabbers of Walton still fresh, I long toyed with the idea that at this point I would anthropomorphize a mud crab and have it stand up, huge dark claw dripping and raised, and clack out a long and earnest speech about strengths, weaknesses and possibilities for creative writing in America. There the crab would stand, on a small stage at the Walton County Fair, red, white and blue bunting bright behind it, the Mayor of Walton, Ade Elwin, standing there grinning beside it, the design of his abstract tie somewhat like the tangled reedy reaches of the upper river, the golden tubas and trumpets and trombones of the town's brass band glittering nearby in the spring sun. The crab, dark with age and, it can be imagined, veneration, clacking out long eloquent sentences about creative writing on the American campus. Through that dark clacker the crab would mount a vigorous defense of 'literary culture', echoing something of the Association of Writers and Writing Programs 50th anniversary conference declaration, while referring to the history of one or other creative writer's presence in a program or 'on campus', along with the founding of several 'literary magazines', each with its fine inaugural editor and their individual vision, and a poignant reference to 'the founding of the writers' workshop'. The personal aspects of the mighty crab's historical points would be grounded in its hinterland analysis of the role of American college education in 'forming the citizen' and in 'providing for the health and prosperity of the individual' and the perhaps more crabby inclusion of 'feeding the motor of the well-schooled mind'.

Much as I enjoy the dramatic, and the comedic even more so, I have largely tempered that impulse to the prolix and discursive in the interests of a more measured, shorter and yet speculative analysis. You'll therefore instead find ahead the elementary word *'Possibilities!'* clacked out before you. It says exactly what it means. What, indeed, are the possibilities? *Clack!* You might imagine this word followed by the sentence 'a crab clatters in the dim upper reaches of a murky river somewhere in America', to add a reference to the decidedly fertile surroundings.... *Clack!* Creative writing and the teaching and learning of creative writing have such opportunity in America.

In some part of each one of these clackings of *'Possibilities!'* there is a question or questions raised about the strengths and weaknesses of current practices and conditions. By inference, therefore, there is a reference to a need for continuity or for change. I would offer the thought that in teaching and learning creative writing here in America there is the potential for global leadership, both in the understanding of the practices of creative writing and its results and in how creative writing is taught and learnt. I do not believe that potential has yet been reached. I do believe it can be. I also believe that it involves together the practice of creative writing, research in and through creative writing, and concerted attention to contemporary teaching and learning in the field of creative writing.

With that said, I'll leave things now to that imaginary crab sounding off in the upper reaches of Michigan's Walton River:

Possibilities! To begin: the current relationship between those who undertake and teach creative writing, and are appointed to do so in American higher education, and those who teach composition often in the same institutions remains unsteady. The historical origins of what can be described as a tension in this relationship have been well investigated but not adequately developed and certainly not positively resolved.

With the USA being the primary location of Rhet/Comp teaching and learning and the largest market for creative writing teaching and learning, this historical disciplinary relationship needs further concerted attention. Attention seems to me to be needed from both sides of the table, or more topically the river perhaps, and the reason for that is simple: the strength in this relationship will be born out of a new forward-thinking exchange. What kind of attention, in what form, and to what ends, are pressing questions. **Bruce Horner, Tim Mayers** and **Patrick Bizzaro and Christine Bailey** touch on elements of this in the pages of this book. **Alexandria Peary** specifically considers the historical conditions and historiographical practices in relation to it.

Possibilities! Can we really wait any longer before we address the question of what now constitutes creative writing culture in America? If not all creative writing has resulted in 'literature' being produced, and if not all those writing creatively are seeking to produce 'literature', why do so many creative writing courses in America rely on modes and models of critical understanding drawn from literary studies? If it is a creative writing organization, why does the Association of Writers and Writing Programs now mention hosting 'the largest literary conference in North America'? No doubt at all that supporting American literary culture is a fine and laudable aim. But is this supporting creative writing culture? Is the difference between 'literary writing' and 'creative writing' mere semantics, or is it more? **Angela Ferraiolo** has something relevant to say in relation to this question, and **Joseph Rein**'s chapter here is notable too. At first this favoring of a literary studies phenomenon seems merely retrograde, harking back to a period when creative writing courses related to creating a stronger foundation for the production of contemporary American literature. Both D.G. Myers (1996) and Mark McGurl (2009) have explored aspects of this, in much more concerted and interesting ways than I am doing here. But the notion of the retrograde also requires some further examination because it begins on closer consideration to look like a cover for a more contemporary issue. That contemporary issue is broadly the challenge to the viability of other disciplines, specifically those in the arts and humanities, in light of an increased emphasis on STEM subjects (science, technology, engineering and math) within American higher education, which is likewise reflective of such an emphasis globally.

Possibilities! American colleges and universities have long shown a stronger commitment to the liberal arts than does tertiary education in many parts of the world, not least because of the sense of American post-secondary education being strongly also the location of personal and civic education. The recent closures of some smaller American liberal colleges has therefore generated concern about the future of the liberal arts in this country. The strength in liberal arts education is worthy of consideration, as is some thought on how this relates to the demands of the 21st-century world, and potentially suggests some weaknesses, not least in terms of modern educational pragmatism. The role of creative writing on campus relates to this discussion. It is useful to read both **Kate Kostelnik**'s chapter and **Dianne Donnelly**'s chapter in light of this American liberal arts context, and the modern threats to it. Specifically, **Kate Kostelnik** considers what we value and **Dianne Donnelly** considers the workings of the human brain.

Possibilities! It is more an imperative than a possibility to say that diversity is a strength and that considering how we approach diversity, equity and inclusion in creative writing education in America is overdue for further development. Certainly, there is work done and done well, though much of it has focused on the end products of creative writing rather than on the practices and understanding of creative writing. In what ways, we might wonder, do the focus of courses in creative writing and their outcomes support all, or support only some? That question includes how we introduce and develop practices, not just introduce and analyze the end products. In other words, questions of diversity go beyond reading lists and discussion topics to the actual acts of creation.

I have not included enough in *Changing Creative Writing in America: Strengths, Weaknesses, Possibilities* on diversity, equity and inclusion, and how we might seek change in our practices in order to be more inclusive in the American context of creative writing education. That relative lightness of touch is my error. It is more suggested here than it is thoroughly explored. That said, both **Angela Ferraiolo** and **Alexandria Peary** do touch on elements of diversity in their chapters, while **Patrick**

Bizzaro and Christine Bailey reference the cultural politics of the poetry slam, in terms of voices not otherwise heard. There is more work to be done, aspects to examine, actions to take. I trust we might use my failure to investigate this further in this book to think on the strengths that can be gained from doing exactly that.

Possibilities! It is true that the specific site called the creative writing 'workshop' has played a role in creative writing education worldwide. But it is intriguing how *much* of a role, and how *much* of a perceived role, this particular teaching and learning environment has played in American higher education. To a considerable extent, the connection here is with the idea of creative writing as one of the studio arts, and thus the workshop as a creative writing studio space. Ideas about creative writing teaching that do not involve reference to the 'workshop' are still relatively scant in America, considering the size of the teaching and learning population here. **Stephanie Vanderslice**'s examination of textbooks and the evolution of textbooks in creative writing also makes reference to the ubiquitous role of the creative writing workshop in American higher education. The connection between how the American creative writing workshop has continued and how creative writing textbooks have evolved is a curious one. **Tim Mayers** touches on the workshop too, in his chapter, as do **Joseph Rein** and **Bruce Horner** and **Angela Ferraiolo**. It is not exactly a ubiquitous part of this book, but its presence has what might be called 'resonance', both in terms of its strengths and in terms of its weaknesses.

Possibilities! The AWP, founded in 1967, is currently the largest and most influential organization in the USA focusing on the practice, understanding and teaching of creative writing. In contrast, the Creative Writing Studies Organization (CWSO) was formally incorporated in the USA in early 2016. Much newer and smaller it was nevertheless launched with considerable enthusiasm. The CWSO noted at the time that 'creative writing studies is an emerging discipline that is currently in the process of defining itself'. Certainly, while the discipline is emerging, the term 'creative writing studies' already has a strong history. **Katharine Haake**'s book *What Our Speech Disrupts* featured the term in its subtitle, *Feminism and Creative Writing Studies*, back in 2000.

In this organizational frame, the strengths and weaknesses of current and past organizational approaches and emphases come to mind, in relation to what constitutes creative writing practice and knowledge. Ownership or co-ownership of this leadership within the USA also bears some consideration, given the different organizations that clearly show an interest in the practice. In that regard, we can add to the CWSO and the AWP at very least the Conference on College Composition and Communication (CCCC), an organization that was founded as far back as 1949 within the National Council of Teachers of English (NCTE), and it has continued to have some interest in creative writing, albeit navigating the reef-filled waters between Rhet/Comp and Creative Writing knowledge and teaching.

Kate Kostelnik, Stephanie Vanderslice, Alexandria Peary and **Joseph Rein** all make reference to the term 'creative writing studies' here in this book. The defining and exploring thus strongly continue, and the recent emergence of the CWSO is seen to be part of that. As creative writing is further explored, the questions of what qualifies someone to teach creative writing, and how their tenure and promotion in the higher-education institutions of the USA become relevant. Formal organizational influence on these professional elements is surely inevitable.

Meanwhile **Katharine Haake**, whose book *What Our Speech Disrupts* was originally published by the NCTE, is today part of the CWSO and has, like most of us who have contributed to the present volume, also been an attendee at more than one AWP conference! Here Kate explores creative writing and the spiritual, combining both a personal and a disciplinary history. As a coda, and given these organizational considerations, I'd also add that **Patrick Bizzaro and Christine Bailey** explore the nature of creative writing knowledge. Like Kate, Pat and Christine, many of us in this book have explored creative writing from the commonplace to the transcendental, looking for understanding of the practice broadly and of our own practices specifically.

Possibilities! New technologies continue to impact on creative writing, not only on the production and distribution of completed works, but in the delivery of teaching and learning. It would be wrong to say that most technological innovations in the USA in creative writing teaching have related to the development of 'low-residency' masters programs that are largely driven by recruitment ideals. But it would be equally wrong to suggest that there is a considerable range and discussion of innovation in the delivery and reception of creative writing learning. The untraveled avenues of investigation are many in this regard. Dare I say, here too there are strengths and weaknesses to discover – many of them more perceived than as yet thoroughly investigated.

Possibilities! It is one thing to say creative writing is an act possibility, and another to say creative writing as a discipline in American higher education is yet to explore all its possibilities. From the chapters here, it'll be obvious that 'changing creative writing in America' has a range of personal and analytical meanings – and of course, that was the clear intention of this book's title, and its subtitle's reference to 'strengths, weaknesses and possibilities'. The subtitle in fact emerged only in the book's drafting, and its inclusion aims to capture a sense that emerged during that drafting of a positive past, questions about where gaps might lie in the present, and conditions through which we might move forward as we travel into the future.

From the work offered here, it is clear that without some changes occurring now or in the near future we will not know what possibilities for creative writing and creative writing teaching and learning there might be. It is clear, too, that, while recognizing the histories and contemporary identities of organizations and institutional structures, we will all benefit from each openly and individually embracing the vibrancy of our current moment. We have a greater ability now to deliver the practices and the results of creative writing to diverse and ever-increasing audiences. The ways in which creative writing is defined today is related to very new as well as long-established forms. And with our ability to offer more opportunities for creative writing learning to more people, it is certain a great deal will be accomplished in the years ahead in American creative writing education.

The contributors to *Changing Creative Writing in America: Strengths, Weaknesses, Possibilities* have explored and envisaged their own, individual senses of strengths, weaknesses and possibilities. None of these writers was asked to write on anything in particular. They were simply told that the book would be titled *Changing Creative Writing in America* and asked to explore something they believe relevant in relation to that broad description. **Dianne Donnelly**'s chapter is a good example of how that approach produced thought-provoking results. While Dianne has written both on the creative writing workshop and on the emergence of creative writing studies as a discipline, here she chooses to write instead on creative writing processes, and to suggest attention to the way the brain actually functions when considering what might be changed for the better in American creative writing education.

Each contributor presented a version of their ideas some six months before completing the penultimate drafts of their chapters. This initial presentation was achieved by a mini-conference in November 2015, held at the University of Minnesota. Contributors to the book either were present in the room or linked in to discussions via video-conference. Each chapter writer took time to introduce their plans. Some had already completed early drafts and read from them; others had notes or draft sections, which they presented. From there, authors worked to complete their drafts, the majority submitting those drafts in February 2016. Drafts were read and returned with notes and thoughts and, following this, the authors submitted their penultimate drafts in mid-2016. Following review in later 2016, final drafts of chapters were returned to me in February 2017.

Individual interpretations of what positive and productive 'change' might mean have been at the core of this book and have informed the overall sense of possibility. *Clack!* While the opportunity to hear and read what the authors were planning was part of the process of the book's composition, each chapter here represents the individual author's interpretation of what they personally believe is proposed by the title *Changing Creative Writing in America*.

References

Bush, W.H.U. (1990) *10 of 10: Best Stories of the Decade*. Houston, TX: Dynasty Press.

Haake, K. (2000) *What Our Speech Disrupts: Feminism and Creative Writing Studies*. Urbana, IL: National Council of Teachers of English,

McGurl, M. (2009) *The Program Era: Postwar Fiction and the Rise of Creative Writing*. Cambridge, MA: Harvard University Press.

Myers, D.G. (1996) *The Elephants Teach: Creative Writing Since 1880*. Chicago, IL: Chicago University Press.

Thomas, M. (1964) *The Pears of Walton*. Detroit, MI: Nosuch Press.

Thomas, M. (1966) *Landscapers*. East Lansing, MI: Imaginary Books.

Thomas, M. (1981) *Perpetual*. Mission Point, MI: Pointed Press.

Thomas, M. (1983) *Mistaken Fear*. Marquette, MI: City Orphanage.

Thomas, M. (1987) *Curious Midnight and Morning Stories*. East Lansing, MI: Imaginary Books.

Thomas, M. (1997) *Greeting Helen*. Troy, MI: Press Press.

Thomas, M. (1999) *The Broad Tree*. Cadillac Forest, MI: Pontiac Books.

1 Histories and Historiography in Creative Writing Studies

Alexandria Peary

Mildewed, crumpled, rusty, disintegrated, illegible, stained, fading, landfilled, incinerated, erased, deleted, in a forgotten box, on a dusty shelf, in a filing cabinet, in a basement/attic/rented storage facility, on rapidly obsolete technology. If we imagine what is lost without historical studies of creative writing in the United States, we gain a sense of what could be recovered if historical evidence were not treated as ephemeral. What might be recovered includes countless invention, revision, feedback and publication practices developed by generations of writing teachers and mentors, pieces written by decades of undergraduate and graduate students, as well as techniques used by the self-taught. What might be restored includes information about a plethora of local and national institutions of creative writing, those formal and informal sponsors of imaginative work – the journals, book shops, community writing programs, university writing programs, reading series, conferences, retreats, publishing houses, textbooks, manuals, blogs, trade articles, correspondence, marginalia – and their accounts of start-up, challenges faced, successes and evolution, and perhaps of closing doors. Certainly, what is lost are the teaching practices and craft knowledge of those writers and scholars who came before us and who were similarly committed to creative writing. Members of other academic fields, most notably Composition Studies, share an increasingly well researched history, but practitioners in Creative Writing Studies encounter a past that is largely blank. This void indicates that we continue to operate more from a creative writing position – defined by scholars such as Dianne Donnelly, Katharine Haake and Tim Mayers as disinclined toward theory or scholarship and preferring to focus on the training of individual writers – than a Creative Writing Studies position – 'an emerging field of scholarly inquiry and research' (Donnelly, 2012: 1; Haake, 2006: 188; Mayers, 2009: 217–219). As a scholarly enterprise, Donnelly adds (2012: 6), Creative Writing Studies values 'collecting, compiling and presenting data' – and surely historical research constitutes one form of this information.

In this chapter, I argue for increased historical and historiographical work in creative writing in the United States. The historical research that has an important role in the pedagogy and theory of the present and future of the field calls for studies of individual teachers and scholars, groups, communities, institutions (broadly defined) and texts related to creative writing. Critically, this historical work means expanding beyond the familiar US stories of origin (i.e. the Iowa Writers' Workshop) and examining creative writing both inside and outside of formal school settings. The research advocated for in this chapter is not disciplinary history per se (that is, it is not about the contested territory inside English departments) but rather the second strand of historical research Tim Mayers identified in 'One simple word: From creative writing to creative writing studies' (2009: 222) – that of theoretical historical research which seeks 'to place the past in a different light' in ways distinct from the hermeneutics of literary studies. Historiography – or the study of historical method that involves critical perspectives on how histories are framed, researched, narrated and distributed – has an important role in the epistemology of our field and the establishment of terministic screens that suit creative writing. Essentially, historiography addresses questions of how to write history by investigating scope, definition, the construction of categories, methods, stance, ethics, subjectivity, reflexivity and the constructed nature of discourse (including the discourse of history).

History increases disciplinary knowledge whereas historiography deepens knowledge practices while also monitoring and safeguarding those practices. Scholars of historiography have long been interested in fact and methodology, tracking how shifts between humanism, positivism, relativism, presentism and objectivism across Western thought influenced historical accounts (Clark, 2004: 17–25; Collingwood, 1946; Higham, 1965). As Elizabeth Clark says (2004: 19) in discussing historian Michael Oakeshott's contention that the past can never be fully reclaimed but only inferred, 'history is not "out there," but is something that historians create'. While a historical study might examine 20th-century correspondence courses in creative writing, veteran participation at the literary journal *0-Dark-Thirty* or community creative writing groups for transgender youth, a historiographical work would explore the ways in which archival research can be conducted on university creative writing programs or examine the discourse used in historical accounts of the Iowa Writers' Workshop. Historiography can serve as the subject of a publication (examining a research practice) or be used as a research method during the writing process (the scholar looking into creative writing correspondence courses would apply a historiographical awareness to her work). It's fairly commonplace for an academic discipline to practice both history and historiographic research, as evinced in publications such as the *Journal of the History of Biology* and *Journal of the History of Dentistry*, along with the *Journal of Art Historiography*, *Historiography in Mass Communication* and the *Journal of Modern Art History and Historiography*.

Historiography, as an epistemological and critical apparatus, is an opportunity to think carefully and collectively on how creative writers want to approach scholarly activity. Rather than a matter of placing the cart before the horse, starting conversations about historiography now in the nascent field of Creative Writing Studies makes a good deal of sense. Indeed, there are real advantages to establishing historiography during disciplinary groundbreaking moments. Chiefly, historiography entails conversations about epistemology that can be deeply impactful in the growth of a field of study, since the methods by which a field conducts its research (historical or otherwise) reveal much about the values and mission of that field. It can be beneficial to allow historiography to be more formative than corrective, to not play catch-up after methodological or epistemological problems arise. If done thoughtfully, historiography can address significant concerns, like those so cogently voiced by Anna Leahy (2016), that the emerging field of Creative Writing Studies risks severing the interplay of creative and critical activity already possible for creative writers working in academia. These conversations about historiography can help creative writers take charge of their disciplinarity – so that scholarly efforts by creative writers steer clear of the overly esoteric and avoid expending energy arguing for university legitimacy. Creative writers are predisposed to the work of historical research, whether it is the close examination of language intrinsic to textual analysis, the development of a narrative in presenting a historical account, remaining open to the serendipity of discovery, or developing alternative points of view, including a more conscious role for the first person. Discussions of epistemology and method can also help creative writing stay true to its extracurricular roots and maintain what Leahy (2016: 9) calls its 'translational' ability to connect academia with the larger culture, to keep the door open to greater communities of writers.

History, Or How Much Do We Know?

The evolution of a field of academic study occurs through a crucial trio of inquiry into history (background), pedagogy (application) and theory (critical perspective on history and pedagogy). Disciplinarity is in the house when scholars develop professionalizing organizations such as conferences, associations, journals, book presses, newsletters, awards, list-servs, and MA and PhD programs. Another barometer of an academic field's vitality is the amount of historical work it sponsors. In the case of Composition Studies, the field floundered for a long stretch between 1885 until 1945, a time in which literature received more attention and 'composition teaching increasingly went on in a sort of twilit underground, taught by unwilling graduate student conscripts and badly paid non-tenured instructors' (Connors, 2003: 205). According to Connors, a gap occurred between the first great historical work of research in rhetoric, Albert R. Kitzhaber's 1953 dissertation, *Rhetoric in American Colleges, 1850–1900,* and the emergence of historians like James Berlin and Donald Stewart in the 1970s. The rapid evolution of Composition Studies in the 1970s was not coincidental but rather a reflection of its efforts toward historical research. Recently, scholars have linked historical research to the establishment of Creative Writing Studies: for instance, Dianne Donnelly (2012: 1) has described creative writing 'unaware of the histories and theories that inform its practice' posed at a crossroads from the 'emerging field of scholarly inquiry and research' of Creative Writing Studies. Moreover, a lack of historical awareness impinges upon the other two legs of the field – theory and pedagogy – such that remaining stubbornly ahistorical is linked to lore-based teaching (Donnelly, 2012: 5) and vice versa. Failing to situate the teaching present in a larger historical and theoretical context, creative writers instead resort to the 'epistemology of individual experience' that Mayers notices pervading conferences of the American Association of Writers and Writing Programs (AWP) (Mayers, 2016: 4). In turn, workshop pedagogy may have played a role in a lack of historical awareness, since, as a 'forum oriented exclusively to the present', the workshop model displays the 'tendency to erase the past on which its authority and practice were based' (Berry, 1994: 63). To perpetuate this cycle, for the most part, whenever historical work has been conducted, it has been to address perceived problems with the workshop model, the hegemonic Goliath frustrating those who would advance the field.

Of the disciplinary triad of history, pedagogy and theory, pedagogy to date has received the lion's share of attention in Creative Writing Studies. In the past five years, we've witnessed an uptick in the publication of several book-length collections on pedagogy after a lag since Joseph Moxley's 1989 *Creative Writing in America: Theory and Pedagogy* and Wendy Bishop and Hans Ostrom's 1994 *Colors of a Different Horse: Rethinking Creative Writing Theory and Pedagogy.* A short list of recent books on pedagogy include Tom C. Hunley's *Teaching Poetry Writing: A Five-Canon Approach* (2007) and several other books in the series 'New Writing Viewpoints' (edited by Graeme Harper and published by Multilingual Matters); Stephanie Vanderslice's *Rethinking Creative Writing* (2011) and Elaine Walker's *Teaching Creative Writing* (2013) from the imprint Creative Writing Studies; Michael Dean Clark and Trent Hergenrader's *Teaching Creative Writing in the Digital Age* (2015); and my and Tom C. Hunley's *Creative Writing Pedagogies for the Twenty-First Century* (Peary & Hunley, 2015). These contributions to creative writing pedagogy have sought to replace lore in the classroom – the near-sightedness that results when teachers fail to critically consider their classroom practices in light of more comprehensive, less idiosyncratic patterns of praxis (North, 1987; Ritter & Vanderslice, 2007). That myopia, however, is directly related to the extent to which teachers are aware of the history of teaching in the field. Lack of interest in pedagogy is lack of interest in history – in anything more long term or sustained than the isolated course, class meeting or individual student draft. Additionally, a peculiarity of scholarly discussions of academic creative writing, one not faced by composition, has been how creative writing is framed either as elitist – such as James Berlin's (1987: 40) early critique of belletristic writing instruction as the stuff of Yale and the Ivy League – or overly egalitarian, such as Anis Shivani's (2011) diatribe against the populace in the workshop. As a result, conversations about academic creative writing have pin-balled between what Paul Dawson (2005: 1) calls the 'Can it be taught' and 'Should it be taught' dispute. A more expansive take on subject in the historic research of Creative Writing Studies could help disband such unproductive binaries.

Historical research is a form of community building that expands rather than narrows the scope of creative writing. For one, it's an acknowledgement of practitioners who preceded us who were similarly committed to the teaching of creative writing. Designing graduate programs in Creative Writing Studies will professionalize younger scholars and burgeon the members of the discipline of the future: likewise, historical work increases the membership by retroactively including those scholars and writers from the past. Card-carrying members of Creative Writing Studies would then include the new assistant professor at a small, historically black college and people active on theory panels at the AWP as well as the 19th-century magazine editor who helped mentor female creative writers, or Brenda Ueland, teaching the classes she describes in *If You Want to Write* (1938). In a similar way, as will be shortly discussed, historiography, or the critical examination of how histories are researched and narrated, is not simply about 'differings in methodology alone but varying perceptions of what ought to be discovered for the good of the community' (Murphy, 1988: 5). Historical research is almost a responsibility we owe to those practitioners and teachers of creative writing who preceded us. Furthermore, a lack of interest in our disciplinary predecessors risks our own obscurity: if the theory and pedagogy of predecessors have become obsolete through lack of curiosity, that's likely the fate of our current endeavors if the next generation of practitioners is equally uninterested in the community which taught, learned and wrote before them.

Historical research in creative writing in the United States should seek to study histories of imaginative literate practice from any era or geographic location, including places and times in which the exact term 'creative writing' may not have been in currency. This research could examine pedagogy, publication and methods of circulation; genre; socio-economic issues of class, gender and race; and cultural perceptions and reception of creative writing and writers as they have developed over time; it could also reconfigure known histories. Such research would eschew literary analysis and biographies of single authors – the purview of literary studies; it would replace questions of interpretation and meaning with questions about the conditions that made a text possible (Mayers, 2009: 222), including writing processes and social context. As will be discussed in the historiography section below, historical subjects need to include those outside of academia by considering both the extracurriculum (informal ways in which individuals learn about writing) as well as subjects who had nothing to do with teaching, not even informally, but who had writing and publishing engagements worth studying. That is, historical research needs to sidestep what Susan Jarratt (1987: 24) called the 'pedagogical imperative', or the compunction to find relevancy by connecting research to the classroom. Creative writing historians could take a cue from composition and rhetoric historians who have written about such outside-the-box-of-academia subjects, including women in the US submarine force, the letters between Queen Elizabeth I and Mary Queen of Scotts, *Life Magazine* and public libraries.

Composition Studies has defined its boundaries as an academic discipline fairly broadly, and subsequently a type of academic mission creep has overtaken histories of creative writing. Assuming names of 'composition studies', 'discipline of composition–rhetoric' or, more encroachingly, 'writing studies', the various texts of Composition Studies – its policy papers, journal mission statements and association position statements – show Composition Studies pushing creative writing under its auspices. For instance, the mission statement of the flagship journal of Composition Studies, *College Composition and Communication*, states that it 'draws on research and theories from a broad range of humanistic disciplines', with creative writing falling under 'English studies' and the phrase 'and others', since many of the articles exploring creative writing theory, history or pedagogy in recent years have been published in this journal. Although creative writing has been claimed by the publications of composition, it's been given a marginal role. For instance, a search in *College Composition and Communication* for the references since 1997 to creative writing-related terms showed the following: 126 references to 'imagination', 58 to 'imaginative', 136 to 'creativity', 115 to 'creative writing', 93 to 'poet' and 29 to 'short story'. The journal has been more invested in composition-related discussions (although creative writing might be folded inside these discussions), evident in the 1345 references to 'composition', 772 to 'rhetoric' and 179 to 'rhetorician'. To date, composition researchers have included creative writing and creative writers in their scholarship, usually as acknowledgement of writing done outside required course work, self-willed writers, to tacitly make a case for the relevancy of written communication. During the first Octalog, in 1987, Susan Jarratt (1987: 9) called for composition scholars to reclaim rhetorical texts that had been claimed by other disciplines, to become 'daring usurper[s] (rather than marginalized hoarder[s])'. Taking a cue from Jarratt, one undertaking of creative writing historians could be the reclamation of creative writing texts and subjects currently explored by composition scholars. An immediate example would be the role of professional creative writers and the *Paris Review* interviews in helping to establish process pedagogy, an oft-told tale passed around in histories of composition, but one never examined through a creative writing lens.

In the past five or six years, a crop of dissertations which conduct creative writing historical work has arisen in US doctoral programs, typically in conjunction with discussions of Composition Studies, including dissertations by Janelle Adsit (2014), Mary Stewart Atwell (2016), Eric Bennett (2010), Mary Elizabeth Fiorenza (2009), Sarah Harris (2013) and Ben Ristow (2012) – not to mention Dianne Donnelly's, later published as a book (Donnelly, 2012). To keep pace with what's been happening on the international front with dissertations, Creative Writing Studies in the United States needs more dissertations as well as book-length macro histories. Article-length publications, due to their brevity and frequency, would afford the opportunity for a larger number of emerging and established scholars to speak on creative writing history. In addition to sweeping historical-theoretical accounts such as D.G. Myers' *The Elephants Teach*, historical research is much needed that focuses on single figures, single programs, single associations, single journals and single institutions – close-ups, so to speak, that take the form of an article. For instance, *New Writing: The International Journal for the Practice and Theory of Creative Writing* has published historical articles on the origins of the creative writing program at the University of East Anglia as well as the Boston-based extracurricular creative writing organization Grub Street – this one a model for investigations of US-based creative writing (Holeywell, 2009; Rolland, 2013). It's a disciplinary Catch-22, since, to date, *New Writing: The International Journal for the Practice and Theory of Creative Writing* has served as the sole provider of a forum for articles in the field, although at the writing of this chapter the *Journal of Creative Writing Studies*, housed in the United States, is underway, along with an annual conference. The *Journal of Creative Writing Studies* thus joins international creative writing organizations in providing both conferences and publications – such as the United Kingdom's National Association of Writers in Education, the Australasian Association of Writing Programs, the Canadian Creative Writers and Writing Programs, and the European Association of Creative Writing Programs.

The discourse of upcoming publications on historical research in the United States will be undergoing a transition in the next five years both as a result of the increasing disciplinarity of Creative Writing Studies *and* as a driver of that disciplinarity. Currently, the primary audience for many of the article-length publications (my own included) that conduct historical work on creative writing is not necessarily creative writers. Much of this research was conducted for a Composition–Rhetoric readership, hoping to pass by editorial gatekeepers at the journals of Composition–Rhetoric – *College Composition and Communication, College English, Pedagogy, Composition Studies, WAC Journal, Rhetoric Review, Rhetoric Society Quarterly* – with creative writing specialists possibly a secondary audience and certainly not with creative writing specialists occupying editorial positions. In the very recent past, a creative writing scholar enjoyed fewer publishing opportunities and depended upon the publication and presentation venues of Composition Studies to obtain lines on a curriculum vitae, tenure and other professional advancements. As rhetoric tells us, intended readership affects interpersonal discourse – and invariably these forums to date have affected how historical research has been conducted on creative writing. With scholarly opportunities inside Creative Writing Studies on the ascendancy in the United States, the rhetorical situation will change for historical research, and that audience change will bring forth changes too in discourse and possibly methodology – key historiographic considerations.

Historiography, Or How Do We Know What We Know?

Historiography is linked with increasing disciplinarity because it entails conversations about definitions, values, scope, purposes and subject position. We need to think critically of how histories of creative writing are framed, researched, narrated and distributed, because failure to examine one's approach to historical work is to take ethical and epistemological risks. As Victor Vitanza counseled (1988: 8) in tones of Hegelian dialectics, 'If there is no consciousness without self-consciousness, there can be no Histories/Hysteries of Rhetoric without historiographies/hysteriographies'. Conversations about historiography have been active between scholars of composition and rhetoric, with at least two full-length books, Michelle Ballif's *Theorizing Histories of Rhetoric* (2013) and Vitanza's *Writing Histories of Rhetoric* (1994), numerous journal articles and, not the least, the highly influential set of public conversations about historiography, held at the flagstaff academic conference, the Conference of College Communication and Composition, the transcript of which has been published in three issues of *Rhetoric Review* as 'Octalog I', 'Octalog II' and 'Octalog III'. In these forums, held in 1988, 1997 and 2010, three different groups of eight prominent scholars provided a prepared statement and then engaged in a dialog on historiography. By reading all three octalogs, creative writing historians can gain a sense of the three-decade-long evolution of the conversations about historiography in the other writing field, including controversies around inclusion and methodology – a history, as it were, of the historiographic practices within this discipline of writing. A similar forum on historiography could be useful in the near future at one of the national or international conferences on creative writing.

While creative writing historians can benefit from the historiography of compositionists, creative writing scholars need to establish the terministic screens particular to Creative Writing Studies, with emphasis on how historical materials might have a bearing on the practices and inquiry of present-day creative writers. Different terministic screens will emerge as Creative Writing Studies evolves, in part because 'creative writing' is a narrower stratum of writing; constructs of imaginative writing and of the literary writer should be at the forefront. Historical research in Creative Writing Studies focuses on belletristic genres – what James Britton (2003) called poetic discourse – rather than the more transactional types of composition that are taught in first-year writing courses, in WAC (writing across the curriculum) programs and WID (writing in the disciplines) programs. As Britton would say (2003: 158–159), it's 'MAKING something with language rather than doing something with it'. Thus, historical investigations of imaginative writing by creative writing scholars will lead to increased understanding of both the invention phases of imaginative work as well as the ways in which engaging with genre have impacted drafting and revision. The identity and the practices of the literary writer need to be center-stage, and the writer's lived experience (the so-called writing life) could become a factor in research (Adsit, 2014). It would be paramount for historical research to take into account the significant differences in audience faced by students in composition classes versus students in creative writing courses. The rhetorical situation of big and small literary journals, writing contests, grants, agents and the book publishing market, of listeners at readings, of fans and reviewers, and of systems of merit and reward surely distinguish the freelance literary writer from the transactional writer, for instance, who instead encounters employers, customers and readers who seek information or argument.

In establishing the scope of historical work, Creative Writing Studies scholars would want to consider a wide range of writing experiences and writers as possible research topics, striving for parity in genre (valuing 'low-brow' and 'high-brow' work from a gamut of aesthetic traditions); process (valuing less polished alongside finished works); and author (valuing the novice alongside the well established writer). For instance, interesting instruction has occurred at smaller programs, low-residency programs, student-run literary magazines, online degree programs, correspondence courses from the earlier part of the last century, not to mention creative writing outside the university – non-degree-granting, informal settings such as community writing groups, blogs devoted to advancing creative writing, networks, e-zines and organizations, regional, local as well as national. Journals soliciting creative writing histories should include this information in submission guidelines; organizers of conference panels could endeavor to include this range. More efficacious perhaps would be a consistent discussion of topic selection in the methodology sections of articles on creative writing history. While critically considering scope, it's important to not disregard seemingly modest student creative production or that of their perhaps less-than-famous faculty – or to overvalue polished works and to downplay drafts. As Graeme Harper advises, we need to be more attentive to creative writing as a human activity occurring in time rather than as a commercialized or polished object. Some scholars overvalue special artifacts of creative writing (the celebrated ones). The field has consequentially limited itself by omitting a wide range of writing experiences:

too rarely do we hear someone refer to all available and distributed evidence of Creative Writing, or to artifacts of Creative Writing other than those deemed to have cultural or societal significance. That is, evidence or artifacts produced solely because of their personal significance to the writer are rarely noted in university classes. (Harper, 2011: 2)

Careful consideration of scope means not disregarding seemingly modest student creative production or that of less-than-famous faculty – or over-valuing polished works and downplaying drafts. For instance, archival research necessitates that hierarchies of this sort be avoided. Less prestigious archives and secondary players, regional and local sources, family or personal subjects, and hidden and digital resources are important components in a comprehensive sense of what constitutes an archival resource (Glenn & Enoch, 2010: 14–16; Kirsch & Rohan, 2008: 3; Ramsey, 2010). As Cheryl Glenn and Jessica Enoch (2010: 17) have said of composition historiographic practice, archival research evolved beyond thinking only of illustrious Harvard- or Yale-like archives, to 'consider what other, lower-case-*a* archives might hold, archives that don't immediately promise insights into the practices or histories of our field'. A good model here is how composition historians have used a range of archival sources, including the acting trunk of a researcher's grandfather, a southern Illinois cemetery and the documents of a rural Nebraska writing club.

The scope of historical research in creative writing should also include extracurricular settings and not be limited to academia. We need to recast historical work as an exploration of the expansive activities of creative writing and not yoke the subject of historical work to departmental or disciplinary clout – more theoretical and less institutional histories. For one, this type of expansive exploration will preserve the extracurricular roots of creative writing – which really began separate from academia and, perhaps more importantly in terms of historical research, continues to thrive outside higher education. As Anne Ruggles Gere (1994) points out, significant learning about writing has long occurred in the United States in the extracurriculum – or in the coffee-shop writing groups, Athenæum and other community writing organizations – alongside formal classroom training. Since the extracurriculum often serves learners disenfranchised by traditional education due to constraints of class, gender, race or geography, it's an important consideration in equitable historical work. When examining a variety of writing settings, scholars should look for alternative sponsors of creative writing – those 'agents, local or distant, concrete or abstract, who enable, support, teach, and model, as well as recruit, regulate, suppress, or withhold, literacy – and gain advantage by it in some way' (Brandt, 2001: 19). For instance, a close look at creative writing sponsors could entail studying the impact of a regional poetry festival in a community or of the online publishing service Submittable. As Gere (1994) has shown, such sponsors may not resemble those who we typically think of as writing instructors: in addition to community writing group facilitators, text-based writing forums should be considered, including self-published books on writing such as Natalie Goldberg's *Writing Down the Bones* (1986) or Brenda Ueland's *If You Want to Write* (1938), as well as online forums for learning, what I've elsewhere called textrooms, essentially classrooms co-constructed by individuals as they write and publish together (Gere, 1994: 80–81; Peary, 2014).

One of the most significant historiographic practices to retain from compositionists is the conducting of historical work as a matter of plurality, not singularity, of *histories*, not a history. First, it's important to expand beyond the known US stories of origin to include unknown moments, sites and people in the evolution of creative writing. Our field has an opportunity to challenge the practice of writing histories mostly about a narrow set of individuals and events, mostly defined by politics, economics and patriarchies. This expansion helps avoid master narratives, the repeated turn to certain institutions and practices that are either glorified or vilified. For Composition Studies, that master narrative has too frequently focused on Harvard in the late 19th century, as presumable site of the beginnings of college instruction in expository writing, to the exclusion of other sites of instruction (Gold, 2008; Skinnell, 2014). The Iowa Writers' Workshop has become a master narrative in the way Harvard has functioned in narratives about Composition history: Iowa is like the brilliant trouble child who receives too much attention in a family. As a side result, historical research in creative writing in the United States should help release scholars from familiar arguments (e.g. whether workshop works). It's worth noting, as Ryan Skinnell (2015) has, that recovery work should be performed critically to avoid the 'broadening imperative', or the inclusion of more individuals and groups into historical accounts as a way to bluntly perpetuate the ideology of the discipline. Secondly, historical research should expand beyond hallmark book-length historical treatises; in Composition Studies, certain authors have become reified such that their axiomatic power goes unexamined – James Berlin, David Russell and Sharon Crowley are three such scholars. For creative writing scholars, we are blessed with this pair of outstanding historical sagas – D.G. Myers' *The Elephants Teach* (1996) and Paul Dawson's *Creative Writing and the New Humanities* (2005) – but their control over the terms of historic discourse needs to be continuously investigated and mitigated (by other histories). One way to develop this critical stance toward the big-block historical accounts in the field is to compose historiographic essays that examine the ways various historians have covered a topic (Brundage, 2013: 89). To further avoid hegemonic narratives of history, scholars should bypass closure and favor multiplicity, even if seemingly fragmentary, to 'discover as many layers of meaning as possible in order to interrogate the interestedness of each version of a given story, not in order to choose one version' (Dolmage, 2011: 113). Similarly, James Berlin (1987: 25) advised in the first octalog, citing Adorno's negative dialectic, 'We can't ever achieve totality. We can't ever explain everything', adding that scholars should continue to strive toward some closure while at the same time realizing that it's only an attempt.

The stance of the historian is also crucial to historiographic work – the extent to which the historian remains critically aware of his or her own positionality in relation to a topic, to the impact on and point of view of individuals researched, and to the rhetorical choices used in composing historical accounts. For R.G. Collingwood, historiography entailed thinking 'about the historian's mind' (1946: 3) and a historical imagination in which the historian needs to be cognizant of the preconceptions he or she brings to historical work (244–246). No matter the research method, whether archival, ethnographic, interview or library based, historical research requires a good deal of reflection and self-awareness in order to perceive what Cheryl Glenn and Jessica Enoch (2010) call one's 'interestedness'. Whether this information about positionality stays a hidden part of the researcher's writing process – a private reflection to gain insights to be used in shaping the piece – or is imbedded in the final draft as a disclosure depends on the researcher. Glenn and Enoch (2010: 21) state:

> In the field of rhetoric and composition, it has become almost commonplace for researchers to devote space in their manuscripts to revealing their standpoint and interestedness in relation to their project.

For example, a creative writing historian exploring the history of poetry contests for children might privately examine his own assumptions about early-life public recognition for creativity, factoring in his own experiences with competition and peers, in order to understand the biases he brings to the subject. A researcher needs to acknowledge the 'intersections' of the personal and academic in the work: 'how a researcher chooses a subject is a subject unto itself' (Kirsch & Rohan, 2008: i). This awareness extends to the discursive choices made by the historian – including the researcher's ethos and narrative choices in framing the account. Creative writing historians would want to circumvent the mistake made by early composition historians who were taken to task by John Schilb in 1986 for failing to notice the rhetoric of their own historical productions: 'I don't find in recent histories of rhetoric clear acknowledgement that authors are composing discourse ... [that they are] shapers of texts rather than passive recorders of a naked reality' (Schilb, 1986: 13). Historical research in creative writing, that is, should remain *writerly*, an act as much dependent on an artful and accurate use of language as it is on a research methodology.

Finally, historiographic considerations and the conditions of writing history suggest there's less of a binary between creative writing/creative writers and scholarship/scholars than some might think. It's not coincidence that in describing the ideal disposition of the historian, compositionists have turned to creative writing, comparing the historian to a mystery author. An important part of historical work, narrative analysis, 'usually takes the form of a detective-style analysis which seeks to highlight the causal impact of particular factors within particular cases' (Lange, 2013: 4). As David Gold (2010: 43–44) has described his archival practices:

> I also read a lot of detective fiction; a standard conceit is the grizzled veteran who always notes the importance of not jumping too quickly to a conclusion based on limited or even overwhelming evidence, lest one ignore clues that don't fit one's theory.

While this exploration may be relatively new to a composition scholar trained to construct literature reviews, identify gaps in existent scholarship and produce thesis-driven work, for creative writers, working off what Kirsch and Rohan describe as a 'simple clue' and following the initial wisps of a story might come naturally (2008: 4). For creative writers, flexibility of point of view – that ability to adopt a first, second or third person or to craft a persona – could dovetail into academic historical work and the consideration of positionality. As Jenn Webb (2015: x) says in making her case for a hybrid identity of 'writer-researcher', reminiscent of Wendy Bishop: 'research practices can invigorate writing, creative practices can invigorate research, and creative writing can operate as a mode of knowledge generation, a way of exploring problems and answering questions that matter'.

Found on a shelf, discovered at the bottom of a wooden box, dust blown off, yellowed page carefully turned, labeled, photographed, transcribed, transferred to a PDF, stored on the Cloud, documented, read and reread, commonalities found, mysteries cleared up, histories known. If we imagine what can be found with historical study in creative writing, we gain a sense of the contexts and connections that can be established between our work now and that of the past. For Creative Writing Studies, a future that includes a well detailed and intriguing past awaits.

References

Adsit, J. (2014) What is a writer? Historicizing constructions of the writing life in composition and creative writing. PhD thesis, State University of New York at Albany.
Atwell, M.S. (2016) Imaginary subjects: Fiction-writing instruction in America, 1826–1897. PhD thesis, City University of New York.
Ballif, M. (2013) *Theorizing Histories of Rhetoric*. Carbondale, IL: Southern Illinois University Press.
Bennett, E. (2010) Creative writing and the Cold War. PhD thesis, University of Michigan.
Berlin, J. (1987) *Rhetoric and Reality: Writing Instruction in American Colleges, 1900–1985*. Carbondale, IL: Southern Illinois University Press.
Berry, R.M. (1994) Theory, creative writing, and the impertinence of history. In W. Bishop and H. Ostrom (eds) *Colors of a Different Horse: Rethinking Creative Writing Theory and Pedagogy* (pp. 57–76). Urbana, IL: NCTE.
Bishop, W. and Ostrom, H. (eds) (1994) *Colors of a Different Horse: Rethinking Creative Writing Theory and Pedagogy*. Urbana, IL: NCTE Press.
Brandt, D. (2001) *Literacy in American Lives*. Cambridge: Cambridge University Press.
Britton, J. (2003) Spectator role and the beginning of writing. In V. Villanueva (ed.) *Cross-Talk in Comp Theory: A Reader*. Urbana, IL: NCTE.
Brundage, A. (2013) *Going to the Sources: A Guide to Historical Research and Writing*. Malden, MA: Wiley-Blackwell.
Clark, E. (2004) *History, Theory, Text: Historians and the Linguistic Turn*. Cambridge, MA: Harvard University Press.
Clark, M.D. and Hergenrader, T. (2015) *Teaching Creative Writing in the Digital Age: Theory, Practice, and Pedagogy*. London: Bloomsbury.
Collingwood, R.G. (1946) *The Idea of History*. Oxford: Oxford University Press.
Connors, R. (2003) Writing the history of our discipline. In L. Ede and A. Lunsford (eds) *Selected Essays of Robert J. Connors* (pp. 202–220). Boston, MA: Bedford St Martins.
Dawson, P. (2005) *Creative Writing and the New Humanities*. London: Routledge.
Dolmage, J. (2011) Octalog III: The politics of historiography in 2010. *Rhetoric Review* 30 (2), 109–134.
Donnelly, D. (2012) *Establishing Creative Writing Studies as an Academic Discipline*. Bristol: Multilingual Matters.
Fiorenza, M.E. (2009) Methods and models of writing and living: Brenda Ueland's writing life. PhD thesis, University of Wisconsin Madison.
Gere, A.R. (1994) Kitchen tables and rented rooms: The extracurriculum of composition. *College Composition and Communication* 45 (1), 75–92.
Glenn, C. and Enoch, J. (2010) Invigorating historiographic practices in rhetoric and composition studies. In A. Ramsey *et al.* (ed) *Working in the Archives: Practical Research Methods for Rhetoric and Composition* (pp. 11–27). Carbondale, IL: Southern Illinois University Press.
Gold, D. (2008) *Rhetoric at the Margins: Revising the History of Writing Instruction in American Colleges 1873–1947*. Carbondale, IL: Southern Illinois University Press.
Gold, D. (2010) On keeping a beginner's mind. In A. Ramsey *et al.* (eds) *Working in the Archives: Practical Research Methods for Rhetoric and Composition* (pp. 42–44). Carbondale, IL: Southern Illinois University Press.
Goldberg, N. (1986) *Writing Down the Bones: Freeing the Writer Within*. Boulder, CO: Shambhala.
Haake, K. (2006) Creative writing. In B. McComiskey (ed.) *English Studies: An Introduction to the Discipline(s)* (pp. 153–198). Urbana, IL: NCTE.

Harper, G. (2011) Back to the future. *New Writing: The International Journal for the Practice and Theory of Creative Writing* 8 (1), 1–4.
Harris, S. (2013) From the fictional to the real: Creative writing and the reading public. PhD thesis, University of Arizona.
Higham, J. (1965) *History: The Development of Historical Studies in the United States*. Englewood Cliffs, NJ: Prentice Hall.
Holeywell, K. (2009) The origins of a creative writing programme at the University of East Anglia, 1963–1966. *New Writing: The International Journal for the Practice and Theory of Creative Writing* 6 (1), 15–24.
Hunley, T.C. (2007) *Teaching Poetry: A Five-Canon Approach*. Clevedon: Multilingual Matters.
Jarratt, S. (1988) Octalog: The politics of historiography. *Rhetoric Review* 7, 5–49.
Kirsch, G.E. and Rohan, L. (2008) *Beyond the Archives: Research as Lived Process*. Carbondale, IL: Southern Illinois University Press.
Lange, M. (2013) *Comparative-Historical Methods*. Los Angeles, CA: Sage.
Leahy, A. (2016) Against creative writing studies and for ish(ness). *Journal of Creative Writing Studies* 1 (1), article 5.
Mayers, T. (2009) One simple word: From creative writing to creative writing studies. *College English* 7 (3), 217–228.
Mayers, T. (2016) Creative writing studies: The past decade (and the next). *Journal of Creative Writing Studies* 1 (1), article 4.
Moxley, J. (1989) *Creative Writing in America: Theory and Pedagogy*. Urbana, IL: NCTE.
Murphy, J.J. (1988) Octalog: The politics of historiography. *Rhetoric Review* 7, 5–49.
Myers, D.G. (1996) *The Elephants Teach: Creative Writing Since 1880*. Englewood Cliffs, NJ: Prentice Hall.
North, S.M. (1987) *The Making of Knowledge in Composition: Portrait of an Emerging Field*. Portsmouth, NH: Boynton/Cook, Heinemann.
Peary, A. (2014) Walls with a word count: The textrooms of the extracurriculum. *College Composition and Communication* 66 (1), 43–66.
Peary, A. and Hunley, T.C. (eds) (2015) *Creative Writing Pedagogies for the Twenty-First Century*. Carbondale, IL: Southern Illinois University Press.
Ramsey, A.E. (2010) Viewing the archives: The hidden and the digital. In A. Ramsey *et al.* (eds) *Working in the Archives: Practical Research Methods for Rhetoric and Composition* (pp. 79–90). Carbondale, IL: Southern Illinois University Press.
Ristow, B. (2012) Creative writing joins rhetoric and the public arts: A comparative study of craft, workshop, and craft beyond English studies. PhD thesis, University of Arizona.
Ritter, K. and Vanderslice, S. (2007) *Can It Really Be Taught? Resisting Lore in Creative Writing Pedagogy*. Portsmouth, NH: Boynton/Cook Heinemann.
Rolland, R.G. (2013) 'Finding the through-line': A portrait of an innovative creative writing organisation. *New Writing: The International Journal for the Practice and Theory of Creative Writing* 10 (3), 272–281.
Schilb, J. (1986) The history of rhetoric and the rhetoric of history. *PRE/TEXT* 7 (12), 12–34.
Shivani, A. (2011) *Against the Workshop: Provocations, Polemics, Controversies*. Huntsville, TX: Texas Review Press.
Skinnell, R. (2014) Harvard again: Considering articulation and accreditation in rhetoric and composition's history. *Rhetoric Review* 33 (2), 95–112.
Skinnell, R. (2015) Who cares if rhetoricians landed on the moon? Or, a plea for reviving the politics of historiography. *Rhetoric Review* 34 (2), 111–128.

Ueland, B. (1938) *If You Want to Write: A Book about Art, Independence and Spirit.* BN Publishing (2008).
Vanderslice, S. (2011) *Rethinking Creative Writing in Higher Education: Programs and Practices That Work.* Newmarket: Professional and Higher Partnership.
Vitanza, V. (1988) Octalog: The politics of historiography. *Rhetoric Review* 7, 5–49.
Vitanza, V. (ed.) (1994) *Writing Histories of Rhetoric.* Carbondale, IL: Southern Illinois University Press.
Walker, E. (2013) *Teaching Creative Writing: Practical Approaches.* Newmarket: Professional and Higher Partnership.
Webb, J. (2015) *Researching Creative Writing.* Newmarket: Creative Writing Studies.

2 Writing as Spiritual Practice

Katharine Haake

> Writing is the intelligent but unbiased heart living in its own beating.
> Breyten Breytenbach

Retirement

Philip Roth has given up writing! At 80, he reports a certain calm at knowing his long struggle with sentences is over.

Naturally, he's not the first writer to do so, to give it all up, to write his last sentence and say 'Enough of that for me'. Enrique Vila-Matas' *Bartleby & Co.* is full of them – writers of what Vila-Matas calls 'the no'. From Herman Melville to Hart Crane, the book, a collection of footnotes on a nonexistent text, regales us with writers who, for one reason or another, succumb to the impossibility of writing. But Roth's announcement he is done has got to be the first such notice ever featured on the front page of the *New York Times*, never mind other such distinguished publications as the *New Yorker*, the *Guardian,* and the *Paris Review*.

Al la la.

Breaking news: WRITER STOPS WRITING.

Oh, save us from these cataclysmic times.

Of course we know cataclysmic times because we live as if we had invented them ourselves. Born on the cusp of the end of the world, it seemed to us in the beginning that anything could happen, and after everything that has, it's fair to say it did.

And so it's hard not to consider my own long struggle with sentences. An early writer of the no and way ahead of Philip Roth, I'd already given up writing by the time I turned 16, when, on the morning of that special birthday and with the stale aftermath of my 'first kiss' still disturbing in my mouth, I stood on the unfamiliar shore of a local lake to which I had been brought the night before as a birthday surprise, dug my toes into warm and clayey sand, and, having finished reading *Moby Dick* just the day before, firmly renounced writing in my heart. For if I took anything from *Moby Dick*, it was that I was neither smart enough nor talented enough to be a writer. Before the year was out, I'd be reading Dostoyevsky and we would have sent a man to the moon.

Today, I wonder: what sweet 16 reads Dostoyevsky anymore?

Is there even such a thing as a sweet 16 anymore?

I did not write again for half a decade and when I did, I was, paradoxically, totally primed (oh, what an outpouring of feeling!) and woefully unprepared (my reading being deeply mired, still, in the distant grandeur of that 19th century).

My path toward *pincha mayurasana* (forearm balance) followed a parallel path, although I did not take up yoga until deep into middle age and had no interest in inversion for a long time after that. When I finally started thinking about going upside down, I was seized by an intense curiosity and primal fear. What must it be like to see the world like that, I thought, your feet in the air and your blood draining into your brain? So when the time came in each class, I doggedly trudged to the wall, where I'd steel myself to kick up, only to fall back, and back, and back against the implacable weight of my own body and the pull of gravity. During this time of leaden humiliation, I often considered giving up. What difference would it make if I chose, instead, to fold up on the floor in *kapotasana* (pigeon pose)? I was old, after all, not like all the others with their Lululemon bodies. I could stop.

I could, like Philip Roth, retire.

One day that will happen. One day, I'll go upside down for what will be the final time (although I likely will not know it when I do), but for now, well I just wish I could give you that feeling as a gift, held out in the cup of my palms – what it was like when I finally let go and went up: here, *fly*!

It's the same with writing: what you do and who you are, which begins with dogged practice and ends with letting go. Of course, it doesn't matter if you fail – you will always fail – you still struggle every day to write, working the words on the page, one sentence after another.

But how did it happen that this struggle fell to me? No one in my family wrote or even read. We watched TV. In Korea, there's a national exam – the state decides. But here in the US, what possesses us to commit our lives to words, the demands of sentences, our love of punctuation? And why are so many of us possessed? And why does any of it matter?

Oh why, Jane Bowles might say, oh why, oh why, oh why? Oh what a hideous riddle.

But not Philip Roth. Roth is done. He's called it good riddance and quits, enough.

Writer is pretty much tempted to quit writing.
Writer is weary unto death of making up stories. (Markson, 2001: 1)

Or so begins David Markson's *This Is Not a Novel*, which deconstructs our idea of the novel in order to give us – surprise, a novel! At the core of this collection of other writers' foibles and habits is a twinned lamentation at both the impossibility and the imperative of writing.

So how about you and what about me? What would the day look like if there wasn't any writing? We might wake up, I suppose, fry some eggs for breakfast, maybe take the dog for a walk (if we had a dog), clean out some drawers or weed some weeds (we do have drawers to clean and, if we're lucky, weeds to weed), do a little breathing meditation.

Unthinkable, we think, no writing.

But we are not Virginia Woolf.

Counsel

I once had occasion to counsel a friend who had fallen in love with a woman not his wife but, newly in love then myself, I found myself dithering irresolutely, until, at last, he turned to me in rage: *I trusted you*, he probably said, *now's not the time to go ambivalent and dewy-eyed on me*. We talked for some time after that. Our terms were plain; our emotions, raw. His rage, his feeling of betrayal, was genuine. He'd wanted me to be his moral compass, but I was flawed, like anyone, and hadn't told him what he wanted to hear; I didn't even know what I should say.

Approaching this project, I've felt a bit as I did then – at a loss and, maybe, as ever, a bit of a fraud. For the longer I work at this business of creative writing scholarship, or theory, or just what Wendy Bishop used to call 'thinking systematically', the more plumb out of answers I feel. And in fact I've been trying for years to find a way to politely desist. Here, at least, I will become one of Vila-Matas' writers of 'the no'. I've said enough, I think. It's time, like Philip Roth, to stop.

But one thing and another, I say yes when I mean no.

Therefore, permit me, if you will, a rant.

Like others in this volume, I've been at this long enough that it's impossible not to look back, to review what I have said and done, to reassess. Is it true I wore socks with that sack-like dress from Berkeley at the first (and last) AWP pre-conference pedagogy workshop I co-led with Wendy Bishop and Sandra Alcosser in 1993? Did we really want to change everything and all at once? Whose speech did I think we were disrupting anyway? When did I grow old?

During these years as I've been growing old, the Creative Writing world has changed, but not in ways we called for when we were starting out and certainly not in ways we could even have imagined then. My father, for example, was dismayed when I chose to study writing at Stanford (in 1975): don't you think, he said, we might be training a few too many creative writers in this country? Oh Daddy, I think now, how prophetic you were, for look at us now, we have become legion. These days, everyone's a writer. Shouldn't you be thinking about writing your memoirs?

So at least part of this story has to do with how much – and how little – has changed. Consider, for example, that old bailiwick of graduate versus undergraduate students. They're not the same, we clamored, they're not the same, you can't treat them the same. We went on like this with a kind of fervor as if – *as if* – no one had ever noticed before. And maybe they had and maybe they hadn't, but we were still splashing around in some fairly small ponds. The world was not yet our oyster.

Now, the AWP (the Association of Writers and Writing Programs, an organization whose annual conference has grown more than 10-fold in these same years of my growing old) has an official set of hallmarks and guidelines for some five different types of writing programs, beginning with the MFA and low-residency programs and including, in this order, the BFA or undergraduate major, the undergraduate minor and, finally, the two-year college programs. (Conspicuously missing: the MA and PhD, the two degrees I hold, but that may only be conspicuous to me.) Here, it's notable that these undergraduate guidelines begin with the disclaimer that few undergraduate students will go on to 'professional literary careers' and they clearly stipulate that the pedagogical practices appropriate for graduate and undergraduate students will be very different.

It was no single voice that brought this about, but all of ours together. The most self-evident part of what might once have counted as a platform now enacted as official policy. This is progress, yes, but is it change?

A closer look at those same hallmarks reveals a stubbornly conventional approach to the literary arts that includes the following praxes and objectives:

> … reading and critical analysis of canonical and contemporary works of literature; practice in integrating the strategies of literary models, especially through isolating a specific craft technique to achieve a particular effect; practice in writing original poems, stories, creative nonfiction, or plays; and peer review of student writing in discussions moderated by the instructor. Students study literature 'from the outside' as readers and critics and 'from the inside' as writers of their own works.

So even if our students are not destined to be writers, we're still treating them as if we hope they might be, an observation that becomes even more pronounced when we consider the also recommended corollary curriculum of tiered workshop (a minimum of four), craft classes and thesis production that is generally consistent with pre-professional training. Maybe the language has changed, but the gig has not: what we're supposed to be doing is teaching, more or less, some passing familiarity with what might look like North American literary writing, along with some basic skills for reproducing it. The same stuff, really, if a little watered down.

And those core assumptions persist even more perniciously at the graduate level, where the hallmarks state that the 'general goal for a graduate program in creative writing is to nurture and expedite the development of the literary artist', by providing 'an enabling progression of both practice and study in the literary arts in order to prepare the student for a life of letters and to equip the student with the skills needed for writing a publishable book-length creative work for the thesis'.

That's what they told me at Stanford, in 1975, and then again at Utah five years later: for your thesis/dissertation, they said, you will produce a 'manuscript of publishable literary quality'. I'm pretty sure they said 'produce' and not 'write', as if writing itself were beside the point, as if I were merely a means of production, which I suppose I am. But I am also a writer, as in a person who writes, and I don't think anything was said back then about what that might mean and be. Between now and then, the focus on *publishability* (whatever that means) remains among the most persistent of our tenets. And while I don't mean to suggest I'm against publishing, which I've pursued as avidly as anyone, (just for what it's worth) I'd like to try out the concept that a life of sustainable literary practice – both reading and writing – may well be incompatible with the end goal of a 'publishable literary manuscript'.

Today, one of my fiction colleagues is a mainstream New York City type, all about agents and 'selling' (even when the places where he places his work pay him nothing for it); another, a radical experimental small-press kind of guy with a genuine affection and enthusiasm for the kind of community fostered by such presses. These two models – one of narcissistic competition, the other of energized collaboration – are well known in today's writing world. And it's hard to argue with either. This is what students *want*; isn't it what students *want*? But all of us know that most of our students aren't destined to publish, maybe one or two a year, maybe a handful. Out of hundreds; over the years, thousands.

This is heartbreaking for students, and for the discipline itself it presents an ethical dilemma of significant proportions, for it says that a particular educational practice consistently sets students up for failure. But it is also bad for writing. There are many versions of this story, from McPoetry to MFA fiction, but here is one from George Saunders himself:

> the perception of homogeneity [may be a] function of the fact that, as CW programs expand so that every town has fifteen of them, more average writers are being let in ... and so what we are really seeing is a bunch of average writers doing what average writers are supposed to do, which is write average. It might also be possible that, in any generation, there are only about two writers who are really great anyway, and it takes time to sort that out, and meanwhile the books keep flying off the presses. (Saunders, 2014: 32)

And herein lies a core of my own ambivalence, for my own dissertation adviser, François Camoin, used to tease me by calling me an elitist in the arts, which drove my hackles up. Later, a student – who was herself a progressive, political activist – described me as the most democratic person she had ever met, which I found profoundly flattering. It's true, what François used to say, that I tend, in my reading, toward texts that are strange, difficult and complex – that aspire toward 'greatness'. But I don't think we're producing average writers in our programs because all the programs and all the writers are average, but because we are parsimonious in our expectations of them and because our own publication fetish promotes principles of – to borrow an old distinction from Barthes – 'readable' over 'writeable' text. So it's always worth reminding ourselves – and our students – of what Virginia Woolf wrote somewhere in her journals:

> I will not be 'famous', 'great'. I will go on adventuring, changing, opening my mind and my eyes, refusing to be stamped and stereotyped. The thing is to free one's self: to let it find its dimensions, not be impeded.

Still, just the other night, I found myself at a dinner party where a new game was invented in which people called out names of dead musicians they admired and others called out 'genius' or 'talent'. I think this was supposed to be fun. But the very idea of 'genius' works in insidious ways to constrain the rest of us (think *Moby Dick* and me), and surely there's a middle path where our ideas of what is possible – what is *necessary* – in writing may instead be generous and expansive. And surely it is possible that creative writing in the 21st century may find a space where such a middle path is clear.

I think that.

And then I don't know what to think, so I don't think anything at all.

Success

When creative writing attached itself to the tug and pull of the marketplace and succumbed to its own commodification, it lost a little bit of what we might once have called its soul. It's also very possible that the hyper-professionalization that has afflicted the entire academy in recent years has been particularly bad for us.

But what I told my worried father in 1975 about my future in it was that if I didn't 'succeed' by the time I was 30, I'd give it up and go to chef school, maybe start a rice and beans restaurant in Berkeley. Fortunately for the culinary world, my idea of 'success' did not extend far beyond publishing a story in a small magazine on the far other side of the country where someone I knew knew someone. Before long I would be discovering what failure, by contrast, looked like instead: like the handful of young men and women I knew who'd already given up writing because they had not been launched, young, into high-profile publishing careers.

In both models, what determines the idea, and experience, of 'success' or 'failure' lies beyond our own control in the complex system of what Foucault would call 'limitations and exclusions' that governs literary publication in America – in other words, a crap shoot. I know I'm not supposed to say so. I'm supposed to say instead, as I did when I was young, that if the writing was good, if you were persistent enough, it would find its way into the world. Later, I'd embrace the idea that every book has a thousand readers, adapted from a book I didn't read and whose title and author I've forgotten – just the idea, as a friend explained it to me, that in today's world we should celebrate, not lament, diminished readerships because a reader is a reader and every reader counts and, anyway, there are more books to go around. These days, it's easy for students to make their own books, but arguably harder to find any readers at all – because there are more books to go around. I'm just trying to suggest how counterproductive a creative writing pedagogy based on the imprimatur of others may be. If we want our students to write – if we value the writing itself – it's time (past time) to reframe our basic thinking about what it is we do – both on the page and in our classrooms – and why we do it.

Let's begin with the principle that a person never simply speaks/writes, but that there has to be a context in which a person feels privileged to speak/write – a virtual light bulb of sudden enlightenment in my own graduate school training – when, by George, all along, I'd thought the deficiency was me. But if I'd found Melville inhibiting, imagine the experience of our students when their worlds intersect with ours. Over the years, I have relied heavily on Linda Brodkey's concept of the 'modernist scene of writing', in which the Great (Male) Author sits Alone in His Attic Garrett furiously Writing by the Light of a Thin Gray Candle – that, or any other idealized scene of writing students might have adopted along the way – to help them confront their own grouchy ladybugs (Carle, 1999), who will always be there taunting, 'oh you, you're not big enough', as in you're not *good* enough, not *you*. I have also worked a lot with Mary Louise Pratt's 'Arts of the contact zone' and her ideas about autoethnography, which are powerfully transferable to creative writing classes (Pratt, 2008). My objective was straightforward – I wanted to introduce students to ways of thinking about writing that would empower them to make writing itself a lifelong practice, a little like yoga, I think now, but I could not think that then because I was still rolling my eyes at yoga.

I became, in other words, a fierce champion of writing itself. I'm not sure I thought it mattered what students wrote, as long as they were writing something. I was, and remain, a great fan of Henry Miller's book *Paint as You Like and Die Happy*. I believed – and believe – in the value of this practice and was utterly convinced that the various silences I'd seen my fellow writers falling into were a grievous loss. For years, my implacable conviction in the enduring value of writing took the form of rejecting the workshop, which I saw as normative and reductive. I was all about process back then. I didn't yet know how to look at Miller's book and think 'Yes, but that doesn't make me a painter'.

Still, I hardly even noticed when all that started shifting and, a few years in to this 'writing only' project (and nearly 20 years ago) I started to worry all over again about content and craft, beyond the narratology I taught. Of course, the world was changing too. Higher education was becoming a consumer-driven site of job skill development and pre-professional training, which writing itself, along with its attendant skills – systematic reading, painstaking craft, revision – aligned nicely with.

Then one day, the world changed, and although this is a story I have never told before, the day after 9/11, I got up, like most of us, and drove to work and stood before a class of creative writing students – not one of whom was absent – who looked to me to explain to them, now what? I don't tell this story because I don't really remember it, what I said to those students that day, not the way I remember the sound of my former husband's voice as he'd called me to the TV just the day before, or the stillness of my middle school son beside me as we watched. We all did this, if we were lucky: moved back into our daily lives, where everything was both the same and different. And maybe not right away, but soon enough, we found ourselves facing the question about what writing could possibly be or mean in this whole new millennium where we now found ourselves.

'Nothing', art critic Linda Nochlin says, 'is more interesting, more poignant, and more difficult to seize than the intersection between self and history' (Nochlin, 2000: 31).

The novel, Mikhail Bakhtin tells us, is the only 'ever-developing' genre because it takes place in a 'zone of contact with the present in all its open-endedness' (Bakhtin, 1988: 53).

It's easy to forget this in the busyness of daily life. Creatures of routine and habit, we fret and seek out small pleasures and comforts; we watch TV. But when an event comes along, to borrow from Grace Paley, to 'jolt or appraise us', if we are to take a good hard look at that interstitial space between history and the open-ended present, we may find that we '*can take some appropriate action*' after all (Paley, 2007: 131).

In every class there comes a moment when I ask what no one ever asked of me: I ask the 'why' of it, I ask the 'what are you doing here anyway' of it, I ask the 'what is the doing of the thing we are doing' of it. Almost without exception, it's an uneasy moment – aren't I the one who's supposed to have answers for them? Students need this class to graduate; they're here – that's not enough? I don't know for poetry, but those of us in fiction come to it, by whatever circuitous paths, out of a love for the story, but stay – if we stay – for the love of the sentence. This is the root of the both/and practice that can keep us honed to the ever-evolving craft of writing. I use the word 'craft' here as Stephanie Vanderslice recently posted it in the burgeoning Facebook creative writing pedagogy forum, where she was quoting Marjory Zoet Bankson (the post itself was quoted by Shannon, 2013):

> According to the OED, the original meaning of craft is 'strength,' 'force,' 'power,' and 'virtue.' In German and Swedish, *kraft* moves beyond 'strength' into 'force of character.' In Dutch, *kracht* implies 'vigor' and 'potency.' It is only in English that there is the association of 'craft' with 'skill.' What if we were to shift our view of 'craft' from being a skill for a few to being a sign of the inner life force in each of us. (Bankson, 2008: xxii–xxiii)

As uneasy as I may be myself with the language of an 'inner life force', it seems I may have sensed this all along, or something like it, for years ago I wrote:

> As a writer, when I came to experience myself not as an 'owner/ creator' but as a kind of locus where language and stories simultaneously occurred, I learned to know another self, constructed in the act of writing, who

nurtures all my other selves. Writing thus became an organizing principle of my identity and a primary experience that is at least of equal value to whatever I produce. (Haake, 2000: 32)

I am reminded also of the phenomenon of 'ostension', at least as Tim Mayers describes Paul H. Fry's construction of it in *(Re)Writing Craft*, in which 'the act of writing occasionally hurls the writer (and by extension the reader) into an ontologically prehermeneutic realm – a "place" where there is no meaning, only existence' (Mayers, 2007: 117). Notably, Mayers does not debate the merits of this position, but does acknowledge that 'Fry may be attempting to articulate something about writing for which there is no room, and no language, within interpretive literary study' (Mayers, 2007:118).

Or, as ever, of Calvino:

... it is the childish delight at combinatorial play that induces the painter to try out patterns of lines and colors and the poet to attempt combinations of words. At a certain stage something clicks, and one of the combinations obtained by its own mechanisms, independently of any search for meaning or effect on some other level, takes on an unexpected sense or produces an unforeseen effect that consciousness could not have achieved intentionally. (Calvino, 1986: 19)

'Then sentence by sentence', Don DeLillo (1993) tells us in a *Paris Review* interview with Adam Begley, 'into the breach'.

Or Trihn Minh-Ha's distinction between 'writing about the self' and 'writing the self' (Trinh, 1989: 28).

Or letting go and kicking up in yoga, as effortless as if you were a bird.

For myself, I like to think that what happens in the act of writing when we are really writing is we that we somehow slip into some interstitial space between being and meaning that can't be either closed or traversed but that enables us to be as wholly present as we can be in these bodies on this planet. I think this is what Lacan calls the 'suture', but that's a lot of theory. More theory of enduring value includes Barthes' writing as an 'intransitive act', or Derrida's elegant demonstration that, the center not being the center, 'coherence in contradiction expresses the force of a desire' (Derrida, 1988: 109).

All of the above – and so much more – remains the lure of writing, that takes us by surprise and takes us up and hurls us somewhere outside ourselves, outside even meaning. Over the years, students have described this in various ways: like stepping off a cliff or taking off their training wheels, like jazz improvisation when you finally let go and let wail.

Naturally, you can't *will* this. You can only *earn* it through the hard – the very hard – daily work of *writing*, of honing yourself to the word.

Dream

Not long ago I had a dream in which I faced a terrible choice. In the dream there was something of enormous importance (possibly another dream) I had to tell my friend, but found myself constrained by language, for in the dream, only two existed. In the first, I'd have had the ability to achieve extraordinary eloquence, that would, however, be entirely devoid of any meaning; in the second, to express exactly what it was that I intended, but be utterly unintelligible to others. Stymied by this paradox, a third option was dance, and so awkwardly, tentatively, I raised my arms and began to spin before my friend, who watched with compassionate eyes, but whether they were comprehending or not, I couldn't say.

The friend in this dream lives several states away, but visits twice a year to teach in a local low-residency writing program. When she visits, we walk. Recently, on such a walk, she asked me to describe my spiritual practice. I think that was the word she used, 'describe'.

Describe, she said, your spiritual practice.

Not surprisingly, just as in my dream, I felt myself seized by a sudden panic, so I cast about dumbly for her. I don't know, I delayed. What do you mean, 'spiritual'?

But what I was thinking was something about connectedness that reaches out beyond our selves, which can happen any time, with no warning. Just yesterday, for example, I drove the length of California's Central Valley stunned into greenness by El Niño rains at last. It's the end of February and a warm and temporarily benevolent sun filled this greenness with a dreamy light and all the orchards were in bloom. The same clutch of co-extensiveness with the world can surprise you at any time – in a banal moment of unguarded exchange with a clerk who is suddenly human, when you're listening to music and time disappears, in *savasana*.

But I didn't think that's what my friend was talking about. I thought she meant something more ritualized, maybe like my mother, who gets up every morning to a half-hour prayer of gratitude. My mother's 94. She wrote the prayer herself. I don't know how she thought to do so – she never prayed before.

But then my friend suggested it might be something as purely human as reaching out to the lowest among us – to homeless men and women – not just with money, but with conversation, compassion – a story.

Yes, I said. I think I get that.

Even so, I still sometimes try to imagine myself like Philip Roth.

Yes, it's true, I would announce with some relief, I am retiring. It was, I might say, a good enough run. I was painstaking and particular; I loved the sentence and filled the hours with what felt like a labor of value, although my former husband called it whiling, as in whiling away the time. Lah dee dah, he said. Right up there with bon-bons and soaps.

You have to do something, I said.

But however much I try to imagine letting sentences like water flow through my hands, I still open my computer every morning just as I still go to the wall in yoga, knowing that what sometimes eludes me there will remain the single most enduring desire of my life. I suppose that might be true of anyone.

It wasn't my father who worried about my plans for PhD school, which followed my MA by nearly five years, but the man who was my lover at the time. This man, a painter, would work all day and would then hold up his new painting next to a piece of art he loved by a great artist. He'd study the two of them together, looking for what he called a kind of humming, and if he didn't find it he'd tear his day's work up and fix himself a drink.

Don't go to graduate school, he warned me. Graduate school will ruin you.

Reader, I went to graduate school. (I wonder: am I ruined?)

While there, I insisted I would never be a teacher.

I became a teacher.

One day the world changed.

Not long after that, two of my closest friends would die young, still in their 50s.

And then, some more years later, another close friend would challenge me to describe my spiritual practice.

I didn't know it when she asked. Or I knew it but I didn't want to say it, or I didn't know how to say it, but after all of that, it turns out what we do – and therefore what we teach – is neither process nor content, neither story nor writing, humanity nor art – these are all false binaries anyway – but both. Like the two sides of a piece of paper, the semiotic sign, or a bonsai (which, it turns out, is both plant and pot), you can't take them apart, but they are different. A long time ago when I was new and starting out, I seized upon Derrida's logic of supplementarity as precisely what it was, what he called it: a logic of writing. As a young woman I fixed writing in this very same force of its Derridean desire, and of course, to some extent, I still do. But more and more, I think of it, also, as the force of a discipline too.

And it's a discipline that far transcends the beautiful sentencing of the world.

A current student, in her 50s and a survivor of a traumatic brain injury, has concluded that her life has no meaning, at least not any that would be of interest to anyone else. Still, she writes, because, as she writes: 'I still feel there is value in attempting to contradict the knowledge that my life has no meaning by constructing a puzzle that is complicated and interesting enough to distract me from that knowledge.'

'In that sense, then', South African poet Breyten Breytenbach (2009: 64) tells us, 'writing is always against death, obliteration, extinction, and non-writing. But writing is also a way of situating yourself in the world we inhabit', which is, as Marcus Aurelius wrote more than 2000 years ago, a 'living being – one nature, one soul. Keep that in mind. And how everything feeds into that single experience moves with a single motion. And how everything helps produce everything else. Spun and woven together' (Aurelius, 2003: 40).

Or a beautiful puzzle.

Which is just to remind us that our lives do matter, after all, even if they just amount to the solving of puzzles. A puzzle is a beautiful thing. The world is a puzzle; a word is a puzzle. The word takes us into the puzzle of us and back out to us.

Grace

This essay has proven to be a tremendous challenge to me. I should have known it would be. I should, as I've long promised myself, have politely declined.

Basta, I could just as well have said.

The idea to write about writing as a spiritual practice came to me instead because I knew at some level that's what I wish I had said to my friend.

'But isn't that what writing is?', I should have asked. Maybe the practice of being aware and present as often as possible is not dependent on writing, but is enabled by it. And writing, in and of itself, is also just such a form of attention – what Breytenbach (2009: 113) calls an 'awareness-enhancing process'.

At another level, I only intuited this, only vaguely sensed it might have something to do with creative writing in the 21st century. But because I was interested to see what I meant, I said yes to writing this essay instead of no. Then the puzzle became a terrible knot. I knew what I knew – I knew something, I *felt* it. But its resistance to articulation was both stubborn and profound. We have all been there – oh well, tra la. I gave it up, wrote something else, considered withdrawing from this project. If I couldn't bring myself to speak of spiritual things to the woman who is among my closest friends, whatever made me think I could espouse some public views? I don't even *like* the term 'life force'. I am a hapless cynic.

And so I packed my bags and went to spend a week with my 90-something parents where, deep into one night in the room my sister slept in while we were growing up, I opened the book I'd brought with me on impulse – Clarice Lispector's *Near to the Wild Heart* – and came across this passage in Benjamin Moser's Introduction:

> This is the core of the fascination of … Clarice Lispector. It was not a matter of style versus substance, nor a simple question of emphasis, that separated her from [other] writers [of stylistic conformity] … it was a fundamentally different conception of art. In [*Near to the Wild Heart*] she summed up the impulse.... 'You see, vision consisted of surprising the symbol of the thing in the thing itself.' The remark was important enough for her to repeat it a hundred pages later – 'the symbol of the thing in the thing itself'– and was the heart of her entire artistic project.
>
> But as the phrase suggests, that project was less artistic than spiritual. The possibility of uniting a thing and its symbol, of reconnecting language to reality, and vice versa, is not an intellectual or artistic endeavor. It is instead intimately connected to the sacred realms of sexuality and creation. A word does not describe a pre-existing thing but actually *is* that thing, or a word creates the thing it describes: the search for that mystic word, 'the word that has its own light', is the search of a lifetime. That search was an urgent preoccupation of centuries of Jewish mystics. Just as God, in Clarice's writing, is utterly devoid of any moral meaning, so does language signify nothing beyond what it expresses: 'the symbol of the thing in the thing itself.' (Moser, 2012: xi–xii)

I'm not going to say I understand this in conventional biblical terms, but I am fairly certain it's what held my knot together, precisely because the knot was the thing itself. And I am also certain that this is what brings me back – and back – to the daily discipline of the page. For, as Breytenbach (2009: 89) has written, 'True works of art happen, I suspect, only when inner and outer come together. That's an important reason they're so rare'.

Long ago, when I first started out, I stubbornly rejected the teaching of my mentor, who insisted writing was not about thinking: don't think, he said, just write. I had something to *say* (that's not how it gets said); I thought writing served a higher moral or political purpose (that's not how service gets done). For it would take a long time for me to figure out writing is less about saying than it is about being.

This is how your purpose is revealed: you set your gaze – what yogis call your *drishti* – and then you write. Which is to say that you write intransitively: you become the writing, the thing, the thing and itself in all its splendid and terrible knottiness. I don't really expect students to accept this, never mind understand it – I hardly do myself – but I want them to worry about it so one day, far into the future, if they are still writing – I *hope* they're still writing – when they fall at last into language, they will remember enough to give themselves permission to continue into what Trinh Minh-Ha might call the coming into being of the structure of the moment. By which I don't mean to imply anything at all like what they think of as 'flow'. It's not automatic writing, stuff doesn't just pour out of you, the 'story' doesn't 'take over.' It is, instead, is a slow, painstaking, utterly attentive engagement with the word that requires years and years of disciplined practice to even to begin to take in enough so you can finally forget all about it and just write.

I think I've been writing around this concept for most of my professional life, but much of what I said before I couched in theoretical terms. Theory seemed both powerful and empowering to me, which it absolutely is. It's powerful, at least in part, because it provides us with a way to think and talk about what writing *is*, even as it helps us articulate the 'poetics' that Rachel Blau DuPlessis claims will give us 'permission to continue' (DuPlessis, 1990: 156). But it may also help that theory lets us sound smart and maybe gives us a chance to hang out with the cool kids. Even so, it brings us only to a close approximation. And the day is always coming when there will be no longer any need to sound smart or hang out with the cool kids.

One way I've written around this is to explore how part of what sustains writing for me is not the thing I'm making so much as it is the person I become when I am making it. In time, I came to think of this experience not as a person but as a space, the 'suture' I talked about above, adapted from Lacan and neither 'thing' nor 'symbol', but the space between. I didn't think that space could be resolved, but I did think – I *do* think – writing takes us into it and somehow obviates it. In this interstice, neither the 'thing' nor the 'symbol' exerts itself, maybe a little like the empty mind of yoga. I thought this – I *think* this – but it's different now: it's not about who I become but somehow about ceasing to be, which may also be described as the moment of connection with everything else.

My friend who asked me to consider my spiritual practice is Sharman Apt Russell, whose recent and very wonderful book *Standing in the Light* examines, among other things, current thinking in scientific pantheism, the essential premise of which is that the 'universe is an interrelated whole that deserves human reverence' (Russell, 2008: 12). No one agrees what this might mean or how we may observe it, only that the universe is singularly uninterested in us. But the more we know about it, the more complex it becomes, until complexity itself achieves the status of divinity.

Years ago, when I was among a core group of founding faculty in the Antioch Low Residency MFA program, I engaged in a six-month online dialogue with another founding faculty member, poet and Buddhist Peter Levitt. The internet was still new then, and our dialogue was public – an exhilarating exchange, in which on a nearly daily basis I wrote to him about theory and he wrote to me about Buddhism. At the end of the six months, when we reconvened with our students in LA, they clamored to explain to us that even though we both used different languages, we were each saying the same thing.

Yes, I said, it's the same. But only to the extent to which we were each struggling to articulate – to describe with language – a thing that, while made out of language, eludes description precisely because it is language itself. And I think Moser is right to suggest that difference between theoretical – or aesthetic – and spiritual thinking, at least in this regard, is that each proceeds from a fundamentally different conception of art.

So let's imagine, for a moment, that Moser is right. Let's imagine a writing in which language signifies 'nothing beyond what it expresses: "the symbol of the thing in the thing itself"'. In lieu of writing as an interstitial space held together by the contradictorily coherent force of the desire that it should – i.e. language – we may think of it instead as the space where no such split exists, the split that is not a split – i.e. language. In such a construction – then the person we become – or cease to be – when we are really writing, the person 'in the suture', is nothing more or other than a person in prayer. Maybe this is a kind of ostension – a hurling out of self and meaning – but I think it's more like a rock. A rock, like the planet itself, contains all its layers in one and simply is.

Like the stone in W.S. Merwin's 'Tergvinder's stone', the rock sits in the center of our living rooms, and like Tergvinder ourselves, we may awaken at night and visit the stone in the middle of our house. When we do, let's hope we, too, can be like Tergvinder, himself, who 'knows its size, its weight, the touch of it, something of what is thought of it. He knows that it is peace. As he listens, some hint of that peace touches him too. Often, after a while, he steps down into the living room and goes and kneels beside the stone and they converse for house in silence – a silence broken only by the sound of his own breathing' (Merwin, 2007: 15).

They say breathing is the most important thing in yoga.

And this, too – this *breathing* – is writing.

I'm not sure what all this has to do with teaching, although I suspect it's as much what brings me back to the classroom as it is what brings me back to the page.

Therefore, let 21st-century creative writing proceed from a fundamentally different conception of art, rooted in the practice of the word and the principle that this practice belongs to all of us. In such a discipline, we may recuperate some of what's been lost of what I called above our soul. And maybe what I had to grow old to discover about what I may always have known is how little this practice shares with public recognition, how intimately it invokes connection. Either way, I think I am convinced that if a sustainable literary practice (AWP's 'life of letters') is even achievable – if we are all not to become writers of 'the no' – the shift occurs here, in our conception of art and what and why we're doing it when we are making it. And I think it's worth at least acknowledging as much in the work that lies ahead, both for us and for the students we will stand before and teach.

That's all I know. I wish there were more, but there's not.

Except maybe for this:

As a girl, I used to wander the outer reaches of my schoolyard below where the others played, looking for just the right stone, or boulder, to sit on. I can't say quite how I would know it but somehow I did. Just, there it would be – the rock, on which I would sit, lay my hand upon its gritty surface, set my gaze upon a distant hill or peak, and fall into what I can only now call the natural meditative state in which I spent most of my childhood. Like the indigenous peoples of this continent who believed that wherever you planted your feet marked the exact center of the earth, or the yogi whose strongly rooted stance sends rising energy up through body, heart and mind – or the writing writer – so much depends on the planting of feet – pen – which, like the stone, find their place on this earth.

Sometimes, in final resting pose – when we most approximate the stone – after a particularly present yoga practice in which everything I've just told you has ceased to mean anything at all, I find myself getting lost in the cosmos, a word I have never used lightly, and especially not since being scolded by a noted cosmologist that my way of thinking is bad for the planet. Nonetheless, at deepest rest I am like the stone hurled through the air on the reverberant sound of Tibetan drums and soon am lost and swirling in the darkness of the universe above. Everything's connected then, breath to moon to galaxy, and even if all this is just a tiny fraction of everything there is, now that I know that, as vast as it is, I am myself composed of those exact same structures, what else can I do in final resting pose other than swirl?

And this – all this – will have to be enough.

References

Aurelius, M. (2003) *The Meditations* (trans. G. Hays). New York: Modern Library.
Bakhtin, M.M. (1988) Epic and novel. In M.J. Hoffman and P. Murphy (eds) *Essentials of the Theory of Fiction* (pp. 48–69). Durham, NC: Duke University Press.
Bankson, M.Z. (2008) *Soulwork of Clay: A Hands-On Approach to Spirituality*. Woodstock, NY: Paths Publishing.
Breytenbach, B. (2009) *Intimate Stranger. Brooklyn*. New York: Archipelago.
Calvino, I. (1986) Cybernetics and ghosts. In *The Uses of Literature: Essays* (trans. P. Creagh) (pp. 3–27). San Diego, CA: Harcourt.
Carle, E. (1999) *The Grouchy Ladybug*. New York: Harper Festival.
DeLillo, D. (1993) The art of fiction, no. 135. *Paris Review* 128. Available at http://www.theparisreview.org/interviews/1887/the-art-of-fiction-no-135-don-delillo (accessed June 2017).
Derrida, J. (1988) Structure, sign and play in the discourse of the human sciences. In D. Lodge (ed.) *Modern Criticism and Theory: A Reader* (pp. 107–123). New York: Longman.
DuPlessis, R.B. (1990) *The Pink Guitar: Writing as Feminist Practice*. New York: Routledge.
Haake, K. (2000) *What Our Speech Disrupts: Feminism and Creative Writing Studies*. Urbana, IL: NCTE.
Markson, D. (2001) *This Is Not a Novel*. Berkeley, CA: Counterpoint Press.
Mayers, T. (2007) *(Re)Writing Craft: Composition, Creative Writing, and the Future of English Studies*. Pittsburgh, PA: University of Pittsburgh Press.
Merwin, W.S. (2007) *The Book of Fables*. Port Townsend, WA: Copper Canyon Press.
Moser, B. (2012) Hurricane Clarice. In C. Lispector, *Near to the Wild Heart* (pp. vii–xii). New York: New Directions.
Nochlin, L. (2000) Of self and history: Exchanges with Linda Nochlin. *Art Journal* 59 (3), 18–43.
Paley, G. (2007) *The Collected Stories of Grace Paley*. New York: Farrar, Straus and Giroux.
Pratt, M.L. (2008) Arts of the contact zone. In D. Bartholomae and A. Petroksky (eds) *Ways of Reading: An Anthology for Writers* (8th edition) (pp. 440–460). New York: Bedford Books.
Russell, S.A. 2008 *Standing in the Light: My Life As a Pantheist*. New York: Basic Books.
Saunders, G. (2014) A mini-manifesto. In *MFA vs NYC: The Two Cultures of American Fiction* (pp. 31–40). New York: N+1/Faber and Faber.
Shannon, M.O. (2013) *Crafting Calm: Projects and Practices for Creativity and Contemplation*. Jersey City, NJ: Viva Editions.
Trinh, T. (1989) *Minh-ha. Woman, Native, Other: Writing, Postcoloniality, and Feminism*. Bloomington, IN: Indiana University Press.
Vila-Matas, E. (2004) *Bartleby & Co.* (trans. J. Dunne). New York: New Directions.

3 We Serve Writing Here

Tim Mayers

Our task is to change creative writing in the US.

How do we do this?

We change creative writing in the US by changing some of the ways in which we *think* about creative writing. We change creative writing by asking why and how it has become what it is (that is, by investigating its history) and by evaluating whether or not past practices are worth continuing. We change creative writing by refusing to allow the static features of writing to blind us to writing's dynamic underlying potential. We change creative writing by thinking of ourselves, in our teacherly roles, not as guardians of propriety but rather as guides to experience. We change creative writing by seeing ourselves as working in service to writing, more so than we are working in service to writers.

What does all this mean?

Let me begin with two scenes, set more than a quarter century apart.

Scene 1

Spring semester, 1990
I sit in a small auditorium, listening to a well known poet read from his work. The university where I am in my final semester of an MA program in creative writing (and hoping to continue on into its PhD program in creative writing) is conducting a job search for a poet who will teach graduate and advanced undergraduate poetry workshops. The search committee has identified four finalists for the position, and each finalist visits campus for an interview that includes (among other things) a workshop with graduate students and a public reading. I watch the third of four candidates read a selection of his poems. He has published three books of poems at this point in his career, two of which have won major prizes. In prestigious literary journals, he has published nearly a hundred individual poems. The other three candidates have credentials similar to his; arguably, two of them are even more accomplished. He reads his poems in a clear, practiced voice. The audience is deeply engaged.

But an uneasy thought intrudes upon my enjoyment of the reading: Three of these candidates are not going to get the job. Three of them. Three poets who between them have published at least ten books and who have won a slew of national and international prizes for their poetry are not going to make the cut: Are. Not. Going. To. Get. This. Job. I try to focus my attention back on the reading, but the thought haunts me. I have not published anything – at least not outside of my high school and undergraduate college literary magazines. Out of the countless poems I've written, I have perhaps a dozen (based on positive commentary from my workshop professors and classmates) that I believe are 'publishable' in national literary magazines and journals, if I can find the right editor at the right time. But I know how gut-wrenching and time-consuming a process this can be. I've gotten a couple of pleasant and encouraging notes from journal editors, along with a small collection of form rejection letters, but no publications yet.

I keep thinking. Let's suppose I get admitted to the creative writing PhD program – either at the institution I'm at (where admission is highly competitive and teaching assistantships even more so) or one of the others to which I've applied – and, along with completing all the coursework, the exams and dissertation, and teaching courses as a graduate TA, I manage to get a bunch of poems published. Let's suppose I'm even fortunate enough to get a book of poems published, which I know is highly unlikely given the time frame in which I would like to finish the PhD. Then what? Will that be enough to qualify me for the kind of full-time academic work I aspire toward? And even if it does qualify me for that kind of work, what sort of competition will I face? I want to be a practicing, publishing creative writer. I also want to be a college or university professor. Is that kind of future even possible? I begin to wonder.

Scene 2

AWP convention, April 2016

I sit in the audience at an AWP convention panel focused on whether or not it is a good idea for creative writers to pursue the PhD degree as a means of seeking a full-time academic career. Unlike most members of the audience, I am not attending the panel in order to decide for myself whether entering a PhD program is a good option or not. I have had a PhD – in composition and rhetoric, not creative writing, which I earned eight years after the event described in Scene 1 – and a full-time academic position for almost two decades. Instead, I am attending this panel because I am interested (partly because of what I described in Scene 1) in the professional issues and questions surrounding creative writing in the academy. The panelists offer a range of excellent perspectives on how such a momentous decision can be approached; they outline reasons in favor of beginning a PhD program as well as reasons opposed to it. Better still, they offer the audience a detailed sense of what to expect in various kinds of PhD programs, including those focused solely on creative writing and those that combine creative writing with scholarly literary study. Although they do not agree on every particular point, the panelists do share a consensus that pursuing doctoral study is the right decision for some creative writers, the wrong decision for others, that it is not a path to be undertaken without serious prior reflection, and that the PhD is not a guarantee of full-time academic employment.

Near the end of the panel's allotted time, during a brief question-and-answer session, one of the panelists says, 'One thing to remember is that if you earn a PhD and have a full-time academic career, you'll spend a lot of time reading other people's work. You'll spend a lot of time correcting their grammar.'

On the one hand, these two scenes seem separated by an almost incomprehensibly large gap of time, learning, questioning and lived experience. On the other hand, they seem linked by the simple reality that creative writing in academia is beset by significant professional issues and problems, especially for graduate students wondering where they will go and what they will do once they finish their degrees, and for undergraduates wondering if graduate study in creative writing is a desirable or viable path. One of those issues is that creative writing courses and programs are most often housed in English departments, and that English departments (for better or worse) are places where the work of 'correcting people's grammar' is expected to take place. It's such a simple insight. But in academia – and especially within English departments – nothing is ever simple.

A little more than 25 years after Scene 1 took place, I look back on it as a key moment for me – but one among many, not necessarily *the* key moment. My choice to weave it into this chapter may confer a narrative weight greater than the moment deserves, or may deny narrative weight to other moments I could have chosen instead. But that moment is nonetheless one that has remained with me all these years. That moment continues to shine forth in its clarity because it was one of the first times I not only knew but also *felt* that the changing realities of the academic world might make it impossible to have a career in academia as a creative writer according to the traditional rules of that game. At the time, I had only the vaguest sense of *why this was*. Yet I wanted to figure that out, and in some ways the intervening years have been an ongoing process of doing just that.

Scene 2, on the other hand, is perhaps only one of the more recent repetitions of a scene that has happened over and over again, not only to me but to almost anyone who has taught English at any level in the United States. In the public mind, the enforcement of proper grammar rules is one of the most – if not the most – important things English departments are supposed to do. An old joke among English teachers goes something like this: *I met someone new yesterday, and when they found out I am an English teacher, they said, 'Oh, I guess I'd better watch my grammar around you.'*[1] As professionals, we may lament that part of our identity, or embrace it with enthusiasm or with resignation or even bitterness. But it is one of the realities we face, whether we teach creative writing or composition or literature. For those trained in composition studies, as I am, a professional identity as a grammar checker and corrector is something to be challenged, not so much so that it can be rejected but so that its meaning can be unpacked. And unpacking its meaning might, just might, help change the larger public's mind about what writing is and how it works. More on this point later. For now, I'd simply like to note that the focus on proper grammar is a focus on a static surface feature of written language. And static surface features of written language have a tendency – in the teaching of creative writing as well as the teaching of composition – to obscure the messy and dynamic experience of writing; to obscure the process, the struggle, the labor of writing; to obscure how writing happens.

Creative Writing: The State of the Art(s)

Few people reading this book, I imagine, would dispute that the situation of creative writing in the academy has changed dramatically over the past several decades. Creative writing faces a series of upheavals that, though distinct from each other in important ways, overlap enough that they cannot be considered purely in isolation from each other. These upheavals are social, technological, economic/institutional and ideological/aesthetic. Together, these upheavals call into question much of what creative writing has historically taken for granted, much of which had gone unquestioned for so long (or, when it was questioned, was dismissed). I hope that my descriptions of these upheavals here indicate some of the ways in which they overlap, how they form an interrelated complex.

In the social realm, groups of people traditionally marginalized – women, people of color, people of differing sexual orientations and identities, the disabled – have challenged their marginalization and invisibility, have advocated for a place in the world of creative writing, have questioned those definitions of 'literature' that traditionally excluded them and have exposed the practices of institutions (such as literary magazines and publishing houses, literary prize committees, MFA programs, and professional organizations like the AWP) that have intentionally and unintentionally fostered and sustained discrimination and exclusivity. These challenges have revealed that creative writing is not – and never was – a neutral practice of trying to produce 'good art'. Such art never exists entirely apart from the ideologies and institutions that sustain it.

In the technological realm, emerging technologies (understood here in the fairly straightforward sense of 'new tools') have changed the way writing is produced, exchanged and distributed. In some ways, this development has merely furthered some of creative writing's traditional practices and ideas (for example, by allowing traditional print journals and book publishers to offer readers digital 'copies' of print works, sometimes at reduced expense, thereby making literary work available to wider audiences). In other ways, this development has actively challenged some of creative writing's traditional practices and ideas (for example, by providing writers previously unavailable compositional modes and textual forms, such as digital hypertext and other multimodal possibilities not available in print, which have the potential to challenge and displace the traditional literary aesthetics and ideologies rooted in print technology). Hannah Sullivan, in her provocative book *The Work of Revision*, argues that the passion for revision articulated by so many of today's creative writers is fundamentally modernist in its orientation, and that it is inherited from early 20th-century writers for whom the available technologies allowed texts to be seen anew in successive forms: handwritten draft, typewritten draft and then page proof (Sullivan, 2013). Each of these successive forms seemed to invite writers to reconsider their texts – to change them, sometimes in significant ways. But our writing technologies in the early 21st century are different from those available to writers a century ago, and our perspective from this point in time allows us to realize that revision (or at least the specific ways in which we practice and think about it) is not a natural part of writing; it is inseparably tied up with and enabled by (though not entirely determined by) the technologies that allow and sustain it.

In the economic/institutional realm, the academic job market that sustained creative writing for roughly the middle third of the 20th century has largely collapsed. Its decline probably began in the 1970s and has dramatically accelerated since then. The influx of students into colleges and universities after the Second World War, and the brief boom in public university funding during the space race and the Cold War, are things of the past. At the same time, the college and university English departments that have most often provided creative writing courses, programs and faculty with an institutional home have themselves undergone a series of upheavals: the challenges to 'canonical' ways of organizing curricula via literary nationalities, time periods and major authors; the emergence of 'theory' as both a generative and a disruptive force; the development and growth of scholarly subfields like rhetoric and composition (now grown and developed enough that many would argue they should now more properly be called 'writing studies'), whose practitioners have striven for viability, visibility and curricular change; and increasing demands for 'accountability' and measurable academic outcomes by politicians and administrators who often seem to be ignorant of or hostile to academic values other than balance-sheet economics and job training. These developments have had an especially harsh impact on the teaching of composition, the one university course most likely to be taught by low-paid contingent instructors without job security or benefits. And many of these instructors are drawn from among the ranks of creative writers with MFA or PhD degrees.

In the ideological/aesthetic realm, the very ideas of what 'creative writing' and 'literature' are have been called into question. In the 1980s and 1990s, those who introduced variously new kinds of 'theory' into interpretive literary study often sought to unmask the ways in which literary works are not purely autonomous aesthetic objects, but are also implicated in systems of exclusion and oppression. Such inquiries have more recently been focused not only on the finished products of literary authors, but also on their compositional practices and the ways in which they are educated. For example, in *Workshops of Empire*, Eric Bennett argues that certain writing practices institutionalized and made to seem 'natural' in early creative writing workshops and programs, especially those administered by key figures like Paul Engle at Iowa and Wallace Stegner at Stanford, are in fact deeply implicated in politics (Bennett, 2015). The preference for concrete description over abstract theorizing in fiction and poetry, for example (which often takes the form of a 'show, don't tell' directive), is in Bennett's analysis tied up with an effort to employ literary production as one among many fronts in the Cold War ideological struggle between individualism and collectivism. An apparently natural and neutral aesthetic preference, then, is shown to be political also, even when – and perhaps especially when – it appears not to be political at all.

If we accept that all of these upheavals overlap, sometimes significantly, we may begin to see that it is possible to focus on one or two at the expense of the others, and thus be at the same time revolutionary and reactionary. To posit just a couple of examples: it is possible to be an advocate for writers belonging to previously marginalized groups but simultaneously to cling to traditional notions of what qualifies people for academic jobs in creative writing (such as print publication in prestigious journals and presses), thereby being attuned to changes in the social realm, but not in the economic/institutional realm. Likewise, it is possible to be an advocate for forms of writing engendered by emerging digital technologies while ignoring or dismissing how new forms may replicate or leave unquestioned discrimination against marginalized groups of people, thereby being attuned to changes in the technological realm but not in the social realm.

To complicate matters even further: while so many things have changed in academic creative writing, others have stayed the same; or, perhaps, people have labored mightily to keep them the same. The workshop, in spite of the many critiques that have been leveled against it, remains a popular and widespread pedagogical model. In many creative writing programs and courses, a preference for literary fiction (and an accompanying distaste for, or outright prohibition of, popular and genre fiction) remains firmly in place. Underneath all of this lies an assumption that, I would argue, has remained largely unchanged since MFA programs began to flourish in the first half of the 20th century and their graduates began to fan out across the US to found new programs and courses at both the graduate and undergraduate levels: namely, that *creative writing exists as an academic enterprise in order to serve individual writers*. For writers *as students*, this means that creative writing courses and programs serve to provide space and time for their development as writers, ideally leading to publication. For writers *as faculty*, this means that creative writing courses and programs serve to provide steady employment, which frees writers from certain kinds of financial worries, which in turn allows time for writing.[2] One of my major arguments in this chapter is that this assumption must be examined and challenged as creative writing – in its incarnation as an academic field – moves forward into the future. Creative writing must re-imagine itself as part of a larger project that primarily serves *writing* more so than it serves *writers*. It will serve writing by acknowledging that many common understandings of writing (of what writing is and how it works) are limited and limiting.

What does it mean to say that the academic field of creative writing currently serves writers more so than it serves writing? Consider the following passage by D.W. Fenza, addressing the state of creative writing in the academy, as he perceived it a few years ago:

> The composition theory-mongers can especially be relied upon for broadsides that seek to force writing programs to surrender their childish pirate flags; creative writing, they argue, needs to codify its pedagogy into something reasonable, systematic, and unified; the theory-mongers offer systems for doing this, of course, even though few of them themselves have published a wonderful book of fiction or poetry. In the academic professionalization of creative writing, there is always the danger that these academic scolds will supplant the poets, novelists, and short story writers. (Fenza, 2011: 212)

Fenza has spent many years as Executive Director of the AWP (Association of Writers and Writing Programs, originally founded as the Associated Writing Programs). He has a history of defending creative writers in the academy from perceived intrusions by people from other subfields of the English departments in which creative writing programs are usually housed. In the 1990s, he perceived a threat emanating from literary scholars and theorists; now, in the second decade of the 21st century, he appears to sense a threat coming from 'theory-mongers' from the field of composition and rhetoric.

My interest here is not so much with a point-by-point rebuttal of Fenza's grumpy mischaracterization of compositionists (which could easily occasion another entire essay) but rather with the unquestioned assumptions that seem to animate his argument. A careful reading of the passage above can tease out a sort of submerged moral position: an implied belief that things *ought to be* a particular way. Academic jobs in creative writing, Fenza appears to believe, rightfully belong to those who have 'published a wonderful book of fiction or poetry'. Secure employment at a college or university is a reward for having written well, and for having published that writing – a reward that the literary marketplace itself so often does not provide. D.G. Myers's widely cited history, *The Elephants Teach: Creative Writing Since 1880*, details how academic employment in the first half of the 20th century became increasingly more common – and increasingly more acceptable – for creative writers whose work was published and praised but (often due to the kinds of small niche audiences to which it appealed) did not provide enough income for a comfortable living (Myers, 1996). On one level, this kind of arrangement makes perfect sense: teachers of writing should themselves be practicing (and, ideally, publishing) writers. On another level, though, this kind of arrangement can be deeply problematic, if publication is assumed to be the *only*, or even the *primary*, qualification for teaching creative writing. There is a vast difference between believing that all teachers of creative writing ought to be practicing, publishing writers and believing that all practicing, publishing writers (and the more widely published, the better) will make good, or even adequate, teachers of creative writing. What seems to trouble Fenza most about the 'composition theory-mongers' is that some of their ideas – that perhaps writing experience alone does not make a great teacher, and that perhaps some great writers make terrible teachers, and that studying and theorizing pedagogy are just as important as publishing 'a wonderful book' – threaten the surrogate market that academic employment has offered a certain class of creative writers. In other words, what seems to trouble Fenza is that creative writing as an academic institution might be transformed so that it serves *writing*, as opposed to merely serving *writers*.

What Is Writing and How Does It Work? Lessons from Composition Studies

It should be clear from what I have written thus far that I believe creative writing in the academy needs to undergo a reorientation of purpose. In order to explain why such a reorientation of purpose is necessary, I will need to take a detour into the history of composition: one of the 'other' types of writing also taught in the academy.

In his majestic and cogent synthesis of many of the available histories of composition teaching at the college level in the US, David Fleming notes a particularly odd disjunction in the ways we tend to think about what writing is and how people learn to do it. According to one fairly prevalent conception, the ability to write well and clearly is a 'basic skill', relatively simple and straightforward, that should be taught and mastered during early years of schooling. When thought about in this fashion:

> [W]riting is simply the transcription of speech, itself merely the outward sign of interior ideas and impulses. Learning to write is thus little more

than learning the rules of graphic correspondence: how to produce and arrange the visible marks needed to represent one's meaning to non-present others. Such skill should be acquired early in one's schooling since it is mainly a mechanical, rather than an intellectual, accomplishment. (Fleming, 2011: 10)

On the other hand, and existing simultaneously, is a conception of writing (often associated with 'literary artists') that holds writing ability not as 'basic' or 'mechanical' but as fundamentally mysterious and impervious to analysis. Fleming explains how this coexistence of dueling and incompatible conceptions of writing has played out over the years in the public sphere:

> Learning to write, in other words, is either basic or wonderful, accessible to all or only a few, a matter of memorizing rules or of tapping into rare talents of expression. There appears to be no middle ground: no course of study stretched over time and leading to the gradual acquisition of a fluency that is schooled but within the reach of all. The set of assumptions that makes such a project unthinkable has served the interests of fluent adult writers because it mystifies their skill, enhancing its value even as it obscures its source. But it has distorted writing for everyone else, treating it as perfunctory, rule driven, and uninteresting. (Fleming, 2011: 10–11)

It would be tempting, and not entirely inaccurate, to claim that the first conception of writing (basic, mechanical, uncomplicated) has traditionally undergirded thinking about *composition* and how it ought to be taught, while the second conception of writing (mysterious, intellectually rich and so complex as to be virtually unteachable) has undergirded thinking about *creative writing*. Yet, as I have hinted at already and argue in more detail below, this distinction has rarely been quite so neat. The first conception of writing sometimes bleeds over into the realm of creative writing, just as the second conception sometimes bleeds over into composition. (Consider, for example, what I described in Scene 2 above: a creative writing professor warning those considering doctoral study that if they eventually find stable academic work, they will spend much of their time correcting other people's grammar.)

The 'middle ground' that Fleming claims has not existed between these two competing conceptions of writing can, in fact, be found. One could argue that countless versions of such a middle ground have been operating within the classrooms of isolated composition and creative writing teachers practically ever since those two subjects found their way onto college campuses. What hasn't really happened yet – at least not on any wide scale – is for those competing conceptions to be articulated and challenged for audiences outside the journals and presses that publish work by specialists in composition studies. What hasn't really happened yet is for the general public – and in this specific context, that includes wide swaths of those who work in academia – to be brought face to face with articulations of its (mis)conceptions about writing and to be challenged to reconcile the contradictions. What hasn't really happened yet is a large-scale attempt to help society at large work toward a revised conception of writing that might finally break the counterproductive cycle of literacy crisis after literacy crisis.

The beginnings of such work have been going on in composition scholarship for a little more than half a century now. Fleming and many other historians of composition note that *as a course required of nearly all first-year college students in the US*, composition has existed since around 1875, when it was instituted at Harvard. Yet *as a field of inquiry and scholarship*, composition *studies* did not come into being until eight or nine decades later. During the last quarter of the 19th century and roughly the first half of the 20th, composition was the major pedagogical responsibility of college and university English departments, but professors in those departments consistently asserted that interpretive literary study and scholarship constituted the rightful intellectual center of English studies. Teaching composition (in keeping with the simplistic and straightforward understanding of writing described above by Fleming) was understood to require no particular ability or training beyond simple familiarity with the conventions of standard written English.

By the middle of the 20th century, though, it was clear to at least a few people that the required college composition course had not solved the problems it was supposed to address. In 1953, a Purdue professor named Barriss Mills published a *College English* article called 'Writing as process'. At the time, Mills was a published poet and translator, chair of the College Section of the National Council of Teachers of English, and – like so many other English professors then and now – a teacher of composition. When the college composition course had been invented at Harvard around 1875, its originators thought it would serve as a temporary stopgap measure to address incoming students' perceived writing deficiencies and send a strong message to high schools and preparatory schools to improve their writing instruction. But the measure proved anything but temporary. By 1900, nearly all colleges and universities in the US had adopted a required first-year writing course, and that arrangement continues, with remarkably few exceptions, even today.

Perception of a 'literacy crisis' – that is, a sense that students do not read and write nearly as well as they should, and that a 'back to basics' approach to grammar and mechanics must be a key facet of addressing this deficit – has been a feature of American higher education virtually since the time, during the middle of the 19th century, when the means of assessing of students' learning began to shift away from oral exams and recitations and toward written work. Indeed, as Mike Rose (1989) points out, evidence of dire complaints about students' writing by professors and administrators can be traced back at least as far as the 1840s, and the complaints have continued virtually unabated since then. The 'literacy crisis' is not a new problem (though many continue to believe that it *is* new, allegedly brought on by new technologies that, detractors believe, weaken minds and shorten attention spans) and the required first-year university composition course has, for more than a century now, been one mechanism for managing that crisis.

Mills, writing more than 50 years after the inauguration of the college composition course, argued that the problem with students' writing could primarily be located in *the ways writing was taught*, and not so much with the deficiencies of the students themselves. Writing in school, according to Mills, was too often divorced from any underlying purpose (except to be assessed and evaluated) and, when evaluated, was regarded only as a *product* illustrating the students' deficiencies that needed to be corrected. Such problems were rooted in 'think[ing] of communication in terms that are static, atomistic, and non-functional. And such thinking will continue to produce unsatisfactory results' (Mills, 1953: 19). Mills offered a wide range of suggestions for writing teachers, arguing that 'purpose' ought to become the center of writing instruction and that virtually all aspects of the written product – including its generic form and the particular grammatical and mechanical rules followed – ought to be treated as subservient to purpose.

But it was not until at least a decade and a half after Mills's article was published that a significant movement toward thinking about – and teaching – 'writing as process' got underway. Available accounts differ about exactly when, where and how the 'movement' started, but noticeable strands of research emerged in the 1960s and pedagogical innovations gained traction in the early 1970s (some time 'Around 1971', in the words of Sharon Crowley).[3] For the purposes of my current argument, the pedagogical practices that came to the fore during the process movement (e.g. freewriting, brainstorming, peer editing groups) are less important than some of the research that was conducted, and what that research seemed to reveal, or at least had the *potential* to reveal, about writing.

Perhaps no single piece of published research better illustrates what the process movement potentially revealed about writing than Nancy Sommers' 'Revision strategies of student writers and experienced adult writers'. Published in 1980, this article centers mainly around a series of case studies Sommers performed over a three-year period (presumably during the mid- to late 1970s) comparing the writing processes of two groups: one consisting of 'student writers' from first-year composition courses at two different universities, and the other of 'experienced adult writers', more specifically 'journalists, editors, and academics ... from Boston and Oklahoma City' (Sommers, 1980: 380). The exigency for Sommers' study, by her own account, was that although significant research on writing processes had been done in the 1960s and 1970s, very little of it focused on *revision*, which Sommers operationally defined as '*a sequence of changes in a composition – changes which are initiated by cues and occur continually throughout the writing of a work*' (Sommers, 1980: 380, italics in original). Sommers found available models of revision inadequate, characterized by 'a theory of writing which makes revision both superfluous and redundant, a theory which does not distinguish between writing and speech' (Sommers, 1980: 379).

Sommers found significant differences between the revision practices of the two groups in her study. The student writers tended to retain the structures of their first drafts and to make changes only at the word level – scratching out one word and substituting a supposedly better one. The experienced adult writers tended to revise much more holistically – moving, removing or adding whole sections of text. But the most intriguing implications of Sommers' study for me has always been that experienced writers not only exhibit different revision practices than the students, but also that these different practices appear to reflect *an underlying understanding of writing – an implied definition – that differs fundamentally from the one the students have.* In other words, writing is a *different thing* for experienced writers than it is for students. Students seem to view the ideas they express as largely static, and as pre-existing the attempt to express them on a page. Thus, once a first draft is complete, the changes made remain on the surface level (the kind of thing experienced writers might call *editing* as distinguished from *revising*). The experienced adult writers, on the other hand, tend to see their ideas as (at least partially) *shaped* or *formed* or *discovered* by the process of trying to express them. One of the adult writers in Sommers' study said, 'In rewriting, I *find* the line of argument' (Sommers, 1980: 384, italics mine). This is not something that would have been said by any of the students in the study, for whom the line of argument was 'found' in their own minds prior to the composition of their first drafts.

One question Sommers does not address in her article (likely because it is beyond the purview of both her focus and her methodology) is where the experienced writers' view of writing originates. How did they acquire it? The experienced writers had once been students themselves, and it seems fair to assume that they (or at least some of them) once approached writing, and conceived of writing, as the students do. So what happened? Experience happened is one plausible answer; the older adult writers had written more, and had had experience writing in situations outside of the school setting, and along the way had figured out that ideas can change during the writing process, and had adapted that knowledge into their own practices. Whatever the case, one possible implication of Sommers' study is that the less-experienced student writers, in order to improve, did not need merely to gain more practice with what they were already doing, nor did they merely need to be taught new techniques. *They needed to undergo a change in how they thought about what writing is and how it works.*

What, we might ask, has all of this to do with creative writing? A great deal, I would suggest. Creative writing, like composition, is hampered when people outside its purview misunderstand and mischaracterize the work of its practitioners and theorists. One of composition's major problems since the 1960s has been its difficulty in bringing the knowledge it has generated about writing to audiences beyond its own disciplinary specialists. Of particular note is composition's inability to 'reach' many students or members of the general public, except in sanitized or distorted ways. Some may be tempted to mock compositionists – who, after all, are closely tied to rhetoric – for allegedly failing to *use* rhetoric effectively in this regard. Yet rhetorical theory and practice show that *context* is a crucial element of any argumentative situation, and that some audiences, under some circumstances, can be notoriously difficult to 'reach', even if the rhetor has a solid argument ready at hand.[4] *Kairos*, a concept well known to rhetoricians in ancient Greece, posits *time* as a key element in rhetorical situations. No matter how potentially powerful an argument may be, no matter how much potentially persuasive evidence can be marshaled in its favor, audiences may not be receptive to it. They may not yet be ready to 'hear' it. It may not yet be the right time.

A range of elements may play into composition's *kairos* problem. For one, composition scholarship has long been yoked (in the work of many of its scholars and in the minds of virtually everyone else) to the required first-year college composition course. If the required composition course is widely regarded as a place where surface-level errors in student writing will (or should) be eradicated so that they do not turn up in later situations (both academic and professional), then any argument not obviously tied to that purpose may be difficult to make. Perhaps one of the many reasons so many scholars turned away from composition's research focus on process from the mid-1980s onward is that the knowledge generated by this research gained so little foothold outside the community of the researchers themselves. Perhaps composition's turn toward ideology critique and cultural studies in the 1990s represented (at least in part) an attempt by compositionists to understand why the knowledge generated by the field's earlier engagements with cognitive psychology had not had more public impact.[5]

Whatever its flaws, whatever its shortcomings, the early process research in composition was valuable because it challenged a prevailing view of what writing is and how it works. That view, excessively static and formalistic, was most often referred to as 'current-traditional' by the process researchers and pedagogues. Writing in 1982 as an advocate for some of the process-oriented research conducted during the previous two decades, Maxine Hairston described the current-traditional paradigm this way:

> Its adherents believe that competent writers know what they are going to say before they begin to write; thus their most important task when they are preparing to write is finding a form into which to organize their content. They also believe that the composing process is linear, that it proceeds systematically from prewriting to writing to rewriting. Finally, they believe that teaching editing is teaching writing. (Hairston, 1982: 78)

Although emerging process research offered a potential alternative to current-traditionalism, Hairston argued, conditions were not yet ripe for a complete overthrow of the old paradigm. For example, many of the people teaching composition were not trained in composition theory and scholarship; they were trained instead in interpretive, academic literary criticism and had either no knowledge of or no interest in composition scholarship. Composition textbooks, Hairston noted, were largely geared toward this kind of teacherly audience and thus did not disseminate any of the findings of composition scholarship (Hairston, 1982: 78–79). And one could plausibly argue that even today, 35 years after the publication of Hairston's article, the situation has changed, but not completely: while English departments may be more likely in 2017 than in 1982 to have a few tenured or tenure-track professors specializing in composition, large numbers of those who teach composition – especially among the adjunct ranks – are still drawn from graduate programs not in composition but in literature (or, perhaps more so now than in 1982, in creative writing). And while people with graduate degrees in literature or creative writing may be more likely today than in the 1980s to have had some exposure to composition scholarship and theory, their level of professional commitment to such scholarship and theory is frequently nil. Thus, current-traditional assumptions about writing still survive (and in some cases thrive) in some composition classrooms and textbooks now.

And, just as elements of current-traditionalism thrive within some composition pedagogies today, and in many parts of the public discourse about writing, it could be argued that similar elements persist and thrive in creative writing pedagogies as well. Any time a workshop discussion proceeds under the assumption that the writer knew exactly what s/he wanted to express or communicate before composing the draft at hand (and merely needs to find the *right words* to do so), or any time such discussion focuses primarily on textual surface features like verb tenses or dialogue tags, we might argue that creative writing pedagogy is operating within its own brand of current-traditionalism – or what, in *(Re)Writing Craft*, I named 'the institutional-conventional wisdom of creative writing' (Mayers, 2005). That this institutional-conventional wisdom sometimes operates in the classrooms of creative writing teachers who arguably *ought to know from their own experience and daily writing practice* that it is bankrupt only serves to underscore its tendency to hide itself in plain sight.

So Now What?

Where is this all leading?
What should we do?
I do not have a specific blueprint, but can offer a broad outline; I can offer a few *ways of thinking* that may help us figure out where to go.

The shared challenge – the common ground upon which composition and creative writing can meet – is to contest excessively static and formalistic understandings about what writing is and how it works. Composition has thus far found that task extraordinarily difficult – at least outside the ranks of its own scholars and researchers. Creative writing has seemed less interested in that task most of the time, taking advantage of the contradictory but often simultaneously held ideas about writing described above by Fleming. Creative writing can be most helpful to composition for its potential to challenge the way of thinking that positions writing as *always* and *only* a form of communication. There is nothing wrong with understanding writing as communication. Writing was most likely invented as a means of communication, and communication is most often what we use writing for. But if we understand writing *only* as communication, or if we allow communication to overshadow other possible understandings, we get into trouble. Writing can be a mode of communication, but it also can be a mode of expression, a mode of discovery, a mode of revelation, among other things.

The first thing creative writers in the academy can do is *begin to see themselves as involved in a common project along with composition teachers and scholars.* This common project is not merely correcting students' grammar. It involves, as I have tried to suggest throughout this chapter, creating learning environments that allow students to experience the dynamic, thought-shaping processes of writing in such a way that they might come to see grammatical correctness as a minor feature of a much more complex enterprise.

A second thing creative writers can do is to focus on our undergraduate courses – especially the multi-genre introductory courses often taken by students not majoring in English or creative writing – as the vital center of our work in the academy. This certainly does not mean abandoning MFA programs or advanced creative writing courses for undergraduates. But it does mean that the works published by MFA holders are not the most important 'public outreach program' that academic creative writing programs have. Instead, the experiences provided to students who have never tried creative writing before, a few of whom may go on to publish in traditional ways and many who will not, are that most important point of contact. Some might argue that the approach I outline here would risk repeating the early history of composition studies, in which (according to some scholars and practitioners) a too-close association with introductory-level college courses constrained the possibilities for meaningful and impactful research. But I would counter that a cooperative project between composition studies and creative writing – a project to help *change the way people think about writing* – is a natural complement to, and extension of, the attempts within composition studies, underway since at least the 1990s, to extend the reach of the field's scholarship and insight beyond the limiting frame of how writing is taught and learned in classroom contexts.

If we can shift our focus from serving writers to serving writing, if we can recognize some of the ways we have already begun to do so and figure out how to continue those efforts and convince others that the effort is worthwhile, we will have changed creative writing in America in significant and lasting ways.

Notes

(1) Astute readers may have noticed that I have here used a construction sometimes called the 'singular they', and that such a construction is often considered a grammatical

error. Yet it strikes me as appropriate here; such are the choices writers must often make.
(2) Of course, the recent deterioration of the academic job market, and the trend toward casualization of academic labor, belies this goal. But it still exists as the imagined ideal state of affairs for many.
(3) Crowley's claim is that champions of 'the process movement' characterize it as a radical change in thinking, which, in her analysis, it actually was not. In Crowley's view, the process movement was grafted rather easily onto the 'current-traditional' model it had allegedly overturned (Crowley, 1998).
(4) Or, to explain this in the terms of Aristotle's famous rhetorical triad, logos alone can rarely carry the day. Ethos and pathos must also work in the rhetor's favor.
(5) There were also other very legitimate concerns about the early 'process movement' research inflected by cognitive psychology, particularly with regard to some of its methodological issues (especially the difficulties inherent in observing writers' processes without altering them) and its tendency to focus on the individual while eclipsing the social dimensions of writing processes.

References

Bennett, E. (2015) *Workshops of Empire: Stegner, Engle, and American Creative Writing During the Cold War.* Iowa City, IA: University of Iowa Press.

Crowley, S. (1998) *Composition in the University: Historical and Polemical Essays.* Pittsburgh, PA: University of Pittsburgh Press.

Fenza, D.W. (2011) The centre has not held: Creative writing and pluralism. *New Writing: The International Journal for the Practice and Theory of Creative Writing* 8 (3), 206–214.

Fleming, D. (2011) *From Form to Meaning: Freshman Composition and the Long Sixties, 1957–1974.* Pittsburgh, PA: University of Pittsburgh Press.

Hairston, M. (1982) The winds of change: Thomas Kuhn and the revolution in the teaching of writing. *College Composition and Communication* 33 (1), 76–88.

Mayers, T. (2005) *(Re)Writing Craft: Composition, Creative Writing, and the Future of English Studies.* Pittsburgh, PA: University of Pittsburgh Press.

Mills, B. (1953) Writing as process. *College English* 15 (1), 19–26.

Myers, D.G. (1996) *The Elephants Teach: Creative Writing Since 1880.* London: Prentice Hall.

Rose, M. (1989) *Lives on the Boundary.* London: Penguin.

Sommers, N. (1980) Revision strategies of student writers and experienced adult writers. *College Composition and Communication* 31 (4), 378–388.

Sullivan, H. (2013) *The Work of Revision.* Harvard, MA: Harvard University Press.

4 Theory and Pedagogy in Introductory Writing Textbooks: Creative Writing Leads the Way

Stephanie Vanderslice

Recently as I was examining Tara Mokhtari's new *Bloomsbury Introduction to Creative Writing* (2015) for a review essay, I was struck by her considered references to creative writing theory as a natural companion to craft, references made as early as the introduction and, occasionally, throughout the book. Mokhtari's stance seems fairly influenced by a multinational background in creative writing (now based in New York City, she received her higher education in Australia, a country with a thriving creative writing culture within higher education in which craft and theory seem to exist side by side). However, I began to wonder if other recent introductory creative writing texts took creative writing theory and pedagogy into account or at least tipped their hats to it.

Theory and Textbooks: Some History

After posing this question aloud at a conference with an audience of creative writers and composition scholars, I learned that in the field of composition, writing theory and the textbook industry have a complicated history. Indeed, research into what has been written about composition theory and the textbook industry reveals this to be the case. In 1989, W. Ross Winterowd pointed out that 'conscientious publishers respond to the need and demand of the market' (Winterowd, 1989: 145), providing what the customers want. As far back as 1982, moreover, textbook authors Arn Tibbetts and Charlene Tibbetts suggested that 'Teachers do not want textbooks based on research in composition'. Rather, 'teachers want what is familiar to them' (Tibbetts & Tibbetts, 1982: 856).

Kathleen Welch's influential article in 1987, moreover, surveyed the state of the field and asserted that 'of the hundreds of pounds of freshman writing textbooks produced each year, few are constructed with any overt indication that composition theory has ever existed' and some seem to even 'deny composition theory' (Welch, 1987: 269). In fact, her review revealed that textbooks at the time focused on the five classical canons and the modes of discourse, promoting an 'unexamined ideology' (271). 'Writing instruction', she maintains, 'as it exists in these textbooks rests not in sound composition theory but on a belief system that is virtually ideological and therefore not easily opened to examination' (271). Such a situation is especially troubling when one considers that it is common knowledge in the field that composition textbooks 'act as persuasive places where new teachers of writing are trained and where experienced ones reinforce the training' (271).

It is difficult to determine how theory has fared in composition texts since then. Scholarship on the subject has declined since this flurry of activity in the 1980s, with the exception of Xin Liu Gale and Frederic Gale's *(Re)Visioning Composition Textbooks: Conflicts of Culture, Ideology and Pedagogy* (1999), a collection of articles which actually forecasts the decline in status of the traditionally published textbook, and reiterates the ways in which the textbook reproduces cultural ideologies and suggests ways textbooks can both challenge and perpetuate social and academic culture. Indeed, the book's introduction calls for an examination of the many roles a textbook can play in both problematizing and reinscribing social norms. But if Google Scholar is any indication, nearly 20 years on, this examination hasn't really happened and we see the world of textbooks has morphed once again, textbook companies merging with stunning speed, open-source texts become increasingly popular and even more writing teachers eschewing textbooks in the composition classroom altogether.

In Creative Writing: From No Textbook to Introductory Creative Writing Texts

So. Whither creative writing's equivalent to the composition text: the introductory creative writing text? Armed with this burst of research about composition texts from the 1980s, and my own involvement in and knowledge of the rise of creative writing theory and pedagogy in the US in the last 15 years, I wanted to find out. As a proponent of both the concept-based introductory creative writing course and the work of Heather Sellers, I've been using Sellers' *The Practice of Creative Writing* since it was first published in 2007, so my first task was to get a sense of other introductory creative writing texts available today. I wasn't able to get my hands on all of them in time to complete this preliminary study, but I was able to review a representative list of American texts, which includes the most recent editions of the aforementioned Mokhtari's *Bloomsbury Introduction*; Sellers' *Practice*; David Starkey's *Creative Writing: An Introduction to Poetry and Fiction*; Stephen Minot and Diane Thiel's *Three Genres: The Writing of Literary Poems, Prose and Plays* (9th edition); Janet Burroway's *Imaginative Writing*; and Lisa Roney's *Serious Daring: Creative Writing in Four Genres*.

Let me reiterate: the purpose of this review was not to judge the quality of the textbooks for use in the introductory creative writing classroom. Indeed, I was pleased to reacquaint myself with what is available to today's beginning creative writing student and teacher. Based on this sampling, they are in very good hands. Moreover, in examining these texts, I was struck more than once at how, in the aggregate, they demonstrate how far our field has come. Twenty years ago, when I first started teaching introductory creative writing, fewer than half of these books were available. Thirty years ago, when I took my first creative writing course in college, we didn't use a textbook at all. As a result, my first college creative writing class, and every one like it until I graduated, as well as most of the ones I experienced in graduate school, were 100% workshop-based. We turned in stories; the teacher and the class critiqued them. That was all. I learned from those workshops and from those critiques of my own work and that of others. But that was the only form of pedagogy available and, as I have often written, I suspect I could have learned more if the workshop had been combined with other methods of instruction, some of which might have come from a textbook. It says a great deal that we have such a selection of introductory textbooks today; it says that we consider creative writing a teachable subject and that there exist, in fact, an array of techniques and strategies, in addition to the workshop, through which to teach it. The benefits that accrue from having textbooks to ground students and teachers in a common pedagogy of creative writing include:

- emphasis on process and drafting that debunks myths about writing;
- development of a language with which to analyze and discuss creative work;
- a framework for the development of the metacognitive skills with which to analyze one's own work and that of others;
- the provision of literary work to exemplify elements of craft.

While it is possible that some enlightened professors may provide these elements without a textbook, just as with introductory composition texts, the fact that most introductory creative writing textbooks provide them delivers a degree of quality assurance for less experienced instructors and provides an outline for a creative writing pedagogy that simply did not exist 30 years ago.

Of the six books I surveyed, half mentioned research and theory as a basis for their instruction: *Bloomsbury Introduction* by Tara Mokhtari, which inspired this piece, Heather Sellers' *The Practice of Creative Writing* and David Starkey's *Creative Writing: An Introduction to Poetry and Fiction*. The degree to which their texts referenced this research varied considerably, however, as I'll discuss later in this essay.

The other three books in this survey focused on craft instruction, instruction which derived its credibility wholly from the author's publication and experience as a writer, with some texts providing additional support in the form of quotes and anecdotes. There is nothing ostensibly wrong with this stance as long as students understand that the instruction they are being given in writing is based entirely on the experience of *one* author/teacher, no matter how considerable. They are, in fact, book-length versions of what Wendy Bishop calls in *Released into Language*, her pivotal book on the teaching of creative writing, 'writer self-reports' (Bishop, 1990). The problem with these self-reports, Bishop asserts, is that they are solely the view of one author/educator among many and may or may not be generalizable. Moreover, it is not unusual, as Bishop suggests, for a writer to 'gild the lily' in a self-report, to exaggerate and to focus on the aspects of the writing process that make him or her look good. As one might expect, therefore, each book presented different versions of singular writerly advice, suggesting that even the most prescriptive book (Minot and Thiel, for my money) was also highly subjective. Each however, was valuable in its own right and offered useful lessons for the beginning creative writer.

It would be easy to argue that, in such a nascent field, research on the teaching of creative writing and writing theory would be difficult to obtain, so difficult as to excuse the fact that three of these books leave it out completely. Nonetheless, such an argument would be mistaken, as the books that do acknowledge creative writing and creativity theory in their advice to writers bolster their case immeasurably.

For Mokhtari in the *Bloomsbury Introduction*, this acknowledgement seems to be part of a highly relevant approach to introductory creative writing that includes chapters on blogging and other digital formats, screenwriting and writing the critical exegesis, all of which reflect an awareness of the *most recent* developments of the 21st-century introductory creative writing classroom. This approach has its appeal to instructors and readers because, more than any other text, it actually focuses on the most current reality in which the students write. I have often suggested that, as writing teachers, we should strive to stay as current as possible in our fields, with the aim of preparing students to enter the *contemporary* writing landscape, not the one we entered a decade or two ago. Mokhtari's *Bloomsbury Introduction* clearly has this contemporary landscape in mind, and it is one that includes writing theory – a combined result perhaps of the fact that her creative writing experiences are not only global but current.

Another text that acknowledges the disadvantages of both reinscribing the outmoded creative writing pedagogy of the last 20 years and of the writer-self report, as well, is Sellers' *Practice of Creative Writing*. In the introduction, she notes:

> For years, I taught creative writing the way it had been taught to me, taking my students through all the prescribed lessons on character, voice, point of view, theme, line breaks, meter and symbol. But after a while, I felt like a fraud in the classroom; I didn't work this way myself. (Sellers, 2012: vii)

Although Sellers refers to her own practice throughout the book, she also explains that she felt her own experience wasn't enough, that 'in writing this textbook ... I researched creativity, play, and the "zone" athletes talk about when every shot swishes, when the goal just vacuums up the ball' (viii). Indeed, evidence of her use of 'research' and theory appears throughout the text, in descriptions and definitions of Csikszentmihalyi's 'flow' and acknowledgements of the recursiveness of revision, a well known tenet of cognitive writing theory referenced by compositionists and creative writers alike.

If I was impressed when Heather Sellers referred to the research she did on creativity to support her own creative writing text, however, I was downright awestruck at the amount of real estate David Starkey committed to writing theory in his book, *Creative Writing: An Introduction to Poetry and Fiction*. I shouldn't be so surprised – David Starkey was a good friend and writing partner of Wendy Bishop, a founder of the creative writing pedagogy movement, and so it's only natural that he would use writing theory to articulate a number of different ideas about creative writing. But I'm not sure that even many first-year composition texts employ this much theory in explaining the discipline-wide values that scaffold introductory composition courses. *Creative Writing: An Introduction to Poetry and Fiction* is clearly written from the perspective of someone with a composition and creative writing background who believes that letting students in on some of this theory can only help enhance their learning.

In fact, Starkey directs his words on writing theory not to instructors using the book but, in his introduction, to *students*, 'A Few Things You Should Know About Creative Writing' (1). Here he reminds students of their composition experiences and asks if composition really is so different from creative writing, noting that Wendy Bishop, one of the 'great creative writing teachers of the late 20th century', (2) 'made a number of innovative connections between the teaching of expository and creative writing' (3). Building on that connection, Starkey explores the 'discipline-wide values' of the position statement produced by the National Council of Teachers of English (NCTE) in 2004, 'Beliefs About the Teaching of Writing', and explains why these key disciplinary beliefs can be useful to them as beginning students of writing (2). These beliefs, he explains, 'underlie the pedagogy, or theory of teaching, behind this book' (2) and, he notes interestingly, your 'instructor … probably shares many of these assumptions' (2). Importantly, furthermore, Starkey emphasizes, 'even if you find yourself disagreeing with one or more of these beliefs, thinking about why can be a critical stage in your development as a writer' (2). He then goes on to devote *six pages* of his book to unpacking the NCTE position statement as it pertains to learning creative writing, including whether the subject can be taught, six pages that read like a brief guide to writing pedagogy and theory in the early 21st century.

Starkey's nod to theory, however, does not end there. Later in the book, in a chapter about revision, he extensively references the work of Nancy Sommers and quotes Donald Murray, two composition all-stars, in 'busting' revision myths (10). He also brings in Nancy Welch's ideas about 'getting restless … with familiar scripts in your writing, recognizing their limits' (10), Wendy Bishop's advice in 'Acts of Revision' that 'You need others to revise wisely. You need to share your work …' and Lester Faigley and Stephen Witte's research on how expert writers revise in 'Analyzing Revision' (12).

What are the implications, then, of the fact that one of the most significant displays of writing and creative writing theory in a writing textbook happens in an introductory creative writing textbook? There are a number of them. One is that the circumstances and/or timing must be right; that a creative writing textbook needs to be written by a colleague of Wendy Bishop who co-authored many theory and creative writing texts with her and, like Bishop, who also wrote creative writing texts, saw no reason why the two couldn't be blended, why students wouldn't benefit from knowing the many posited 'whys' behind the 'hows' of craft. However, I suspected, the reasoning went deeper than that. So in getting a better sense of the story behind his integration of theory in *Creative Writing: An Introduction to Poetry and Fiction*, I interviewed the author himself, via email, in 2016.

An Interview with David Starkey

SV: You've written or edited a lot of books with unique ideas about writing theory, including some with Wendy Bishop. Did this impact your thinking that it would be natural to introduce some theory into your textbooks?

DS: Absolutely! It's hard to imagine my career as a teacher/writer without Wendy's encouraging influence. Of course, as you and I both know, you have to come across theory at the right time in order to find it useful. I met Wendy Bishop early in my teaching career, and I was probably far more receptive to her ideas that I would have been as a graduate student or as a more advanced teacher.

You write about meeting Wendy Bishop in '"There's an essay in that": Wendy Bishop and the origins of our field', and the two days you spent with Wendy in 1999 were remarkably similar to the visit she made to my campus in the early 1990s. I always felt that when she was sitting across from me, she was giving me her *full* attention – and, man, that was a powerful experience. Like you, I felt inspired to go out and try and do what she was doing.

Collaborating with her was a whirlwind experience. She was always juggling three or four or five projects at the same time, trying out and developing her ideas on the fly. I was very much the junior partner in everything we did, so when she passed away early in our work on *Keywords in Creative Writing*, I pretty much stopped doing anything related to theory or pedagogy for over a year. There was a tribute to her at CCCC the year after she died, and I still have a very visceral memory of weeping the entire time I was reading aloud her last email to me.

Again, to reference your article, it's amazing the influence she had on people. I only ever saw her a couple of times a year, but, like hundreds of others, I corresponded with her online, and she usually responded within a couple of hours, no matter what time of the day or night it was. That energy was tremendous. If I can convey just a fraction of her passion for writing to my students, I'm probably doing a decent job.

It's lucky for creative writing studies that people like you and Anna Leahy and Graeme Harper have done so much to carry on the work Wendy started. For a while, I was worried that she was such a powerful *individual* influence, that her passing would leave the field empty. Fortunately, that hasn't happened.

SV: Do you use theory when you teach creative writing? Do your students respond to it?

DS: I probably use the word 'theory' more in my book than I do in the classroom, even when I'm employing theory to explain ways to generate, craft and revise writing. In class, I'm more likely to say 'strategies', 'approaches', 'tactics', maybe even 'tricks'. Some theorists probably wouldn't approve, but ultimately what I'm trying to do is just get students to ask themselves, *Why did I make this decision rather than another?* Once they realize that they have, indeed, made a decision – consciously or not – they are often open to exploring how and why they got where they are as writers and thinkers.

SV: How did the publishers and your editor respond to your inclusion of theory in the book? Did they want you to take it out? Were they okay with it? I ask because it was 'explained' to me by compositionists (and supported somewhat, but not completely, by my research) that publishers don't like to include theory in textbooks because it's not 'what teachers want' and they want to cater to teachers.

DS: I happily credit Steve Scipione, my editor at Bedford/St Martin's, with not only allowing me to incorporate theory into my textbook, but nudging me to include more.

I suspect the argument that teachers don't want theory applies to something more complex and heavy-handed than what is found in my book. No teacher wants to look foolish or under-informed in her students' eyes, but the theory I think you and I are talking about is designed to help both students *and* teachers reflect on their practices as writers in positive, non-threatening ways. Who wouldn't want that?

SV: At the end of my article I'm going to call on Creative Writing Studies to be the leaders in including more of what's happening in the field in our textbooks in the future. What is your opinion on that?

DS: I think that's a great idea. Whether we acknowledge it or not, theory is embedded in everything a textbook author does, so it makes sense that writer/theorists would be at the center of that enterprise.

I would add that it's important to include two-year college colleagues whenever possible. I spent the first 10 years of my career at four-year schools, where there was more time and institutional support for theorizing, and I don't know that I would have been able to make a go of the sort of writing I do at my community college if I hadn't had the decade head-start. The two-year college creative writing instructors you meet at AWP are overworked, but they sure have a lot of good ideas!

Textbooks: Creative Writing as a Teachable Subject

In terms of including two-year colleges more in the conversation about teaching creative writing, I think it's important to point readers to Starkey's essay about teaching creative writing in the two-year college in Dianne Donnelly's collection *Does the Writing Workshop Still Work?* (Starkey, 2010). It's been a touchstone in my Teaching Creative Writing course at the University of Central Arkansas, where some of the students in the course come from the community college system and find the essay makes important points about a form of education and thus a creative writing classroom that encompass large numbers of students but about which little has been said. Discussions of the two-year college creative writing classroom can also shed light on important issues of diversity and social justice.

What Starkey – and Sellers and Mokthari's *texts* – can teach us, however, is that the American creative writing textbook market in the 21st century is actually one that is quite favorable to the ideas and theories that scaffold creative writing as a teachable subject. And it is one that has followed a quite different history from the field of composition in the US. At a 2017 panel on the influence of their books ('The influence of creative writing textbooks', AWP panel presentation, Washington, DC), three of the top-selling introductory creative writing texts in the country, Burroway, Sellers and Starkey, all agree that their work might be used differently by creative writing teachers than the way composition textbooks might be used by composition teachers, for example. Burroway ventured that it is the choice of a textbook that reflects the teacher's philosophy rather than dictates it; that is, an instructor might choose from among Burroway, Sellers' or Starkey's text based on the extent to which it extended and supported their own theories about creative writing, rather than influencing them. Sellers, moreover, added that she sees the textbook as a 'chorus' that the instructor directs or employs to support own goals or purposes in the course, rather than the driving force. Starkey went so far as to guess that some creative writing instructors, especially graduate students, were so independent as to 'thumb their noses', at creative writing textbooks recommended to them, using them sparingly or only in parts in teaching their courses.

How reflective, then, is the creative writing text of current creative writing theory? How influential is it, as the composition text is purported to be, in the teaching of creative writing? In spite of these useful remarks from the authors themselves, we still don't really know. To move this inquiry beyond lore, several empirical studies are possible: a comparative examination of introductory creative writing texts and the syllabi for the courses on which they are used, along with interviews of instructors, would yield illuminating information about what seems to be a chicken-and-egg question. Similarly, a broad-based empirical study of the kinds of introductory creative writing textbooks that yield the best results for nascent writers would also shed light on the kinds of theories and exercises that prove most useful for students. Finally, a comparison of courses and instructors who hew closely to textbooks to those who teach more free-form creative writing courses and their end results might also begin to give our discipline some data to build on in determining how young writers might be best taught. All of these could be the significant but highly worthy undertakings of a field laying the groundwork for an empirical, theory-driven pedagogy.

The current expansion of the creative writing studies movement in the US (the movement is already well established in the UK and Australia), which Wendy Bishop, David Starkey and others began so long ago, with the founding of the Creative Writing Studies Organization, the *Journal of Creative Writing Studies* and the annual conference, dovetails perfectly with this favorable environment. As a 'theory' of creative writing in the US, or 'strands' of theories of creative writing not necessarily labeled creative writing studies continue to mature through work published in important outlets such as in the Multilingual Matters series and others, and in the *New Writing* and *Text* journals, and the *Journal of Creative Writing Studies* (produced by the National Association of Writers in Education, NAWE), as well as the *Journal of Creative Writing*, new ideas around how creative writing is taught and learned will emerge. Now that these ideas have arrived and begun to establish themselves in our discipline, it will be our responsibility as writers and teachers to ensure that they are researched and examined if they are to endure, and that we continue to lead the way as a field in establishing a reciprocal relationship between research and learning so that it becomes a hallmark of the creative writing discipline.

References

Bishop, W. (1990) *Released into Language: Some Options for Teaching Creative Writing*. Carbondale, IL: NCTE. Available at http://eric.ed.gov/?id=ED326879 (accessed June 2017).

Burroway, J. (2010) *Imaginative Writing: The Elements of Craft*. Upper Saddle River, NJ: Pearson.

Gale, X.L. and Gale, F. (1999) *(Re)visioning Composition Textbooks: Conflicts of Culture, Ideology and Pedagogy*. Albany, NY: SUNY Press.

Minot, S. and Thiel, D. (2011) *Three Genres: The Writing of Literary Poems, Prose and Plays* (9th edition). Upper Saddle River, NJ: Pearson.

Mokhtari, T. (2015) *The Bloomsbury Introduction to Creative Writing*. London: Bloomsbury Academic.

Roney, L. (2014) *Serious Daring: Creative Writing in Four Genres*. New York: Oxford University Press.

Sellers, H. (2012) *The Practice of Creative Writing: A Guide for Students* (2nd edition). Boston, MA: Bedford.

Starkey, D. (2010) The creative writing workshop in the two-year college: Who cares? In D. Donnelly (ed.) *Does the Writing Workshop Still Work?* (pp. 148–159). Bristol: Multilingual Matters.

Starkey, D. (2013) *Creative Writing: An Introduction to Poetry and Fiction*. Boston, MA: Bedford.

Tibbetts, A. and Tibbetts, C. (1982) Can composition textbooks use composition research? *College English* 44 (3), 855–858.

Vanderslice, S. (2016) There's an essay in that: Wendy Bishop and the origins of our field. *Journal of Creative Writing Studies* 1 (1). Available at http://scholarworks.rit.edu/jcws/vol1/iss1/2 (accessed June 2017).

Welch, K. (1987) Ideology and freshman textbook production: The place of theory and writing pedagogy. *College Composition and Communication* 38 (3), 269–282.

Winterowd, W.R. (1989) Composition textbooks: Publisher–author relationships. *College Composition and Communication* 40 (2), 139–151.

5 The Print Doctrine

Angela Ferraiolo

Last year, I was approached by a group of film students who were adapting a Chekhov short story for the screen. The students were advanced filmmakers who knew a lot about cameras, lenses, blocking, even working with actors. But their screenwriting skills weren't as strong, and their script did not quite take into account how an atmosphere of suspended, unspoken and prolonged tension, so typical of a Chekhov opening, had been lost in their use of the camera, an oversight that might undermine their project overall. In fact, these students seemed to have not much context for Chekhov whatsoever, other than the knowledge that his work was in the public domain. When I suggested they learn more about Chekhov's narrative strategies, or even take their film script to a writing workshop, the students hesitated. They were making a movie, they explained, not writing a short story. They were filmmakers, not writers.

Likewise, after describing the long, iterative process behind the development of avatars for her interactive scenarios, a student game developer told me her six-hour sci-fi epic about a small group of explorers in a distant solar system wasn't writing, but design. She had no plans to take her game ideas into a writing class, because as a designer, not a writer, what would she do in the workshop setting? Draft outlines? She reminded me of a graphic novelist I knew who stayed frozen on one of his more complicated projects for years. The through-line of his story was perpetually out of reach, but he'd never workshopped the piece because he was an illustrator, not a writer. Illustrators, he explained, 'don't do sentences'.

Filmmakers, game designers and illustrators aren't the only people who think this way. Novelists and poets can be just as orthodox. Even in great creative writing programs, teachers as well as students have led me, sometimes with a great deal of patience, through the categories of who and what the workshop process serves, how 'real' writers work in either fiction or poetry, how in specific cases a writer might feel a need to put forward a collection of essays, but how the serious work of writing, its exhausting process and ultimate outcome, is the paper artifact, the manuscript, the book or, in the case of experimentalists, the book-like thing, and how this printed object ultimately signifies the fact that the work of writing has occurred.

This concept is reinforced by industry, where an absence of paper usually means some kind of negation of writing in general and writers specifically. Take the early days of film production. Directors went out on location and shot stories of whatever came to mind, or whatever they thought an audience might want to see. Since this style of moviemaking did not necessitate a text, no writers were engaged. Instead, after a movie was in the can and on its way to theaters, somebody in the studio's publicity office, often one of the secretaries, would spend a lunch hour writing a scenario intended to make sense of the jumbled assortment of scenes constituting the film. Those scenarios were then sent to theaters along with the film reels, not as scripts but as collateral material. A contemporary version of this kind of production situation is to find yourself with the job of creating an interactive story or video game, a forward-moving, progressive experience which plots events over a beginning, middle and end, maybe several endings actually, including anchor and supporting characters and several layers of interactive plot. As long as the story of that game goes unprinted on paper, you may have a difficult time convincing producers to even consult a writer. The thinking goes something like this: We need game code to make the computers run. We have therefore budgeted for game programmers. However, there is no need at all for a game script printed on paper. In fact, the story of the game, all that dialogue stuff, that's going into a text parser, making the story a parsable feature of the code, so we've decided to 'let the programmers write it'. In other cases where there's no provision for a printed script, producers and directors may decide to 'use existing sources', meaning some kind of script is being 'gathered from the environment'. People will also 'let the actors write it', 'let the internet write it' or, a current favorite, 'let the audience write it'.

Again, although there's a need for characters, setting, plot and some kind of forward-moving narrative strategy, unless it is necessary to evidence words on paper, it's possible to think there's no writing going on, therefore no need to know about writing, understand writing or have a writer on hand. It took several years and thousands of dollars for those early movie people to admit that shooting anything that came to mind is expensive and produces mediocre films, but finally film production moved to a process where shoots were thought through ahead of time, scenario writers began to write scene outlines for everyone on the crew, and those outlines were printed and distributed before the work day began. Once writing was seen as a way to regulate costs and producers accepted the need for a printed document, secretaries became screenwriters and movie summaries became screenplays.

The key to understanding these situations, their futility and waste, lies in observing a long-held idea that writers work with language alone and that every writer's goal is to produce some kind of text. We might call this the print doctrine, the belief that writing occurs when writers write books – and only books. This ideology identifies the storyteller not by the creative role he or she performs – it's probable that anyone designing a plot, events or characters is in some sense writing – but by the medium through which that story is ultimately expressed. Thinking this way, filmmakers make films, designers make games, illustrators create comics and cartoons, and writers work in print, putting text on paper in the form of novels, stories, essays and poetry. Above all, according to this idea, writing manifests itself not in gesture, image or agency, but in language and language alone. Everything else is merely some form of media production. If the print doctrine were to be restated as a slogan it would be some sort of short clever phrase that would look good in type, maybe something along the lines of 'no paper, no writer'.

Writing in the Expanded Field

Meanwhile, production in all media forms has been constant, expansive, in some ways overwhelming. Storytellers flood film schools, game programs and art studios, giving us accounts of meat boys whose girlfriends are band aids, dad's transition from Mort to Maura, Stalin's morphogenesis as a claymation figure, a rat's survival in the Jewish ghetto. These stories depend on pictures, footage, animation, visualization, simulation, sound and interaction to engage audiences and transform experience. Their creators rely on a range of practices that are distinct from print endeavors and production methods, and which include techniques from the visual arts, the stage and algorithmic processes.

Taken together, these channels of production constitute an expanded storytelling practice we might call media writing, the origination point for a range of new narrative forms, from unusual works of collaborative fiction to video games. Media writing can be visual, oral, graphic, interactive, distributed or textual. Many media stories appear as hybrid forms combining text, sound, image and animation, while blending narrative devices from fiction, cartoons, filmmaking, the visual and performing arts. From text installation to virtual reality, media narratives have given us hundreds of works that cannot be categorized in one discipline or another, that instead range across multiple media forms and platforms.

The forces behind the expansion of media writing are more than familiar. First, there have been large cultural gains in narrative itself. The cognitive sophistication of post-modernist, speculative and modular writing forms has created audiences interested in and able to follow non-hierarchical fictions, the meta-story and conceptual exploits in language. This fundamental evolution in the capacities of the audience has fostered the viability of speculative and hybrid forms in general. Next, as we are by now weary of admitting, digital production offers writers the ability to include many kinds of media in stories, moving writing beyond print and towards assemblage and collage. The web page, which can scroll to infinity while carrying text, image, footage and sound, while linking itself to other equally media-driven pages, insists on redefining the concept of page, navigation, possibly reading itself, if not for the print generation, then for successive generations of people who have been termed 'digital natives'. Technologies of computer graphics are about to engender completely new genres of story such as augmented and virtual reality, and 360-degree immersions. The media tropes of the television serial and the episodic webcast are adapting to an explosion in digital distribution as well as to the demands of computation. From a practical, hands-on point of view, the expense of working in animation, video, film or ink is no longer a barrier to many writers. In addition to media's increasing affordability, the skills needed to make a competent independent game, video or color publication are now within reach of most students. In many cases, even self-educating writers can with a little money and perseverance produce a worthwhile film or online comic.

Finally, the delivery systems of all media forms are converging. Ten years ago, a person who wanted to see a movie would go to a movie theater. Once there, he or she would chose a movie, buy a ticket and enter the theater. Now, thanks to mobile devices, set-top boxes and internet delivery, a large part of the audience seeks story through device, not location. Through this single and constant reference frame of the device, a viewer can pick up a book, magazine, film, game, graphic novel or almost any other kind of media, all at the same access point, all equally available, all equally accessible. This media ubiquity is in turn encouraging audiences to be more adventurous, more pluralistic, to give games, graphic novels, zines and interactive works a larger part of their attention and, in some cases, a measure of appreciation that's been overdue.

What is implied here is something deeper than the teaching of screenwriting, blogging in the classroom, or the addition of video clips to an essay about the ocean. It's an admission of substance. Writers have always taken print as a given. Unlike other artists, sculptors or painters, we have not had to spend much time thinking about material. On the contrary, writers tend to assume a material and, by assuming the page and avoiding questions of the studio, we also avoid certain materialities of production like space, paint, plaster, casting, location and light, all of which are fundamental to other artists.

Does a refusal to consider material push writers toward other disciplines? Forced to choose between a technical education and the exploration of story, many students will choose the practicality of learning their equipment. Many will be buried in an avalanche of technical information. Forced through oddly divided departments, some students begin to mirror that divide within themselves. Institutionally discouraged from developing a context for work that might have traversed many media forms, some students may find they are less understanding of each individual form.

In other situations, writing becomes a one- or two-week phase of pre-production, unconnected to a literary present or past, or proceeds through the use of how-to manuals intent on reducing storytelling to just another production element. A recurring discussion among writers of serious fiction and poetry concerns the sometimes repetitive and limited fiction of popular forms – movies, comics, video games – much of which can feel like bad drafts of a B-movie. But the authors of those popular forms are, or will be, in many instances, either educated according to a purely technical agenda or self-taught through a hit-or-miss grab bag of whatever comes through while wandering around online. This is why so many game designers have read nothing but Tolkien, and how we arrive at the student film director who has never read Chekhov. Both of these are in a way instances of the same problem. In even worse trouble is the student who believes Tolkien is the only writer who has anything to offer a designer, the student who is a master camera technician yet somehow has no sense of story, plot or character, or the student who is so media xenophobic she is unable to see that her narrative ideas would work better on film than in a book.

The fact that paper, a surface, has been the primary medium writers have relied in the past does not mean writing will continue on paper in the present, or in the future. If we as writers define ourselves as producers of the printed form, what happens to us when technology pushes storytelling beyond the page?

Letting Go of the Page

One of the first things that happens, or that might happen, is that media inclusion could bring more kinds of storytellers into the workshop.

We have the ability, culturally and technically, to imagine any story in any medium, and to consider the resources of each medium relative to a specific story. Along with new kinds of writing and writers, we could also take the opportunity to help students understand the ways narratives are ultimately shaped by the medium they inhabit. In that process, narrative qualities specific to each media type are almost certain to emerge. By teaching writers the way stories are continually created in and move from one medium to another, we might also teach how that inception or migration has significant effects on the feel and nature of their discourse, making it easier to see how fiction, nonfiction, films, graphic novels and games accomplish their goals in different ways.

A more inclusive writing program might also be an opportunity for all writers to reconsider some basic questions about narrative. What are the principles and constructions of media-specific creative writing? What are the resources each medium offers? What are their limitations? What are their unique narrative constructs? From narrative point of view, what do we actually understand about media forms? Movies are close to oral storytelling. They often require strong plots and clear character arcs viewers can hold in their minds for an extended period of time. In other approaches, films may be imagistic and impressionist, using visual metaphor to produce meaning that may not be articulated in dialogue, using image to create a dream state for the audience, and casting narrative as if it were a spell. The film dissolve, for example, is a cognitive device of narration that expresses something uniquely human and right, while remaining a specific feature of film. Likewise, the nature of time as it flows, disjoints, amplifies and contracts in the panel sets of a graphic novel is unique to the form of sequential art. Manga uses use strong, iconic compositions, chunking time into panels. Plays insist on a series of dramatic actions as their basic building block of expression. Creative nonfiction must engage the reader while retaining intellectual credibility through attribution and an evidential fact pattern. Games are stories with outcomes, wins and losses. They require allowances for user agency and input, sometimes on the scale of hundreds of thousands of players simultaneously. Playable media – interactive narratives – may not require goal states, but do require a kind of story that flows through algorithmic routines almost as a kind of data, allowing computation, simulation and transformation.

Just this handful of examples implies that writing may be an art of dual natures. On the one hand, certain aspects of storytelling act independently of the medium through which they are delivered. On the other, it seems all stories are importantly dependent on that medium. All writers will need some understanding of character, plot and setting to create stories, even if only to write against those concepts. These narratological constructs may, to some degree, have the ability to travel across media types. We might conclude, then, that almost everyone would benefit from a fiction workshop. To some degree, what is taught there is global, useful to all media types. This seems close to the model we have now, with departments sectioned into fiction, poetry and nonfiction, and with the expectation that all people who want to study writing will benefit from that model of study. Nonetheless, what is valued in specific media, the visuality of film, the agency of interactive design, are often exactly the qualities that go unexplored in print-directed courses, despite the fact that they are of deep concern, not to directors, designers or illustrators, but to writers.

These questions are not about technology, but about writing. The successful understanding of story as it works across media boundaries is properly the business of writers, not scholars, producers or engineers. It is possible we have reached a kind of golden age of narrative, where many more aspects of story can be brought forward, developed, considered, imagined and re-imagined, and where we could offer narrative ideas not only to fiction writers and poets, but also to graphic novelists, filmmakers, game writers and media designers, revising and expanding the idea of creative writing throughout a post-print society.

An Ongoing Split

Of course, to look at the split between print and media exclusively, to describe and in that way continue some binary categorization of writing, to focus attention there, might tend to perpetuate the representation of the last 50 years of creative expression as the story of several narrow, unrelated avenues of production. In reality, there is much to be said for viewing each of these fields as having undergone its own intense period of acceleration. Advances in social and political thought, as well as the recent phenomena of globalization, financialization and technological disruption, have initiated enormous changes in every field, demanding significant amounts of innovation from practitioners, teachers and students within, let alone across, every creative discipline.

One result, though unintended, of that acceleration is that while asking students to read cogently within an area and to join the long tradition and history of their respective fields, we have also shaped generations of writers who identify themselves according to the technology of their canon, rather than their ability to tell stories or to shape narrative expressively regardless of a story's final state. These are writers who exclude forms of storytelling, even quite close to their home disciplines, from their education. Playwrights ignore screenwriting, filmmakers ignore poets, poets sidestep fiction and nearly all of these groups exclude game designers. Rather than building diversity, there can be the feeling that studying other forms will diminish one's education, robbing students of valuable time. In addition to defining themselves by what they make, students may also define the education they pursue by the equipment they would like to be trained to use. Writers use word processors and maybe pencils, or ballpoint pens. Directors, however, will need cameras, lights, color grading software, actors, green screens and special effects. Illustrators have the tools of concept art, typography and color theory. Game designers need computers, huge ones, and algorithms, affordances, avatars and interfaces. So many skills to learn, so little time.

Also contributing to these divisions is an old media faith in the 'expert', the idea that a person can master only one field well, or do only one kind of practice with achievement – and that a real 'master' is by definition focused and narrow, much in the same way a devotion to capitalist efficiency demands a strict division of labor. As creatives, we have many different ideas about what mastery looks like and what a master might be, but one of the most persistent is the monogamist, the writer who believes he or she must remain faithful to one form of expression, for better or worse, or sacrifice proficiency. This model of writer defines himself or herself as a one-discipline master, a super-specialist, an expert, in many ways the consistent and pervasive model of achievement in the Western world. For the monogamist, writers write books, or at times magazines and journals, but not other things. Poets are educated in a room filled with other poets, experimentalists alongside other experimentalists, playwrights alongside other playwrights.

Likewise, experimentalists read other experimentalists, poets read other poets, playwrights read other playwrights. This is one contributing reason why, although they turn out ever more dazzling and expressive stylists and narratologists, creative writing programs that remain focused on poetry, fiction and, more recently, literary nonfiction may find the audience for their work is also condensing over time. Today, the most likely readers of literary fiction are other writers of literary fiction. One danger of these smaller, more specialized and more condensed audiences is a kind of turning inward, a convolution in which change and innovation are increasingly bound to a medium of representation and increasingly circular. While filmmakers borrow from games, and game designers are informed by theatrics, print writers can remain bound to the page, reading and knowing mostly other print writers, being read and known by mostly other print writers, working and innovating, but limiting their innovations according to the capacities of print.

So that many writers will earn their degrees without ever learning how to put a build into dialogue, design a sector level or set an establishing shot. Just as only a handful of directing students could tell you what a framing device is, or explain the difference between a flat or round character, somewhere along the line many writers will get the idea that visual storytelling is something they will never need to know, or need to be able to do, when, in fact, writing with images is a means of expression which, in our media-saturated times, might be considered a kind of basic narrative literacy. One of the reasons for the long, perhaps over-elaborated stage directions in Eugene O'Neill's *The Iceman Cometh* is that the script, written in 1939 and published in 1940, was initially intended to be read by a large general audience. The play wasn't actually produced until 1946. One of the text's weaknesses, as many a fiction writer has noted, are O'Neill's long, flat and overly tedious stage directions. He is the definition of a playwright who might have benefited from a fiction workshop. In this respect, it is also interesting to note that the large canvas serial, a Dickensian form, is currently making its comeback not in the world of the novel, but as the 'concept that revitalized television' through the binge releases of Netflix and Hulu. Is it possible that it isn't the audience for writers that's shrinking, so much as the audience for print as a medium?

For their part, media writers may not feel unwanted in workshop so much as intimidated. For all their technical skills, media people do tend to be further from language than poets and fiction writers. They may feel overwhelmed even in Poetry I. Media writers may also reveal a dependence on sources that writing programs discourage or even exclude. Feeling somewhat overlooked by, or somehow out of place in, a traditional writing program, media writers will then often reinforce their own prejudices, moving toward traditions formed by subculture, or industry, operating on sensitivities and techniques somewhat unfamiliar to or misunderstood within the workshop. Media writers are also open to choices in genre, pop culture, fringe subjects and extreme emotional registers that print writers often view as simple bad judgment. Where knowledge and deliberation might guide others, media writers may proceed on faith, intuition, chance and a consistent reliance on precedent. They are people who teach themselves to write by watching television, or by playing games, watching cartoons, reading manga and comic books – which is fine, until you realize that this kind of education is largely delimited by the media of the time. Downton Abbey, but not Jane Austen. Straight Outta Compton, but not Ralph Ellison.

Writing Everything

What makes these divisions among creative storytellers so surprising is that they continue through a time of unprecedented engagement with story. At the moment, there are thousands of writers in print, but also hundreds of television and screenwriters, game designers and graphic novelists in production. There has been, in last 30 years, an unprecedented expansion of media in all forms. There are dozens of college-level training programs for storytellers of all vocations. There is a complex online network of writers and readers who support themselves and each other through private donation, crowd-sourced funding, grants, fellowships and subscriptions. It seems not an exaggeration to claim that there have never been so many stories told in so many different ways, so many kinds of storytelling so widely available.

If the kinds of writing being produced are expanding along with their delivery forms, if the audiences for stories is expanding with those features, and if the forms and elements of narrative are changing, then perhaps the definition of writing is changing as well. If it may be that writing is no longer exclusively bound to words printed on a page, then the idea that writers might define and educate themselves for a specific medium, like paper, may feel comfortable, but may no longer be sensible. If we accept a new definition of writing, and by extension a new definition of what it means to be a writer, then we are also accepting a redefinition of what it means to be educated as a writer. If all of this has been evident for a long time, even decades, then a better way to address the current situation of writing may be to consider the ideas that this accelerating availability and accessibility of culture and technology is making various forms of media writing possible for almost everyone and more than familiar to our students and audiences, that the written page is giving way to the networked screen, and that this may be the point at which we agree to teach more forms of writing to more kinds of writers in our classrooms.

Continuing those ideas, the recognition of media composition as a form of writing, and the admission that creative writing is no longer a form of communication intended solely for the printed page, will probably mean admitting that the practice of writing may now encompass aspects of both a global and a media-specific approach, and that, as a practice, creative writing is now varied and mature enough to be understood as having both abstract principles and material realities, each of which can be observed, learned, applied, interpreted and therefore taught, in a classroom. It seems that, to some degree, a new awareness should be possible, one which respects narrative as a universal condition while acknowledging each medium as a form unto itself, rather than a simple delivery system. There are too many stories occurring in media other than paper to forgo the workshopping of those forms. By privileging print, the book and the page, we are, in some respects, asking media writers to look within the print model for guidance, or move on, a position which sends many to the technical hands-on approach of media production.

Whatever kind of media presence young writers might want to achieve, we might allow them to feel that they all have a home in the creative writing department, that there is room to study with other writers, under the auspices of writing, all kinds of storytelling and narrative – print, visual and interactive – and that we agree they should have the opportunity to see whatever kind of work they produce understood by a community of writers specifically as story. This new position on the part of creative writing programs would connect media writing to the heritage of writing practices as well as the workshop model. In addition, we might ask young writers to think of themselves as writers, not producers of paper objects, to understand that a story can be migrated across a number of different media, each with its own strengths and shortcomings, without losing any of its essential characteristics.

This is not to say that young writers will abandon the page, but that they might be encouraged to look beyond paper to something trans-disciplinary, hybrid, and able to tolerate production across many fields. Writers can be educated to the competencies of a growing technical and commercial realm, and be trained to feel capable outside the structure of traditional forms and positions. They can be taught to consider new areas of experience, yet still remain sensitive to the pursuit of the elusive and indeterminate.

It may also be time to consider the idea that the writers whom programs leave to their own devices may diminish the field as a whole. Nothing replaces the desire to get the story right, that motivation will outweigh much in terms of preparation – but self-education, especially for writers, belies a few weaknesses. First, there is a value in working with an accomplished writer, someone whose experience can put setbacks, or what seem like setbacks, into perspective, someone who also has a long acquaintance with a field, who understands how the field has changed and shaped itself over time, and who has read widely and is able to connect Clueless to Emma. Second, it's easy for a self-educated writer to be satisfied with a general grasp of concepts. Without knowing anything more than television police dramas, it's hard to imagine what writers like Poe, Simenon or Manchette have accomplished in the form. Third, the study of creative writing often helps young writers see relevance in a work that lies outside their immediate needs. It is often no more than this simple position: I am studying creative writing – that makes a larger world relevant. You may want to write television, but as a student of creative writing suddenly Proust is relevant, Shakespeare is relevant, Steinbeck is relevant. Creative writing, like any other art, is bound to its community and traditions. If our past declines, we will fall with it. If we allow our traditions to be marginalized in the education of young writers we will in turn be marginalized ourselves. One of the surest ways to erase culture is to leave it in the hands of a commercial sector operating for profit alone. It's destructive to abandon the education of young writers to those forces. Just as they have marketed and worked toward the end of high culture, serious drama and contemporary music, they are intent on maintaining an environment hostile to serious work. As all of the arts struggle to survive the great media shifts of the 21st century, abandoning media writers to 'education by the market' is stupidly shortsighted. More than ever, words and images are how our society produces meaning. Losing media writers from the classroom means losing influence over the way our society communicates and over who or what shapes our culture's sense of language and therefore thought. It means agreeing to an era of writing designed to meet the mindset and criteria of those who feel the role of the writer is to address the individual as one of the nameless thousands and understanding narrative primarily as a tool of persuasion meant to serve politicians, corporations, spin doctors. As the present guardians of a tradition of intellectual inquiry, and as those who follow the example of so many writers who expressed with surety their moral dissent from totalitarianism, nihilism, fascism and madness, it seems unthinkable to abandon the most powerful communication systems in the history of mankind to those whose ultimate motivation is power, money and control. As writers and educators, we should acknowledge a public trust to words and our ongoing responsibility to narrative.

An Attempt at Some Guidelines

With these concerns in mind, it seems a gesture toward media writers could benefit writing programs in several ways. First, it would recognize media writing as a creative endeavor, one that deserves a legitimate home within the academy, and one that has a critical narrative, as well as technical base. A media presence in creative writing would also expose serious students to both conventional and new forms of expression, hopefully not as an obligation but as a range of approach, as modalities, just as a visual arts program might teach drawing, painting, sculpture and digital art. This inclusion would also create commonalities with the fine and performing arts, offering a range of perspectives on aesthetic criteria, in some cases even creating new communities of study, practice, production and performance.

Although the field of creative writing is already significant in size, an inclusion of media forms would reach large numbers of new writers, and acknowledge forms of writing that at the moment seem to slip past us into a purely commercial realm. The study of narrative across media, the lessons of that intellectual context, are likely to broaden and deepen our knowledge of creative writing overall. Finally, the inclusion of media writing along with fiction, poetry and other text practices of print would stave off the technological aging of these fields, and keep creative writing as a practice not only accessible but in some cases relevant to many kinds of audience.

Some of the resistance to expanding the field of teaching comes from the recognition that there is already too much to know and teach. Thoughtful media competence would strain all resources, especially time, across an already weakened system. Another barrier to including media writing is to cast its appearance as a giant shadow, the monolith, the seismic paradigm shift that, as it advances on every aspect of human experience, threatens to drown language in an over-saturated, hyper-mediated world which reshapes many existing aspects of pedagogy.

An easier way to begin might be to outline certain media sensitivities that could be beneficial to all writers of the media age. These might be visual storytelling, process, simulation, navigation, spatialization, networking, interaction. Here, we might also note that the workshop model itself is a contested model. An agreement that media processes are worth studying in depth, as features of a specific medium, with examples of each provided on a case-by-case basis, may influence approach as well as content and technique. Other forms of expression may bring additional approaches to instruction, such as models of the studio, atelier, charette, feminist or devised group practices, as well as an expanded view of important works that might be considered as literature. With these ideas in mind, we can list some principles, though no more than initial thoughts, and a few ideas that seem most immediate to the recognition of media writing:

- beyond the page, other media are literary forms which have developed features, devices and logics with narrative aims;
- while some aspects of narrative design are global (character, plot, setting), others are local or specific to their media type (paragraphs, dissolves, game states, panel inserts);

- each type of media has its own local resources, and the study of narrative in that media form should take these resources into account;
- local features of one media type (print) cannot be imposed on another media type (film);
- the ability to derive meaning from media's specific local features is a form of cognition;
- as different kinds of writers are brought to work together, traditions from other forms of creative expression may widen the nature of instruction, offering surprising alternatives to an at times contested workshop model;
- as new forms of media are developed, new instances of narrative cognition may be observed.

From these principles, it's possible to make an initial attempt at some guidelines for critical media awareness, or a theoretical underpinning that might act for the basis of some educational response:

- if other media constitute literary forms, then studying those forms increases our understanding of literature itself, and a complete understanding of literature would require sensitivity to all media;
- a study of narrative across many kinds of media would give writers a greater context for all narrative behaviors and, therefore, more insight into narrative effect;
- understanding the resources of many kinds of media might reduce an ideology of dominance from any one narrative form, an idea that would serve all writers well in the era of the decline of print media;
- it is essential to the pursuit of literary thought for writers to understand and be able to communicate expressively through popular forms of media.

A pedagogical response to these ideas will require some vision. They signal a fundamental reappraisal of literary practice, implying a legitimation of narrative across all media, and a broadening of aesthetics which would require a significant evolution for creative writing programs across the board. Taking up that evolution means opening our current programs to new people and new modes of thinking about storytelling. It may also mean accepting the lateral growth of writing, a willingness to let writing spread outward, in branches, or networks, creating an intricate, interdependent structure across disciplines. While this may sound pluralistic, including more kinds of media also means asking programs to accept more and different types of responsibility, multiple approaches to teaching, possibly a re-examination of certain embedded beliefs. Evaluation and consistency become more complicated. As in the case of any undertaking, the move from idea to practice is likely to be confusing, open to misstep. However, as literary thought finds expression in more and more forms and technologies, writers, especially young writers, should not place constraints on their abilities or their capacity to create or, at the very least, those constraints should not be artifacts of their creative education.

In Conclusion

After spending centuries within the boundaries of the printed page, it's important to acknowledge the new kinds of narrative made possible by technology, the effects media are having on creative writing and the ways in which storytelling is continuing to evolve.

Comic strips, movies and games produce stories that have meaning. They establish common narrative experiences. They contribute to communal identity. In other words, media creation is a technical enterprise, but it's also a literary practice. Part of our job then as writers – and teachers – is to uphold not only the integrity of language and narrative invention, but also its diversity of expression. That will involve an expanded awareness of reading and writing, but also a new recognition of image making, process and simulation. To define the quality of an idea or experience by its delivery medium is superficial and escapes our commitment to real thought as artists. Limiting the avenues of narrative expression is, in some aspects, a way of limiting the diversity of culture itself. Likewise, salesmen, spin doctors and hustlers want to manage language and emotion, rather than inspire thought and feeling. They're controllers who produce strategy over thought. To abandon media narrative to the commercial world, to replace the study of short fiction with the art of the elevator pitch, fails both language and society. Instead, our sense of who we are, our construction of that identity, our tolerances for our own imaginations and our domains of the literary might expand along with what is new and expressive, even if those modes of discourse have only recently become legible.

The printed page is one self of a writer, a mirror of inner sincerity and a field of personal truth. But it does well to remind ourselves that we are each of us a combination of creative impulses, sensory experiences, media temperaments and cultural desires. We read, but also see, sketch and imagine. Our relatable experiences are an archive of words, images, sounds and processes, one which must be written and revised, but also captured, framed, drawn and designed in order to be understood.

6 The Convergence of Creative Writing Processes and Their Neurological Mapping

Dianne Donnelly

The creative processes of writers comprise an integrated convergence of confluences, connectivity, composting, inquiry, insight and the intuitive practices associated with the acquisition and accumulation of well practiced domain-specific skills. While anecdotal evidence and social cognitive studies point to the role of less controlled and unconscious processes in advancing creative thinking and its performative practices, little is known about how the initiation and inception of creative ideas, insights and intuition arise in the brain. With a particular interest in the ways in which creative processes map on the brain, the ways in which the brain sciences are producing insight about the creative processes, and the ways in which this insight might have meaning for the changing of creative writing in America, I explore the integration and convergence of creative processes and the fundamental neurobiology of creativity and the means by which creative cognition recruits the activation and deactivation of regions of the brain to respond to and increase creative processes.

While insightful research/scholarship has explored the epistemology, pedagogy, taxonomies and theories underlying our creative writing practices (e.g. Bizzaro, Donnelly, Harper, Vanderslice, Mayers, Haake), few studies (e.g. Doyle, 1998; Magee, 2009; Wirtz, 2011) have investigated the *distinguishing* domain-specific creative processes of writers beyond those established by scientific paradigms (the most influential being Wallas' 1926 model of creativity, which divides the process of creative thinking into four to five stages: preparation, incubation, *intimation*, illumination, validation). Moreover, recent research findings (e.g. Kaufman, 2013; Jung *et al.*, 2010, 2013; Limb, 2010; Liu *et al.*, 2012) and technology – specifically, functional magnetic resonance imaging (fMRI) – now provide us with a relational context for how the brain responds to creativity, particularly the kinds of processes creative writers engage with in relation to inception, incubation, insight and intuitive performances of well-practiced craft.

In this chapter, I explore the combinatorial creative processes of writers with an aim to emphasize their performative practices (rather than to promote/clarify discrete 'stages' of creativity) and to link, where possible, specific neurological implications so as to offer a more comprehensive account of the relationship and interplay between imagination and experience (and all their variable components) in Creative Writing. Moreover, my goal is to make connections between the combinatorial nature of creative processes and their coinciding neural correlates as concrete as possible so as to propel the growing field of creative writing research forward in America and to situate this knowledge within the larger creative writing domain in the US, within its academic creative writing communities, and within the scope of new understandings that can translate to new ways of thinking about writing and the teaching of writing.

Initiations and Inceptions

> But, of course, there is nothing mystical about these kinds of thoughts. Unless you are away with the pixies, or fall for Cartesian ghosts hiding in dopamine synapses, you must concede that creative ideas are, like all mental processes, mechanical beasts that are computed – yes, computed – in a 3-pound, mushy pile of electrified biochemistry that is your brain. (Dietrich, 2012: 2)

'Where do ideas come from?' is not a question that creative writers generally want to answer, mostly because writers (and other creatives such as choreographers, artists, musicians, composers, mathematicians, scientists) are not always sure what triggers an idea. The sound-bite answers to this enigmatic question, often asked by our students, don't help very much: from 'a mail-order house in Schenectady' (Harlan Ellison in Le Guin, 2000: 97); 'from a dusty old book full of ideas in my basement' (Gaiman, 2011); or, if you're a songwriter like Willy Nelson, 'The air is full of tunes', so 'just reach up and pick one' (in Le Guin, 2000: 98). Pragmatically, it is often difficult to talk about idea-creation concepts because the conventional language and metaphors that have been used for these triggering moments (e.g. miraculous flashes, muse visitations, divine gifts, magical inspiration) and for sudden bursts of new insight (eureka! and a-ha moments, strokes, epiphanies), while subjectively provocative and 'rhetorically florid', not only present an apocryphal view of idea-creation and insight as these 'wonderful illuminating moment[s]' (Johnson, 2010), but they also perpetuate the romanticized notion that still exists in the minds of many of our students (and still remains a component of a stubbornly sweeping creative writing lore) that the emergence of an idea represents a *single* signifier for creative development in the sense that 'a writer "gets" (takes into the head) an "idea" (some sort of mental object) "from" somewhere, and then turns it into words and writes them on paper' (Le Guin, 1987: 194) or the falsified notion that insight comes to a writer without any preexisting data/memory sets from which to draw.

Liken an idea to a small fragment, which is not yet formed, one which may never fully materialize, might be dismissed entirely, or might, after much pondering, evolve into something completely unrelated to the initial urging. Indeed, these triggering moments *may seem* magical, sparked by literally anything – an image, conversations, a scent, a gesture, a shift in tone, a sighting, movement, a read passage, a painting, a description, a sound, a news event; and as Ursula Le Guin (1987: 193) reminds us, they 'may not [even] involve ideas in the sense of intelligible thought', surfacing rather as a 'mood, resonances, mental glimpses, voices, emotions, visions, dreams' or perhaps as a rhythm. Based on experience and imagination, 'writers tend to train themselves to notice when they've had an idea' (Gaiman, 2011), and to remain open and aware, 'always looking', as Marcella Polain (in Magee, 2009) reflects, 'for something that resonates, shocks or triggers some kind of deep response'.

At an elementary neurological level, these fragments initiate the creation of a 'new network of neurons firing together in [the] brain' (Johnson, 2010), 'merely something to hold on to as you begin' (Gaiman, 2011), 'something that drives you' (Thomas Demand in Aitkin, 2013); and at a deeper level, our creative cognitive processes can be revealed as a neurological product, engaging dynamically configured neural networks in *both* hemispheres of our brain, which can now be studied scientifically via functional neuroimaging technology (fMRI). The latest neuroscientific findings (e.g. Mark Beeman, Rex Jung, John Kounios) reveal creativity as a *whole*-brain activity, 'distributed in multiple, independent streams of processing that are, at no time, synthesized in one central location into a coherent image for the mind's eye' (Dietrich, 2012: 4), not one involving 'a single brain region or a single side of the brain' (Kaufman, 2013) as we once thought, with the results of researcher Roger Sperry's split-brain experiments in the 1960s (which earned him a Nobel Prize in 1981) kicking off the left/right brain dichotomy, and the theories of right-brain dominance later popularized by Richard Florida (2003) in *The Rise of the Creative Class* and by Daniel Pink (2005) in *A Whole New Mind: Why*

Right-Brainers Will Rule the Future. Consider that the neurotransmission across the broad spectrum of the brain's functionality engages interactions between what is estimated to be 200 billion neurons in our brain. Discarding the misinformed theory of hemispheric dichotomy, we now know that there is a back-and-forth communication among multiple neural correlates within and across brain regions, with 'different patterns of neural activations and deactivations' occurring 'at different stages of the creative process' (depending upon the activity and how this activity unfolds over a period of time), so that the 'entire creative process ... consists of many interacting cognitive processes (both conscious and unconscious)' (Kaufman, 2013).

Acquiring this new knowledge about the mechanisms associated with idea-creation and the neurotransmission of creativity can only help our students, who are often clouded in the mystification of the creative act. As we have opportunities to shift perspectives in our US creative writing culture, to tell truths as we know them, and to share knowledge as we acquire it, then perhaps we can expand our predominantly practice-related field to include practice-based research in which we seek new knowledge and spiral these outcomes into the field and into our classrooms.

Confluences, Connectivity and Composting

Beyond being in a state of readiness (as observers of the world, inquirers, readers of variable texts), what Alison Croggon (in Magee, 2009) likes to call 'keeping fit', writers engage in the combinatorial nature of (1) *confluences* – the flowing or merging of ideas; (2) *connectivity* – concluding, as Steve Jobs (1996: 7) does, that 'creativity is just connecting things', the intersecting or perhaps colliding of two or more ideas that Neil Gaiman (2011) suggests 'haven't come together before or haven't been seen together before'; and (3) *composting* – what Gary Snyder refers to in his poem 'On top' as the turning, watering, waiting, sifting of new stuff in our minds (Snyder, n.d.). A writer's experience and imagination have taught her to intuit the internal spaces where this waiting, listening, feeling, *composting* reside, so as not to grasp too quickly, neither 'grabbing' or 'pushing'(Le Guin, 2000: 99); it requires 'no action', director/screenwriter David Lynch (2014) insists but, rather, the receptiveness to receiving what surfaces. Marcella Polain (in Magee, 2009) allows the triggering complex to 'sit in a place', a recognized 'writing space' that she 'can almost feel physically'. She refers to this as a 'psychic space' that 'just turns over'; she 'can feel it doing some kind of work', but she qualifies this space as 'pre-conscious', noting that later in the process, when 'we're casting around for words and feel that space, it's the same one'. Similarly, sculptor/photographer Thomas Demand (in Aitken, 2013) knows he has to 'Get out of the way and see what happens', to 'wait for the picture to come'. Understanding that fragments reappear in different ways, in different configurations and mental sets or glimpses, artist Phillipe Parreno (in Aitkin, 2013) agrees, as he discounts the notion of an epiphany and instead refers to the triggering that 'comes back and then back and then starts to become more repetitive' as it takes 'shape and form', as if it were 'a new piece of land that can be formed'. The understanding that ideas come in small fragments as the 'seed of a shape', like 'bait on a hook', prompts Lynch to share his idea/fishing metaphor in an interview with Paul Holdengraber (in Aleph, 2016):

> You can pull them in, and if you catch an idea that you love, that's a beautiful, beautiful day.... And that idea might be a fragment of the whole – whatever it is you're working on – but you have even more bait. Thinking about that small fragment – that little fish – will bring in more, and they'll come in and they'll hook on. And more and more come in, and pretty soon you might have a script – or a chair, or a painting, or an idea for a painting.

The 'thinking' Lynch intuits in the above context is not the conscious, analytical kind associated with the cognitive control networks of the brain (which help us with complex problem solving and reasoning) but, rather, the *creative* 'thinking' that continues even when we're not consciously aware of these activities. This offline process occurs when there is a 'downregulation of externally directed cognition and upregulation of exploratory idea spaces' (Jung *et al.*, 2013) that arise when our brain falls into default mode and engages in 'complex, evaluative, and unconscious forms of information processing' (Kuhn, 2013: 153). It is during this mind-wandering state that the subconscious neuro-mechanisms associated with the default network spontaneously tap into the pathways that are unique to us: our experiences, memories, future imaginings, perspectives, alternative scenarios, facilitating in this linking the construction of new meanings, connections and patterns that previously had escaped detection or recognition, to emerge into our consciousness as *insight*.

Contrary to circulating anecdotes associated with inspirational accounts of eureka episodes and sudden bursts of insight/a-ha moments (e.g. Darwin, Archimedes, Coleridge, Kekulé, Poincaré) the subconscious interplay, while random, makes connections among external triggering ideas in this compositing circuit and the details/abstracts associated with our data and memory sets. Indeed, Arthur Koestler (1964: 20) insists that the creative act 'does not create something out of nothing; it uncovers, selects, reshuffles, combines, synthesizes already existing facts, ideas, faculties, skills. The more familiar the parts, the more striking the new whole.'

Charles Darwin, for example, wrote about his discovery of his basic algorithm of natural selection in his autobiography, noting 'Ah, at last, I had a theory with which to work' (quoted in Johnson, 2010). The research of scholar Howard Gruber, however, shed new light onto Darwin's sudden revelation when it explored Darwin's detailed notebooks and unearthed the reality that Darwin's theory of natural selection had been all but defined for months before his eureka moment (see Johnson, 2010). Many of us have heard the story of Greek scientist and mathematician Archimedes, who had been asked by King Hiero to determine if the crown he had commissioned had indeed been constructed of pure gold or a combination of metals, as he had feared. Archimedes had been pondering how to measure the gold in the crown and the solution surfaced after he had entered a full tub of water and the weight of his body displaced a particular amount of the bathwater. Knowing these displacement properties could be applied to the weight/material composition of the crown, Archimedes jumped from the tub, shouting 'Eureka! Eureka!' (Archimedes did go on to prove that other metals had indeed been mixed with the gold in the crown.)

While Samuel Taylor Coleridge's poetic vision of Xanadu came to him in an opium-induced reverie, his preface to 'Kubla Kahn' clarifies that Coleridge had been reading about Kubla Kahn beforehand. German chemist Friedrich von Kekulé had spent years trying to work out the structure of benzene. While thinking about the problem, he had dozed off by the fireside, dreaming about a coiled snake grabbing its own tail. This ring-link image further suggested the idea of the cyclic structure of benzene (coincidently, it is said that Kekulé had seen a similar image of a snake devouring his tail seven years earlier, at an 1850 murder trial). Similar to the others, Henri Poincaré's enlightened moments were precipitated by the same subconscious neuro-mechanisms that continue to evaluate and process information when our attention is not on task. Poincaré had struggled to solve a particular mathematical construct, and later, upon boarding an omnibus to attend a geological excursion, the idea now known as 'Fuchsian functions' came to him; he described his ideas as 'colliding until pairs interlocked ... making a stable combination'. In his work *The Foundations of Science*, Poincaré (1913: 393) compares these less conscious ideas, the freer interplay of neural networking, to atoms:

> During a period of apparent rest and unconscious work, certain of them come unhooked from the wall and put into motion. They flash in every direction through the space where they are enclosed.... Then their mutual impacts may produce new combinations.

These 'unhooked' atoms, in other words, may appear as unprovoked sudden insight as they merge into our consciousness, but there is now evidence that points to the back-and-forth neural network transmission that sets in motion the quieting of the cognitive control network and the activating of the default mode with a subsequent feed-forwarding of new patterns/possibilities that we either accept, disregard or return to the default network for more composting, for more 'unhooking' of atoms from the wall.

Insight and Inquiry

The combinatorial processes of creativity happen when the fusion or synthesis of an idea is perceived simultaneously in two or more 'matrices of thought', what Koestler refers to as an act of 'bisociation' and what Le Guin assigns as the 'comingling' of 'sound, syntax, images, feelings', all present 'in some degree', and working together, so that what arises in the mind are from 'psychic contents' that may start with 'a feeling':

> [that feeling] begins to connect itself to an image that will express it, and that image leads to an idea, until now half-formed, that begins to find words for itself, and the words lead to other words that make new images, perhaps of people, characters of a story, who are doing things that express the underlying feelings and ideas that are now resonating with each other. (Le Guin, 1987: 195)

In other words, when creativity operates on more than one plane as Koestler (1964: 20) suggests, there is a juxtaposition of formerly unrelated ideas (a 'bisociation of matrices') that occurs in a 'double-minded, transitory state of unstable equilibrium where the balance of both emotion and thought is disturbed'. As a general mechanism for the creative act, Koestler describes the characteristics of bisociation in this way:

> The moment of truth, the sudden emergence of a new insight, is an act of intuition. Such intuitions give the appearance of miraculous flashes, or short-circuits of reasoning. In fact they may be likened to an immersed chain, of which only the beginning and the end are visible above the consciousness. The diver vanishes at one end of the chain and comes up at the other end, guided by invisible links. (Koestler, 1964: 211)

While we need our whole brain to be creative, neuropsychologist Rex Jung tells us that 'there are particular regions in our brain that are important to certain aspects of certain stages of creativity' (Jung, 2012), and this means that in order for idea-generation and the synthesis of patterns and connections to take place, we need to temporarily calm (downregulate) the rule-based frontal lobes of our brain so that the neural networks of the default mode can be upregulated. Jung and his colleagues, who use brain imaging to study the differences between intelligence and creativity, refer to this frontal lobe disengagement as 'transient hypofrontality' (in Tippet, 2015). He explains that by 'tilting the various control mechanisms in the brain to leverage activation in a concerted way', we're permitting 'a freer interplay of different networks in the brain so that the ideas literally can link together more readily' (Jung in Tippet, 2015). The analogy that Jung uses to distinguish the neural properties associated with intelligence and creativity is useful. He refers to 'this superhighway in the brain' which gets us to our destination, 'Point A to Point B'. With creativity, he tells us, 'it's a slower, more meandering process where you want to take the side roads and even the dirt roads to get there, to put the ideas together'. Summarily, he suggests that these off-track diversions that create frontal downregulation and hypofrontal states are important to 'allow [our] ideas to link together in unexpected ways' (in Tippet, 2015). Structural brain research in the form of brain imaging (e.g. Jung *et al*, 2013; Kuhn, 2013; Limb, 2010) has provided some measurements of intelligence and creativity output (i.e. less controlled processes in creative thinking that influence creativity compared with the intelligence outputs) as it relates to the positive correlations between well established creativity measures and cortical thickness in the brain and the extent of white matter integrity. Results demonstrate the presence of greater cortical thickness and white matter with intelligence and less cortical thickness and white matter associated with creativity. What the structural brain research reveals may help us to understand how the architectural environment of our brains responds to creativity as well as emphasize the importance of self-inducing these hypofrontal states so as to facilitate the bisociation of matrices in these exploratory spaces. This relationship between creative processes and the inducing of brain states that create spaces for exploring ideas and inciting the convergences of confluences and connections allows us to view Creative Writing through a different lens, opening pedagogical opportunities for the field.

While there are, of course, important apportionments of raw materials that precede the downregulation of frontal inhibitions and exploration of possibilities, the ability to disinhibit cognitive resources, to create these spaces for exploring ideas and to incite the convergences of confluences and connections is particular to each creative writer and dependent on those techniques that s/he recognizes as avenues for guiding thoughts in new and creative directions. Whether it be warm baths (Archimedes), long walks (Beethoven, Shelley, Thoreau), playing the piano (Einstein), jogging (Joyce Carol Oates), meditation (David Lynch), daydreaming (Neil Gaiman), ironing (Margaret Atwood) – the list is endless but, oftentimes, patterns and connections show up when we're doing something else, when we're distracted. Many writers and other creatives find the technique/approach that best facilitates the exploration of creative spaces. For instance, Einstein, Edison and Dalí found working naps to be beneficial in facilitating hypofrontal states. More specifically, they experienced a guided creative cognition wandering by inducing the transitional state that exists between wakefulness and falling asleep, the state when the brain is subtle and hyperassociative. Sitting in a chair, each held an object in the palm of his hand, beneath which was an upside down saucer/plate. In each case, when his hand relaxed, the object fell, hitting the plate, and this caused a stirring just before the onset of sleep and precipitated new thoughts and creative directions. Many of us also recognize those lucid moments at the onset of wakefulness as a time when our mind is primed for making creative connections.

Once we have something that resonates (an image, a notion, a mood, the glimpse of a character), we look for the ambiguities so that we may discover something new. Amy Tan, in her TED talk 'Where does creativity hide?', says 'like scientists, writers need to develop a cosmology of their own universe – to be a creator of that universe' by asking these questions: 'Why do things happen? How do things happen? How do I make things happen?' In her search to discover something new in her creative work, she finds value in the observer effect of quantum mechanics and the inequalities associated with uncertainty principles. Once Tan has a question framed, it becomes, for her, a focus, and she recognizes the 'hints' and 'clues' that have 'been obvious and yet that have not been'. She explains this cosmology in this way:

> And all these things that seem to be flotsam and jetsam in life actually go through that question, and what happens is those particular things become relevant. And it seems like it's happening all the time. You think there's a sort of coincidence going on, a serendipity, in which you're getting all this help from the universe. And it may also be explained that now you have a focus. And you are noticing it more often. (Tan, 2008)

Tan suggests inquiring about what is not known and the subsequent making of associations through life looking, listening and feeling.

Questions such as 'What if?', as Neil Gaiman (2011) asks when ideas light, may help to lead to this discovery of what is not known.

John Keats also makes reference to this willingness to embrace uncertainty and ambiguity – what he calls 'negative capability' – rather than trying to reconcile contradictory aspects in the closed rationality of our cognitive control mind (see Popova, n.d.). This search for the unknown requires what Margaret Boden (1991: 12) refers to as the 'skilled and typically unconscious deployment of a large number of everyday psychological abilities such as noticing, remembering and recognizing', each comprising 'interpretative processes and complex mental structures'.

My hope is that my inquiry into the writer's processes and the functionality of the brain can translate into ways in which we can guide our students through these ambiguities, these uncertainties, these boundaries between what is known and unknown, helping our students to unlock hidden voices of creativity that often contain the answers.

Intuitive Practices Resulting from the Acquisition and Accumulation of Well Practiced Domain-Specific Skills

> Sit down. Be quiet.
> You must depend upon
> affection, reading, knowledge,
> skill – more of each
> than you have – inspiration,
> work, growing older, patience,
> for patience joins time
> to eternity....
> (Wendell Berry 'How to be a poet', 1934, in Tippet, 2011)

> There is just the obstinate, continuous cultivation of a disposition, leading to skill in performance. (Le Guin, 1987: 193)

Well practiced domain-specific skills

There's an anecdote about Picasso sketching in the park, and a woman walks by, recognizes him as the *great* Picasso, and pleads with him to sketch her portrait. He agrees, sets about sketching, and a few minutes later he hands her the portrait. She's overjoyed, gushing about how lovely it is, how perfectly it captures her very essence. She thanks him and asks how much she owes him. '$5000, madam', Picasso says. The lady, aghast, outraged, asks how that could be possible as it only took him a few minutes. Picasso looks up, and matter-of-factly replies, 'No, madam, it took me my whole life'.

On a somewhat related thread, when graphic designer Paula Scher was asked how she could create the famous Citi logo in a second after her talk with Citi executives, she responded, 'But it IS done in a second – it's done in a second and 34 years. It's done in a second and every experience, and every movie, and everything in my life that's in my head' (Scher, 2005).

The accounts of Picasso and Scher emphasize that beyond the passion and motivation engaged in cultivating craft, it takes a lot of time to change the structure of our brains before there is the seemingly seamless construct of intuitive practices resulting from the acquisition and accumulation of well-practiced domain-specific skills. Vincent Walsh (2011) refers to this domain-specific obsession as a necessary 'bedrock of preparation', and what psychologist Malcolm Gladwell specifies in his book *Outliers* (2008) as the 10,000 hours of practice rule to achieve 'mastery' in a field, what M. Csikszentmihalyi (2004) suggests as 'flow', the coinciding of 'skills and channels', what Yusef Komunyakaa (in Wirtz, 2011: 21) speaks of as 'the process of moving from the conscious development of craft (i.e., constant rehearsal) to instinct and intuition', and what poet William Olsen (in Wirtz, 2011) sees as 'making', 'seeing' and 'learn[ing] one's craft', so he can 'rely more on intuition' so as not, he insists, 'to sit on a two-legged chair'.

On flow and domain-obsession

Csikszentmihalyi (2004) talks about a composer who expresses the 'ecstatic state' he is in when composing, to the point where he feels as though he 'almost doesn't exist'. The composer describes this state accordingly:

> My hand seems devoid of myself, and I have nothing to do with what is happening. I just sit there watching it in a state of awe and wonderment, and [the music] just flows out of itself.

While this sounds magical and mystical, totally out of the control of the artist, Csikszentmihalyi offers a scientific explanation for this kind of experience, which 'can only happen to someone who is very well trained and who has developed technique'. I find it compelling that our nervous system can process only about 110 bits of information per second, and our concentration in one area uses all 'available bandwidth', so that 'there's none left over to monitor' the 'sense of self'(Csikszentmihalyi, 2004). I suggest that this spontaneous flow happens in the writing realm as well, as the writer's sense of self becomes less monitored and as intuitive practices unfold. Marguerite Duras (1993: 25) is clear to clarify, however, that this *flow* is 'not a matter of passing from one state to another' but, rather, 'a matter of deciphering something already there, something you've already done in the sleep of your life, in its organic rumination'. If I understand Duras correctly, she suggests that writers don't channel personas or characters or enter into a dimension in which they have no control while writing, but rather that the objectivity and subjectivity of writers merge so that a space is created, one which Jennifer Harrison (in Magee, 2009) attests she cannot clearly 'discern ... between what [she's] thinking and what [she's] writing'.

Csikszentmihalyi (2004) describes this concept of flow as 'opening a door that's floating in the middle of nowhere and all you have to do is go and turn the handle and open it and let yourself sink into it'. Poet Alison Croggon (in Magee, 2009) can relate, noting that it feels as 'if there's a door in there', as if she's 'listening to some other part of me, that's not always available'. Novelist Faye Moskowitz likens the concept to 'an archeological dig', noting that 'I carefully remove one layer of memory and go down deeper and then deeper.... At a certain depth ... I uncover what I could not have predicted, and then, flow begins' (see Perry, 2009: 214).

Improvisation and how the writing proceeds

Writing is a performative act, not one that situates the creative act as defined at any point, except, perhaps, as it evolves and completes in its final presentation, and even then it is open to the interpretation and reader response of those who engage with the writing across so many perspectives/realms. So the point here is that writers do not necessarily intend the shape of a piece while they are writing. For instance, rather than having an intention in mind, Croggon (in Magee, 2009) 'wait[s] for the poem to intend itself'; she is uncertain, while she is writing, of the poem's final shape. Instead, because of the convergence of processes, which are clearly recursive, nonlinear and iterative, and because of the intuitive practices resulting from the accumulation of well-practiced skills, writers can allow the creative work (in whatever form it exists) to evoke something new in the creative work that the writer might not have imagined at the onset. This practice – in the deepest sense that practice is associated with domain knowledge, flow of matching skills and challenge of task, as well as an awareness of the simultaneous convergence of images and other connections associated with the creative work – informs the receptiveness and development of the writing.

Jenny Harrison (in Magee, 2009), for example, concludes that it's possible that the visual image comes first, 'yet other connections are arriving simultaneously, immediately, not coming later'. For Marcella Polain (in Magee 2009), 'it's about hearing something and it's about the rhythm of that'. Polain contends that 'once [she's got] the rhythm of the first line, [she feels] a propulsion into the poem'. Virginia Woolf (1926) also felt that the matter for her was related to rhythm, suggesting that 'once you get [the rhythm], you can't use the wrong words'. She lamented in her letter to friend/poet/lover Vita Sackville-West the complexity of her manner of proceeding:

> But on the other hand here am I sitting after half the morning, crammed with ideas, and visions, and so on, and can't dislodge them, for lack of the right rhythm. Now this is very profound, what rhythm is, and goes far deeper than any words. A sight, an emotion, creates this wave in the mind, long before it makes words to fit it.

The improvisational component of creative writing helps us to loosen our associations. Komunyakaa (2004), who has recorded improvisational performances of his poetry in concert with jazz musicians, concludes:

> There is an element of improvisation in poetry. Getting down the urgent energy of the piece is improvisation, then comes the shaping and revising. But the surprises happen in the moment of improvisation.

This improvisational component offers value to our creative writing pedagogical culture and inquires: in what ways might we draw upon/introduce such improvisation techniques to our classroom and/or merge/intersect/combine our practices with the practices of other performative disciplines?

Other creative writers, like Aileen Kelly (in Magee, 2009), have compared the role-playing of characters they engage in with their writing to method acting. Kelly notes, 'Acting for writing poetry is more like that – you feel your way through the experience and the words get generated in the process'. Jan Owen (in Magee, 2009) also suggests the similarity of the ways in which writing is similar to method acting, noting 'you are in a sense playing a part ... like the Stanislavsky method, where you become the person'. But to be clear, these 'parts' are not someone else doing the talking/thinking for writers, it's an intuitive process, not, as Polain (in Magee, 2009) protests, 'another subjectivity', but rather 'different parts', what Duras (1993: 25) refers to as 'sub-personalities', rather than the 'conjuring up of characters that speak for the writer'.

We see this creative improvisation mapped on the brain. Indeed, recent research on the improvisation of jazz musicians (Limb, 2010, 2013; Liu *et al.*, 2012) and rappers (Limb, 2010) suggests that when these musicians improvised, 'activity in their brains' inhibition centers slowed down' (Castillo, 2011), inducing the same transient hypofrontality we've discussed earlier as it relates to creative writers. Liu *et al.* (2012) compared performances of freestyle (improvised) to conventional (rehearsed) performance using fMRI and discovered that the spontaneous improvisation, as a complex cognitive process, shares features with the characterization of the '*flow*' state, with the frontal lobe playing a central role in the improvisatory process', in particular, the freeing up of the 'self-generated action ... from the conventional constraints of supervisory attention and executive control, facilitating the generation of novel ideas'.

Re-envisioning and Reflecting and Final Thoughts

Current pedagogical approaches in the US do not perceive revision as a correlated brain function. In other words, what is being taught about revision is not in tune with the actuality of brain function. We have opportunities to make these connections and draw important pedagogical implications about these relationships. As writing is a recursive process, it is important to note that while transient hypofrontality is critical for the temporary downregulation of the control cognition networks of our brain so as to explore and generate novel material, it is also important later on to upregulate these frontal lobe networks when it comes to revision processes.

We can see the cognitive functioning of this revision/evaluation process in brain studies/imaging. For example, in a 2011 study led by cognitive neuroscientist Melissa Ellamil (in Bryce, 2014), 15 art students were asked to produce illustrations for a book while lying in an fMRI scanner and then to evaluate five drawings in the course of six trials. The study, which revealed the evaluative process rather than the generation of creative ideas, indicated that 'during the evaluation phase, the brain recruited the regions of the temporopolar cortex and prefrontal cortex associated with executive function' as areas that 'support critical thinking and decision making' associated with revision processes.

The reflective nature of re-envisioning, a process that occurs in the development of creative work *often* at *many* points along the way, may engage researching what it is the writer does not yet know. Case in point, Jan Owen (in Magee, 2009) may 'begin a poem because [he] know[s] something and want[s] to know more', and as a result he will 'do some writing and then check the facts afterwards'. At any point in the writing process, the writer may be authenticating the credibility of her characters, imagery, dialogue, language and the course of the story's/poem's direction. If there is some abandoned direction, something that seems untrue to a particular character development, anything that relates to a break in pattern, theme, rhythm or more, the writer revisits the combinatorial process of creative writing, those convergences of domain-specific creative writing processes that now have even more legitimacy given the evidence of their neurological mapping.

My hope is that this research-based inquiry provides new ways of thinking about Creative Writing teaching, learning, research and knowledge in US Creative Writing programs and opens opportunities for more dialogic inquiries.

References

Aitkin, D. (2013) Conversations with Doug Aitkin. *The Source*. Available at http://dougaitkenthesource.com (accessed June 2017).
Aleph, F. (2016) David Lynch: On the art of fishing for ideas. Available at http://www.faena.com/aleph/articles/david-lynch-on-the-art-of-fishing-for-ideas-video (accessed June 2017).
Boden, M. (1991) *The Creative Mind: Myths and Mechanisms*. New York: Basic Books.
Bryce, N. (2014) Creativity – The aha! moment. *Scientific American Mind* 25, 36–41. Available at http://www.nature.com/scientificamericanmind/journal/v25/n4/full/scientificamericanmind0714-36.html (accessed June 2017).
Castillo, M. (2011) Study: This is your brain on improve, TIME Transcript. Available at http://healthland.time.com/2011/01/20/study-this-is-your-brain-on-improv/ (accessed June 2017).
Csikszentmihalyi, M. (2004) Flow, the secret to happiness. Presented at TED2004 Creativity: Flow and the Psychology of Discovery and Invention. Available at http://www.ted.com/talks/mihaly_csikszentmihalyi_on_flow (accessed June 2017).
Dietrich, A. (2012) You're gonna need a bigger boat. *TEXT Special Issue: Creativity: Cognitive, Social and Cultural Perspectives*. Available at http://www.textjournal.com.au/speciss/issue13/Dietrich.pdf (accessed June 2017).
Doyle, C.L. (1998) The writer tells: The creative process in the writing of literary fiction. *Creativity Research Journal* 11 (1), 29–37.
Duras, M. (1993) *Practicalities*. New York: Grove Press.
Gaiman, N. (2011) How creativity works: Where ideas come from? Q & A post, Wheeler Center interview. Available at https://www.youtube.com/watch?v=-C48jAkVlI0 (accessed June 2017).
Gladwell, M. (2008) *Outliers*. London: Penguin Books.
Jobs, S. (1996) The next insanely great thing. *The Wired Interview*. Available at http://archive.wired.com/wired/archive//4.02/jobs.html?pg=8&topicp (accessed June 2017).
Johnson, S. (2010) Where good ideas come from. Presented at TEDGobal. Available at http://www.ted.com/talks/steven_johnson_where_good_ideas_come_from?language=en (accessed June 2017).

Jung, R. (2012) Transcript with Fleming – Uncut. To the Best Our Knowledge at http://www.ttbook.org/book/transcript/transcript-rex-jung-uncut (accessed June 2017).

Jung, R., Segall, J.M., Bockholt, H., Flores, R.A., Smith, S.M., Chavez, R.S. and Haier, R.J. (2010) Neuroanatomy of creativity. Available at https://www.ncbi.nlm.nih.gov/pmc/articles/PMC2826582 (accessed June 2017).

Jung, R., Mead, B.S., Carrasco, J. and Flores, R.A. (2013) The structure of creative cognition in the human brain. *Frontiers in Human Neuroscience.* Available at http://journal.frontiersin.org/article/10.3389/fnhum.2013.00330/full (accessed June 2017).

Kaufman, S. (2013) Beautiful minds: The real neuroscience of creativity. Scientific American blog network at http://blogs.scientificamerican.com/beautiful-minds/the-real-neuroscience-of-creativity (accessed June 2017).

Koestler, A. (1964) *The Act of Creation.* New York: Penguin Books.

Komunyakaa, Y. (2004) An argument against simplicity. At https://www.poets.org/poetsorg/text/yusef-komunyakaa-argument-against-simplicity (accessed June 2017).

Kuhn, S. (2013) The importance of the default mode network in creativity – A structural MRI study. *Journal of Creative Behavior* 48 (2). Available at http://onlinelibrary.wiley.com/doi/10.1002/jocb.45/pdf (accessed June 2017).

Le Guin, U. (1987) Where do ideas come from? In *Dancing at the Edge of the World: Thoughts on Words, Women, Places* (pp. 192–200). New York: Grove Press.

Le Guin, U. (2000) Where do you get your ideas from? In *The World Split Open: Great Authors on How and Why We Write* (pp. 97–120). Brooklyn: Tin House Books.

Limb, C. (2010) Your brain on improv. Presented at TEDxMidAtlantic. Available at https://www.ted.com/talks/charles_limb_your_brain_on_improv?language=en (accessed June 2017).

Limb, C. (2013) Your brain on jazz. Charles Limb interviewed by Chet Cooper. *Ability Magazine.* Available at http://abilitymagazine.com/Charles-Limb.html (accessed 14 March 2016).

Liu, S., Chow, H.M., Xu, Y., Erkkinen, M.G., Swett, K.E., Eagle, M.W., Rizik-Baer, D.A. and Braun, A.R. (2012) Neural correlates of lyrical improvisation: An fMRI study of freestyle rap. *Scientific Reports* 2. Available at http://www.nature.com/articles/srep00834 (accessed June 2017).

Lynch, D. (2014) David Lynch on where ideas come from and the fragmentary nature of creativity. Presented at BAM Howard Gilman Opera House, 29 April. Available at https://youtu.be/Fxr-7O1Bfxg (accessed June 2017).

Magee, P. (2009) Is poetry research? *TEXT* 13 (2). Available at http://www.textjournal.com.au/oct09/magee.htm (accessed June 2017).

Perry, S.K. (2009) Writing in flow. In S.B. Kaufman and J.C. Kaufman (eds) *The Psychology of Creative Writing* (pp. 213–214). Cambridge: Cambridge University Press.

Poincaré, H. (1913) *The Foundations of Science.* New York: Cornell University Library (2009).

Popova, M. (n.d.) The art of 'negative capability': Keats on embracing uncertainty and celebrating the mysterious. Brainpickings, at https://www.brainpickings.org/2012/11/01/john-keats-on-negative-capability (accessed 2 February 2016).

Scher, P. (2005) Graphic designer: Paula Scher. Artist Series, at https://vimeo.com/18839878 (accessed June 2017).

Snyder, G. (n.d.) On top. Available at http://www.poetrysoup.com/famous/poem/23510/on_top (accessed June 2017).

Tan, A. (2008) Where does creativity hide? Presented at TED 2008. Available at http://www.ted.com/talks/amy_tan_on_creativity?language=en (accessed June 2017).

Tippet, K. (2011) 'How to be a poet' (to remind myself) by Wendell Berry. On Being with Krista Tippet, at http://www.onbeing.org/program/ellen-davis-and-wendell-berry-the-poetry-of-creatures/extra/how-to-be-a-poet-to-remind (accessed June 2017).

Tippet, K. (2015) Rex Jung: Creativity and the everyday brain. On Being with Krista Tippet at http://www.onbeing.org/program/rex-jung-creativity-and-the-everyday-brain/1879 (accessed June 2017).

Walsh, V. (2011) Neuroscience and creativity. Presented at TEDxAldeburgh. Available at https://www.youtube.com/watch?v=UyU-AbYiEd0 (accessed June 2017).

Wirtz, J. (2011) The poet's receptive stance as an invention heuristic. *International Journal for the Practice and Theory of Creative Writing* 8 (1), 13–24.

Woolf, V. (1926) Letter to V. Sackville-West 52 Tavistock Square, London, W.C.1., 16 March. Available at Woolf Online, http://www.woolfonline.com/?node=content/contextual/transcriptions&project=1&parent=48&taxa=49&content=6344&pos=7 (accessed June 2017).

7 Rewriting Creative Writing

Bruce Horner

Much of my professional work focuses on the history as well as study and teaching of college composition in the US and the problematics of composition's institutional location, using as my point of departure the question of work in composition – its constitution, status, conditions and effects. Applying that same point of departure to creative writing, in this chapter, I will approach creative writing in America (hereafter, CWIA) as a material social practice that manifests as an institutional phenomenon of postsecondary institutions, albeit one with inevitable ties to other cultural institutions, such as presses, bookstores, awards and review journals (cf. Pope, 2005: 40). More specifically, I argue that the work of CWIA is located in those practices, by students and teachers together, rather than strictly in the textual products of the faculty or in the publications of programs' alumnae: that is, I locate CWIA in the concrete labor conducted at that institutional site, not with commodifications of that labor taking the form of publications and careers, while recognizing that typically the work of creative writing is identified precisely with such commodifications and not with those practices, which are seen as mere precursors to those commodifications. In other words, from the perspective I'm advancing, the actual work that is CWIA goes largely unrecognized, as its work is occluded through and by its commodification. It follows that the kind of change that I'll argue CWIA might undertake is not a change through expansion of its charge through a broadening of the range of materials in which its commodities take form or in the nature of those commodities as, say, an abstracted entity dubbed 'creativity'. Instead, I'll argue for a change to CWIA in how it understands the work of CWIA.

More specifically still, I argue that we need to recognize the writing undertaken in creative writing programs by students and teachers not as precursive to actual creative writing but as itself work on and with language and language differences in writing. In one sense, this might not seem overly controversial: as I discuss below, students strive for difference in the writing they do for creative writing courses in order to distinguish their writing from that of their peers. But here I will advance a more controversial position, namely, that difference in language, as well as in communicative practice more generally, is not a deviation from the norm but, rather, is itself the norm, a position that emerges once we recognize writing as always located not only spatially but also temporally. Thus even a 'repetition' is not merely the same as what is repeated but also inherently different, changing the significance of what's repeated as being subsequently understood, as a consequence of its repetition, as the earlier version of the repetition that follows.[1] What makes this perspective on difference in language controversial is that, from this perspective, creativity cannot serve as an attribute distinguishing some writing from other writing as 'creative' versus 'noncreative', or even as 'more' creative. Instead, creativity is an inherent, inevitable feature of all writing (and all communicative practice).

I should acknowledge (and warn) at the outset that I make this argument with only second-hand knowledge of current creative writing programs, and with at best a lay knowledge of what might be called professional creative writing productions – contemporary imaginative 'literature'. The target of my argument, then, may not match the experience and concerns of those active in such programs and such productions. Nonetheless, it may be of use in demonstrating the understandings and myths of creative writing with which those who are active in such programs and productions must contend.

* * *

The focus on technê in creative writing represents a key, perhaps the key, point of intersection with composition, especially insofar as the technê in question has to do with the production rather than the reception of writing, a concern that distinguishes both creative writing and composition from their more esteemed departmental sibling, literary study, in the dysfunctional academic institutional family known as English studies (see Mayers, 2007). More specifically, the concern with what is called 'craft' in creative writing has its parallel in the concern with language 'skill' in composition, though the latter concern is typically relegated to the more subordinate realms of composition studies – so-called Basic Writing and ESL composition – as a 'lower order' matter. More on that in a bit.

But what also links creative writing with composition, despite their significant differences, is the treatment of matters of craft and skill as abstractions – entities that exist outside time and space but inside individuals as abilities and, therefore, entities that are to be instilled – taught, inculcated, transmitted – via coursework for those individuals to then apply subsequently in other settings. For composition, this manifests in the common charge to and perception of composition courses and programs as the means of teaching general writing skills applicable to the writing that will be demanded of students in other courses in other disciplines and in the workplace: composition as 'general writing skills instruction' (Petraglia, 1995). For creative writing, this manifests in the common perception of creative writing courses and programs as the site for instilling craft ability that students will apply when engaging in subsequent writing – either any and all writing, or at least in writing forms recognized as 'creative' – most commonly fiction, poetry and plays. That is to say, both composition courses and creative writing courses are understood as having a primarily preparatory function.[2]

Composition and creative writing are distinguished from one another by what either is meant to prepare students for – respectively, writing in other academic disciplines and the workplace, or the production of the high-status commodity of contemporary Literature (*sic*). Composition programs, insofar as they are preparatory for any and all academic work and employment, are seen by and large as fulfilling an at best remedial function: teaching students to do what, by rights, it is thought the students should have already learned to do before admission to college as part of the 'college and career readiness' that Common Core education insists K-12 education is to provide students with. Typically, what ostensibly should have already been learned is couched in terms of basic literacy, or 'college' literacy. Current students are deemed, by the standards of an imaginary yesteryear, to be illiterate or subliterate, and thus to constitute a serious, if always hopefully temporary, 'crisis' (Rose, 1985). Those assigned to solve this crisis – that is to say, composition teachers – enjoy all the negative status of the putatively illiterate they teach, and suffer all the poverty in working conditions that attend such status as the cannon fodder occupying the trenches in the literacy wars. In contrast, insofar as creative writing programs are charged with preparing students to join the ranks of producers of a high-status commodity, those programs and those affiliated with them enjoy the greater status within and outside the academic realm assigned such pre-professional programs as law, journalism and engineering. If composition is institutionally situated and mandated to meet the needs of everyone for all writing, creative writing is institutionally situated as and mandated to be a haven for an elite.

As some of my comments above have already hinted, the payoff for compositionists of embracing the official charge of general writing skills instruction has been slim enough, and for so long, that many in composition have started looking for alternatives. Specifically, compositionists have attempted to improve their professional academic disciplinary standing, and thereby (it is hoped) their working conditions, by: (1) adding other fields with greater status to their own or renaming themselves as something other than composition; or (2) adding other forms of composition to the turf of composition's disciplinary purview; or (3) attempting simply to escape composition altogether. So, for example, as I've argued elsewhere, those I continue to call compositionists, in the field I continue to call composition, have named the programs charged in part with training people to teach composition, not programs in Composition, but in: Rhetoric and Composition; Writing Studies; Writing, Rhetoric and American Culture; Rhetoric, Composition and Literacy Studies; Critical Studies in Literacy and Pedagogy; Language, Literacy and Rhetoric; or Composition and Cultural Rhetoric (Horner, 2016).[3] Or the field, it is argued, should be renamed 'writing studies' (Bazerman, 2002; Dobrin, 2011; Trimbur, 2003).

Concomitantly, some have argued for broadening the range of media and forms of composition to be taught and studied to include those identified as 'multimodal' by incorporating, or even drawing exclusively from, images and sounds and materials other than ink and paper (or their digital equivalents), on the theory that a focus on verbal composition alone (alphabetic print texts) is too narrow, especially in light of the rise of digital communication technologies and students' ostensible fascination and expertise with those technologies (e.g. Selfe, 2009; Wysocki *et al.*, 2004: Yancey, 2004). Or, in light of the seeming failure of research to demonstrate the transferability of writing skills (as well as other skills and knowledge), or to identify any 'general' writing skills applicable across domains of writing, the whole charge to teach these is dismissed as futile, and alternatives are posed of either focusing instead on discipline and worksite-specific writing instruction, as in programs of writing in the disciplines (e.g. Smit, 2004), or abandoning the teaching of writing altogether, in favor of studying writing as an object of purely 'academic' interest, without any pedagogical agenda for any site in or outside the academy (e.g. Dobrin, 2011).

All such efforts, I have argued (Horner, 2016), are futile. First, by suggesting that composition is in need of expansion, the strategy of adding other terms to composition or other media and forms to be studied as composition reinforces the legitimacy of negative valuations of composition and of the conventional forms it takes as limited, missing. Second, such attempts at redefinition by addition ignore the ongoing presence of other longstanding disciplinary traditions concerned with the production and study of other forms of composition – such as departments of graphic design, music, film and so on – departments whose interests are understood to be ill served by any affiliation with composition. Third, and more subtly, such efforts participate in the continuing denigration of composition by acceding to the occlusion of composition's own longstanding engagement with matters of modality and medium, rhetoric, writing study and so on. That occlusion results from recognizing only some forms of engagement with such matters as legitimate – ignoring, for example, students' perpetual engagement in rhetorical study, writing studies and the transmodal character of their conventional alphabetic print compositions. Finally, such efforts ignore the ways in which the kind of professional academic disciplinarity that composition aspires to achieve is itself losing ground under the pressures of the current regime of flexible accumulation, a.k.a. fast capitalism (see Ohmann, 2003).

All these point to composition's failure to understand or accept itself as a material social practice located in a specific institutional landscape: composition as an ongoing event and practice rather than timeless entity.[4] In this one way, it's important to admit, composition is in alignment with other professional academic disciplines and subdisciplines – creative writing included. The ideology of professional academic disciplinarity requires that those working in those disciplines misrecognize their work as operating outside material social history, whose daily intrusions are then seen at most as annoyances interfering with that work rather than its necessary, shaping conditions (cf. Keller, 1995). Composition's low status in the hierarchy of academic disciplinarity has to do with its difficulty denying its location in material social history as an institutional entity, and thus its annoying reminder to other disciplines that their own denials are, in fact, hollow.

CWIA arguably has less incentive to challenge itself; its courses fill, and at least for those high in the pecking order, the living is relatively good, with faculty positions in creative writing offering a few the equivalent of sinecures that allow them to continue writing what their colleagues in similar positions can admire or attempt to surpass. So long as those involved in creative writing lower in the pecking order believe that their advance in that order will, in time, come, little is likely to change. In other words, changing CWIA may not be something that CWIA, or at least the dominant among CWIA, wants.

There are, nonetheless, several intersecting pressures on CWIA that are leading at least some working in CWIA to seek some kind of change. First, there is the pressure posed by the emergence of forms of writing (stretching the definition of 'writing') that many in creative writing may currently lack any recognizable expertise in producing, combined with an explosion in the population of those who can claim expertise, or at least significant experience, in producing: the various hybrid and/or digital forms of writing with which the Web is now awash.[5] To 'keep up' with the tsunami of such forms of writing, it would seem that those in creative writing at least need to add the production of those forms of writing understood as new (and, it is often presumed, therefore better) to the work they already do. After all, in the face of 'multimodal' productions, who would want to herald monomodality? Second, there is the apparent promise, or lure, that those in creative writing might be able to cash in on the growing interest in creativity – or, more precisely, innovation – as itself a significant ability or form of intelligence for which there is, ostensibly, growing demand in the new knowledge economy. If creative writing is defined as that writing that differs from the norm of writing, with its difference constituting innovation, then creative writing programs might be understood as incubators of an ability to innovate, or to be 'innovative', and thereby to contribute to the production of the now highly sought-after class of so-called 'creatives'.[6] So, for example, while the demand for those with functional literacy – that is, those deemed able to produce writing that efficiently communicates information – remains strong enough to justify the continuation of composition as a universally required first-year college course, at least in the US, the new interest in adding to these writers those with the ability to produce recognizably different, a.k.a. innovative, writing is growing, and such production carries the additional cachet of promising to help establish and maintain an elite class – again, the 'creatives'.

It is of course possible that creative writing programs might, in fact, be able to sell themselves as producers of such an elite. However, those taking such claims seriously enough to investigate will find their enthusiasm severely tempered by the scholarly literature on transfer, the overwhelming majority of which calls into radical question the transferability of such specific abilities and skills, to the point of insisting on rejecting the transfer model altogether.[7] Following such findings, it would seem that, alas, the creativity that creative writing programs might somehow foster is restricted to the creativity in producing writing deemed creative, and no more: creative writing programs that teach, say, the writing of poetry and fiction foster writers with experience writing poetry and fiction. So, just as composition programs find themselves unable to fulfill their institutional charge to produce students with an all-purpose universally applicable skill at writing – a.k.a. 'general writing skills' – creative writing programs might not be able to deliver on any claims they're tempted to make to produce all-purpose 'creativity' in students, just a highly particularized, specific form of writing recognized by dominant culture as 'creative'. Moreover, any ventures by creative writing programs to add to their remit other forms of work also recognized by dominant culture as 'creative' – such as work in the visual and performing arts as well as, say, business and engineering – face the same barrier of the specificity/particularity and, more generally, un-transferability of the creativity that creative writing programs might more legitimately claim to foster or allow for, while also risking a backlash for threatening to impinge on the remits of longstanding traditions of disciplinary work in these other areas – for instance schools and departments of engineering, business, and the visual and performing arts. The territory they would expand into and cultivate, it appears, is already inhabited and well tilled by others. No need to learn to write novels or poems in order to write, or hack, software, or start businesses. Further, to pursue such ventures is to participate in dominant culture's occlusion of the transmodal character of the work that creative writing programs already engage in – for example, the ways in which conventional print text fiction and poetry engage the full sensorium rather than only the cerebrum, the ear or the eye. Finally, by participating in that occlusion, and in indulging in the pretension to being able to produce a class of 'creatives', creative writing programs would contribute to supporting the sleight of hand of neoliberal, fast-capitalist commodifications of creativity as something transferable without friction or, more importantly, concrete labor, and its fetishization of 'the new', encapsulated in incessant calls for innovation that ignore the specific values realized by what passes for the new and the social relations within which particular innovations might carry such values: typically, the castigation of what is deemed conventional and current, in favor of what is marketed as the new and improved, leading to the fracturing and hierarchizing of the market into ever more finely graded niches, and the treatment of tastes as individual rather than sociohistorical and, along with the individuals themselves, located in a naturally occurring hierarchy. In contributing to such notions of creativity, creative writing programs might, in the short term, add to their value as ostensible incubators of a generalized creativity in an economy of knowledge innovation. However, in the long term, their own professional academic disciplinary status would be diluted, since competition from other, more privatized, institutions (whether designated public or not) could, it can be persuasively argued, be more efficient than creative writing programs at producing the same commodified creativity, that is, doing so with greater speed and less cost, just as those disciplines attempting to improve their lot through claims to teach 'critical thinking' now face competition from private entities (e.g. Foundation for Critical

Thinking, 2013) with marketing programs offering to do so more quickly and at lower cost.

Note that I am not arguing that those who gain experience producing writing currently recognized as 'creative' cannot also perform other kinds of work recognized as somehow 'creative', such as software creation or business start-ups, nor those forms of work more closely related to novel and poetry writing, such as film scripts or opera librettos. But the 'creativity' that these might entail, like the 'creativity' entailed in writing a novel or poem or play, is an abstraction from a specific instance of practice rather than a discrete ingredient added to that practice and susceptible to friction-free introduction into other practices. Creativity, in other words, cannot be imagined as a resource on the shelf of the writer's mind, to be drawn on at will for a variety of activities. Rather, it is the always emergent outcome of specific practices, and subject to the whims of recognition as 'creative' or 'not'.

So far, I have been explaining what CWIA should not do, based on parallels I've drawn between what it is currently tempted to do and the flawed strategies composition has been pursuing to improve its own professional academic disciplinary status and, it is assumed, thereby its working conditions (so far to no avail). It remains, then, to be determined what it is I think CWIA might do instead of yielding to the temptations outlined so far. As before, I will use parallels to what composition might do to identify what CWIA itself might justifiably do, keeping in mind that I speak as an outsider to CWIA (my perspective is that of someone in composition). But drawing such parallels first requires that I make the case for composition's own alternative to the strategies it has so far pursued for improving its position, e.g. adding other forms of study or forms of composition or yielding to teaching site-specific kinds of writing à la writing in the disciplines (WID) and writing across the curriculum (WAC) programs, or abandoning the teaching of composition altogether in favor of boutique pursuit of theories of writing.[8] And to make that case requires that I first consider what a recognition of composition (and creative writing) as material social practice entails.

What that entails is, first and foremost, recognizing the work that occurs in such programs as itself the work of the programs rather than as preparation for subsequent work elsewhere: locating the practice of composition and creative writing in the activities and material (physical and institutional and social and temporal) conditions of composition and creative writing programs. Admittedly, this might at first glance appear to be both obvious and beside the point: of course such programs are where people 'in' composition and creative writing work, hence their work is identified with such programs. But typically, such an admission is accompanied by a failure to identify the value of what those programs produce with the activities engaged in by students in the courses such programs offer – with the writing they produce in composition courses, for example. Instead, the work – in the sense of the 'output' – of those programs is defined in terms of abstracted skills whose value is realized subsequently, in writing undertaken elsewhere. Thus, student writing *qua* student writing is not understood as legitimate writing at all but, rather, as precursive to legitimate writing, identified with the writing undertaken at other, usually subsequent, sites.[9]

Creative writing might be exceptional here: the writing students produce for the workshops ubiquitous in creative writing program curricula may well be intended ultimately for and show up in publications as, well, instances of 'creative writing': poems and short stories in literary magazines, for example. That is, insofar as creative writing programs are 'pre-professional', the work students undertake in those programs may well constitute earlier versions of their work as 'professional' creative writers, a status that publication itself contributes to conferring. But insofar as such occurrences are the exception to the rule, the writing produced by students as part of their coursework retains the status of being preparatory to creative writing recognized as professional rather than 'student' work. Likewise, the work of the teachers in creative writing programs is typically identified not with that teaching but, rather, with the literary and literary-critical publications they produce that circulate primarily outside their institution, just as their earnings from such publications constitute, from the perspective of the US Internal Revenue Service (IRS), instances of their work as businesses independent from their work at their college or university.

James Slevin succinctly presents the contrary view. He asks us to imagine the following:

> the moment a student walks into our classroom, the first day of class, the student would be seen – and see himself or herself – as a full participant in the work of the discipline. *Just for showing up.* She would not have to *negotiate* entry; she would not have to *earn* the right to speak and participate. She has already entered and by definition has that right. The discipline includes her as a *given*, and the intellectual work of the discipline includes her work and our work with her. (Slevin, 2001: 44–45)

In Slevin's picture, the work of composition and creative writing (and, for Slevin, all disciplines) is what is done by students as well as teachers in and during and through programs of courses, rather than something that programs of courses prepare students to do somewhere else at some other time. Slevin's picture opposes the prevailing treatment of academic disciplinary work as a commodity whose value is a function of the range of its circulation. This oppositional relation arises in part from how difference in writing and knowledge are commonly conceived. I have argued elsewhere (Horner, 2016) that composition is the name given to work done in colleges and universities, mostly in the US, by students and teachers as they engage and mediate differences in written language. But for that definition of composition to have any force requires that we redefine difference in written language itself. And in redefining difference in written language, I come to what I think will be another potentially rich point of intersection between the projects of composition and creative writing.

For both composition and creative writing are charged with mediating language difference in writing, but from opposed directions. Creative writing is charged with producing difference in writing as it is conventionally understood, whereas composition is charged with eliminating difference as it is conventionally understood. In both cases, however, difference is defined as formal deviation from a norm of sameness in language, which itself is located in space but outside time, and hence to be identified only with form. Stereotypically, creative writing programs are charged with and focused on enabling the production of formal innovation in writing, and composition programs are charged with and focused on enabling the production of writing that is conventional in its form through the teaching of what is often called 'grammar'.[10] To the extent that both types of programs accept their charge, both maintain a common understanding of difference as deviation from a norm of sameness, with the distinction between the two being that, in creative writing, formal difference is taken as a sign of creativity breaking from convention, whereas in composition formal difference is taken as a mark of deficit – ignorance of or cognitive inability or lack of training in how to produce 'correct' writing.[11] The power of this view of difference is such that even those in composition who wish to defend the language rights of those denigrated as ignorant or cognitively deficient typically do so in terms of the acceptability of forms recognizably different from 'normal' writing – writing that deploys what are identified as mixtures of multiple languages or language varieties, for example, or that deploys syntax identified as deviating from conventional, a.k.a. 'standard', a.k.a. 'Native English' syntax (e.g. Canagarajah, 2006, 2009; Lu, 1994; Severino, 1994; Young, 2009).

Such defenses expand the range of language practices that might be deemed acceptable, in or outside the academy and in or outside writing, in terms of both language rights and the restrictions that English-only monolingualism places on the production, circulation and reception of knowledge. The argument is therefore largely an argument for replacing the dominance of English-only monolingualism with multilingualism in terms of the languages and varieties of English to be accepted, including variations identified with uses of English as a lingua franca (Jenkins, 2014). Multilingualism, it is argued, replaces intolerance with tolerance and advances knowledge and communication, thereby serving the interests of justice, learning and, as well, global commerce (Dor, 2004).

But again, these arguments retain a spatialized conception of language, differing from arguments for English-only monolingualism only in arguing for an expansion of the territory designated as English, or Standard English, through the incorporation of a broader range of forms. That is to say, the range of forms identifiable with 'the norm' is expanded, but that norm itself remains a stable, ahistorical entity, with difference still defined as deviation from that norm. The alternative to this is, then, not so much to expand the range of what counts as 'the norm' but, rather, to understand difference itself as the norm, with any sense of sameness in need of explication. That alternative arises when we acknowledge the temporal location of language itself as always emergent in practices. That is, rather than seeing practices as pale manifestations of an entity – language – that exists prior to and outside time and space, language must be understood as the always emerging product of practices (e.g. Calvet, 2006; Pennycook, 2010). And insofar as language thus always exists in time, moment to moment, difference is one of its inevitable, defining features.

Alastair Pennycook (2007) illustrates this by reference to the notion of repetition. While, from a purely spatial, formalist perspective, repetition of a text represents an instance of sameness, acknowledging the temporal dimension to the repetition demonstrates the difference of the repetition *as* a repetition from that which preceded it (in time) and hence its different valence. It is both the sameness and difference of the repetition from what it repeats that gives both it and what it repeats their particular significance. (Repetition in music illustrates this.) Those pursuing this understanding of language and creativity see the latter arising insofar as the repetition recontextualizes what is repeated. As Pennycook argues (2007: 593), 'It is the recontextualization of sameness or difference that matters'. So, for example, Rodney H. Jones (2010: 467) has argued that whereas most work in applied linguistics and sociolinguistics defines creativity in terms of 'words and how they are put together to form texts', it is possible to identify creativity in language not in terms of 'the novelty of the linguistic forms deployed' but in terms of 'how language can be used in strategic ways in concrete social contexts to create fundamental changes in the world'

(Jones, 2010: 468). From Jones's discourse analytic perspective, creativity resides not in language understood as a discrete set of forms but 'in the actions people take with language', and thus writing might be creative that entails 'no "language play", no metaphors or puns or other rhetorical devices' but that creates 'a new way of dealing with a situation or a new set of social relationships' (Jones, 2010: 472). For Jones, creativity inheres not in specific 'clever' or 'inventive' changes to language but in 'changing the world', such as by producing shifts in power relations or creating 'new kinds of social identities and new ways of seeing the world', as when 'a gay man in China ... uses the label *tongzhi* (comrade) to refer to himself and other gay men, [and thereby] appropriates a piece of discourse from the very ideological system by which in the past he has been oppressed in a way that cleverly disarms the oppressor' (Jones, 2010: 473).

But I would push this argument further. Jones (2010) retains the criterion of 'newness', albeit in social relations, to designate some language practices as creative: for Jones, if no social change occurs (however minute), then the practices cannot qualify as creative. But insofar as change, or 'newness', is the norm of both language practices and the contexts those practices contribute to constituting, and is therefore inevitable, then even those language practices that, say, work to sustain existing social relations, including those social relations we might deem to be ethically noxious, can be defined as creative (and recreative) in the root sense of the term. As James Gee (2000: 190) has observed, 'Situations (contexts) do not just exist ... [but] are actively created, sustained, negotiated, resisted, and transformed moment-by-moment through ongoing *work*', explaining that '[a] word or deed takes its meaning from a context which it, in turn, helps to create'. This applies not only to the creation of recognizably 'new' situations and social relations but also to the sustaining and (re)creating of what are recognized as status quo situations and social relations, which are changed by being further confirmed and sedimented through such work. Thus conventionalized language that produces conventional social relations is creative, in the root sense of the term, in the work that it performs. As Raymond Williams (1977: 112) reminds us, a lived hegemony does not 'just passively exist as a form of dominance. It has continually to be renewed, recreated, defended, and modified.'

In making this claim, and in introducing the term 'work' into my discussion, I am of course upending the longstanding ideological distinction between work and 'art' achieved through the idealization of artwork (*sic*) through its removal from the material social process, an idealization Williams (1977: 156–161) has traced to the 19th-century resistance of craftsmen to the commodification of work within capitalist production.

But that idealization no longer carries force under current conditions of the commodification of art (and 'creativity') as symbolic capital with exchange value. On the contrary, those designated *creatives* now exemplify the new entrepreneurialism in which innovation adds economic value. I am arguing, then, that 'creativity' is inadequate to distinguish some kinds of writing and writers from others, in terms of either form or quality, though the practice of invoking 'creativity' to do just that remains dominant. Instead, creativity is an inherent feature of all writing – a feature worthy of our attention, to be sure, but for its effect, not its rarity.

The view of creativity as an inherent feature of all utterances differs in important ways from arguments for the creativity to be found in ordinary language by such scholars as Ron Carter (2015) and Paul Willis and his colleagues (1990). Admittedly, my argument is aligned with the arguments of such scholars in explicitly challenging the view that creativity is a characteristic distinguishing an elite from the rest, and instead in heralding the agency and creativity of those deemed ordinary – the agency and creativity in what Willis *et al.* (1990) herald as 'common culture'. However, my argument differs from these in its identification of creativity not with specific formal features of language use – such as the use of metaphor, irony and humor – nor with the production of what is recognized as culturally new, but, rather, with the agency and responsibility of all language users for the ongoing *re*-production/re-creation of language, and languages, regardless of whether the formal features deployed are recognizable – that is, correspond to what we are disposed by our training to recognize – as 'creative' rather than 'ordinary'. So, whereas Carter (2015: 11) aims to explore the creativity to be found 'in' ordinary language practices, and Willis *et al.* (1990: 2), following Raymond Williams, herald the extraordinary *in* the ordinary, I aim to help recognize the inevitable creativity *of* ordinary language, the inevitable extraordinariness *of* the ordinary. To do so requires recognizing not only the temporally different character of any iteration but also that iterations – including iterations that appear to sustain hegemonic social relations – are themselves creative, however socially noxious we may view the results of that creativity to be. In other words, we have to recognize the agency and responsibility of production operating in social reproduction, the creative in the re-creative. Such a conception of the creative, as Rob Pope (2005: 88) argues, unlike conceptions identifying the creative with 'the "new", the "novel" and the "original" in their narrowly "modern senses" … leaves more room for conserving and sustaining as well as recasting and refreshing'.

Of course, this perspective implies changes in the questions that might be asked of writing (whether published or in draft) in a 'creative writing' workshop, as well as, consequently, the kinds of writing that students might produce in those workshops. From this perspective, to ask about the creativity of writing is not to ask about what marks it as different in form from other writing but, rather, to ask what that writing might do to the context which it is in co-constitutive relation to, and whether that is a worthy aim, with one possible answer being that it works to sustain, and thereby strengthen and help to perpetuate, current social relations, and therefore might be challenged (and subjected to revision) on such grounds. By way of illustration, we might consider how difference in creative writing is ordinarily marked in the flyers for 'readings' by creative writers that are ubiquitous in college campuses, and how it might otherwise be marked. I trust readers will find the following a familiar template for such flyers:

> _____ is the author of _____ ([name of press, year]), a finalist for the _____ prize. Her poetry has appeared in many prestigious journals, including _____, _____, _____, _____, _____, and _____, among many others, and her fiction has appeared in _____, _____, and _____. She holds an MFA in ___ from the University of _____ and a PhD in ___from the University of ____, where she edited _____. She has been appointed as a fellow at the [famous artist summer colony], and is currently on the faculty at _____.

The template for such flyers identifies the value of the writing, and the writer, in terms of their exchange value as commodities in competition with other commodities: the writing, and writer, have been successful in winning real estate in the pages of prestigious journals and presses, as a consequence of which the writer has beat the competition in securing various positions. Whether s/he teaches or not, let alone what s/he might teach and what she strives for in her teaching, is not worthy of mention. Moreover, what s/he writes about, and what that writing does, attempts to do, or might do to or for readers in their relations to one another and what is written about – how it might affect, for example, how readers might learn to think about or act regarding that subject, and why – are, according to the flyer template, immaterial. In the ideology shaping such flyers, what matters is not what is written about, and its possible usefulness, but rather simply that it has been published, and the status of its publication venues.

Alternatively, we might imagine writing being questioned and valued (or critiqued) for what it does in response and relation to social relations and our thinking about these, with writing being attended to precisely in just such terms. Questions at public readings would shift from those about craft – 'Where do you get your ideas?', 'What's most helpful to you to get started?' – and toward those ideas represented and the social aims and strategies by which those ideas are being advanced. The inevitable social 'relevance' of writing – its engagement in the (re)production of social relations – could itself once again be engaged.

Historically and typically, intense attention to the social relevance of writing has been associated with totalitarian and autocratic regimes – think here of China, North Korea, the former Soviet Union, Saudi Arabia, as well as, of course, Shakespearean England.[12] But it is possible to engage in that attention from an insistently non-totalitarian ethos. Against totalitarian regimes' doctrinaire rejection of some writing (and writers) and praise of others in terms of conformity – in form and content – to the reigning political dogma, writers and readers might debate the possible effects of particular representations – in all senses – of particular characters, events and so on. But such debates would have as their operating assumption the recognition of the inherently contingent nature of the effects of particular forms of representation, and of the ideal social relations to be achieved, contingency that the histories of the reception of parodies illustrates (see for example Novak, 1966). Indeed, that contingent character is, paradoxically, precisely what makes such debate necessary.[13]

To make such a shift would change fundamentally both the work of 'workshops' and the population of those who might enroll in such workshops. More fundamentally still, it would shift our sense of those workshops from being sites for predominantly preparatory, or pre-professional, training in producing commodities identified as 'creative' (and therefore, not coincidentally, understood as by definition apolitical) to being occasions in which writers work actively and deliberately on producing and reproducing and revising language and the social relations that language plays a fundamental role in (re)creating.

Of course, creative writing workshops have always and inevitably been sites where this latter kind of work takes place. In that sense, what I am suggesting is nothing new at all. But this is not at all how creative writing programs have been justified nor how their work and its value have been understood, for to have understood them in this way would require granting recognition and value to the labor of other language users as well: what is instead ideologically misrecognized as – like mothering – not work at all, and hence of no real productive (i.e. exchange) value. 'Democratizing' creative writing by recognizing the inevitably creative character of all writing – regardless of whether or not it evidences what we are disposed to recognize as 'language play' – also entails recognizing the labor of ordinary language, and its value in the ongoing creation, recreation and revision of social relations.[14]

Such recognition would undermine current dominant practices of commodifications of 'creative' writing and writers and of 'creativity' itself that obscure that labor and its value. Of course, insofar as creative writing programs have a vested interest in maintaining such commodifications, I see little chance of them changing in the directions I am pointing.[15] But insofar as ordinary users of language are coming to recognize their role as re-creative, creative writing programs may need to come to terms with the contradictions in which the commodification of creative writing has entangled them, and to turn away from asking, and trying to teach, how to be 'creative' and toward investigating and experimenting with their students, as fellow users of language, what we might attempt to create, how, and why.

Notes

(1) Further exploration of this perspective can be found in Lu and Horner (2013).
(2) As Mimi Thebo (2013: 37) observes, 'Of all the humanities, creative writing tends to be most seen as vocational in nature'.
(3) I myself hold the position of Endowed Chair in Rhetoric and Composition at the University of Louisville's graduate program in rhetoric and composition, whose graduate students teach in the composition program.
(4) Cf. Tim Cresswell's (2002: 25, 26) argument that 'Place as an event is marked by openness and change rather than boundedness and permanence.... [It] is both the context for practice – we act according to more or less stable schemes of perception – and a product of practice – something that only makes sense as it is lived.'
(5) For a judicious presentation of this perspective, see Williams (2015).
(6) For articulations of this argument, see Donnelly (2013) and Healey (2013).
(7) On transfer, see Beach (1999), DePalma and Ringer (2011), Nowacek (2011), Wardle (2012) and Yancey *et al.* (2014).
(8) I take the 'boutique' characterization from Jeanne Gunner's (2012) critique of Sidney Dobrin's (2011) argument in his book *Postcomposition*.
(9) I present this argument more fully in Horner (2010).
(10) This is, of course, a bastardized if widely accepted understanding of grammar.
(11) See Bartholomae (1987). A growing but still minority position in composition has pushed for formal innovation as a means of advancing knowledge (e.g. Annas, 1985; Bridwell-Bowles, 1992; Frey, 1990; Schroeder *et al.*, 2002; Tompkins, 1989, 1990; Torgovnick, 1990; Zawacki, 1992). There is also a growing concern with the role of language politics in knowledge production (e.g. Ammon, 2007; Canagarajah, 2002; Flowerdew, 1999; Horner *et al.*, 2011; Jenkins, 2014; Lillis & Curry, 2010; Silva *et al.*, 1997).
(12) Recall here Bertolt Brecht's ironic quip, in response to East German censorship, 'Where else in the world can you find a government that shows such interest in and pays such attention to artists?' (quoted in Jones, 2001: 292).
(13) There is a longstanding tradition in rhetoric and composition, often traced to Orwell (1946), on which those pursuing such an approach might draw, of having student writers explore the politics of style (see, for example, Coles, 1978; Lu, 1994; Ohmann,

1979; Seitz, 1993), though that tradition is often marred by a failure to recognize the contingent character of the effects of particular stylistic features (see Faigley, 1992: 89–104; Lu, 1994; Ohmann, 1982).
(14) See Swann and Maybin's (2007: 495) observation that 'the extension of "creativity" to everyday contexts has been seen as a process of democratization that challenges old elites', and Willis *et al.*'s (1990: 1) call to recognize the work accomplished in the 'vibrant symbolic life and symbolic creativity current in everyday life, everyday activity and expression – even if it is sometimes invisible, looked down on or spurned'.
(15) Cf. Donnelly and Harper's (2013: xvi) observation that 'little pressing professional impulsion exists at the academic level for creative writing teachers to engage in the critical study of creative writing'; and Thebo's (2013: 45) observation that the allegiance of the academic staff of creative writing 'to the academy is not as strong as their allegiance to the publishing industry'.

References

Ammon, U. (2007) Global scientific communication: Open questions and policy suggestions. *AILA Review* 20 (1), 123–133.
Annas, P.J. (1985) Style as politics: A feminist approach to the teaching of writing. *College English* 47 (4), 360–371.
Bartholomae, D. (1987) Writing on the margins: The concept of literacy in higher education. In T. Enos (ed.) *A Sourcebook for Basic Writing Teachers* (pp. 66–83). New York: Random House.
Bazerman, C. (2002) The case for writing studies as a major discipline. In G. Olson and L. Worsham (eds) *Rhetoric and Composition as Intellectual Work* (pp. 32–38). Carbondale, IL: Southern Illinois University Press.
Beach, K. (1999) Consequential transitions: A sociocultural expedition beyond transfer in education. *Review of Research in Education* 24 (1), 101–139.
Bridwell-Bowles, L. (1992) Discourse and diversity: Experimental writing within the academy. *College Composition and Communication* 43 (3), 349–368.
Calvet, L.J. (2006) *Towards an Ecology of World Languages* (ed. and trans. A. Brown). London: Polity. Original publication *Pour une écologie des langues du monde* (1999).
Canagarajah, A.S. (2002) *A Geopolitics of Academic Writing*. Pittsburgh, PA: University of Pittsburgh Press.
Canagarajah, A.S. (2006) The place of world Englishes in composition: Pluralization continued. *College Composition and Communication* 57 (4), 586–619.
Canagarajah, A.S. (2009) Multilingual strategies of negotiating English: From conversation to writing. *JAC* 29 (1–2), 17–48.
Carter, R. (2015) *Language and Creativity: The Art of Common Talk* (2nd edition). London: Routledge.
Coles, W.E. (1978) *The Plural I: The Teaching of Writing*. New York: Holt, Rinehart, and Winston.
Cresswell, T. (2002) Introduction: Theorizing place. In T. Cresswell and G. Verstraete (eds) *Mobilizing Place, Placing Mobility: The Politics of Representation in a Globalized World* (pp. 11–32). Amsterdam: Rodopi.
DePalma, M.J. and Ringer, J.M. (2011) Toward a theory of adaptive transfer: Expanding disciplinary discussions of 'transfer' in second-language writing and composition studies. *Journal of Second Language Writing* 20 (2), 134–147.

Dobrin, S.I. (2011) *Postcomposition*. Carbondale, IL: Southern Illinois University Press.
Donnelly, D. (2013) Reshaping creative writing: Power and agency in the academy. In D. Donnelly and G. Harper (eds) *Key Issues in Creative Writing* (pp. 3–29). Bristol: Multilingual Matters.
Donnelly, D. and Harper, G. (2013) Introduction: Key issues and global perspectives in creative writing. In D. Donnelly and G. Harper (eds) *Key Issues in Creative Writing* (pp. xiii–xxvi). Bristol: Multilingual Matters.
Dor, D. (2004) From Englishization to imposed multilingualism: Globalization, the internet, and the political economy of the linguistic code. *Public Culture* 16 (1), 97–118.
Faigley, L. (1992) *Fragments of Rationality: Postmodernity and the Subject of Composition*. Pittsburgh, PA: University of Pittsburgh Press.
Flowerdew, J. (1999) Problems in writing for scholarly publication in English: The case of Hong Kong. *Journal of Second Language Writing* 8 (2), 243–264.
Foundation for Critical Thinking (2013) The critical thinking community, at http://www.criticalthinking.org (accessed 15 January 2016).
Frey, O. (1990) Beyond literary Darwinism: Women's voices and critical discourse. *College English* 52 (5), 507–526.
Gee, J.P. (2000) New literacy studies: From 'socially situated' to the work of the social. In D. Barton, M. Hamilton and R. Ivanič (eds) *Situated Literacies: Reading and Writing in Context* (pp. 180–196). New York: Routledge.
Gunner, J. (2012) Disciplinary purification: The writing program as institutional brand. *JAC* 32 (3–4), 615–643.
Healey, S. (2013) Beyond the literary: Why creative literacy matters. In D. Donnelly and G. Harper (eds) *Key Issues in Creative Writing* (pp. 61–78). Bristol: Multilingual Matters.
Horner, B. (2010) Re-valuing student writing. In J. Harris, J. Miles and C. Paine (eds) *Teaching with Student Texts: Essays Toward an Informed Practice* (pp. 9–23). Logan, UT: Utah University Press.
Horner, B. (2016) *Rewriting Composition: Terms of Exchange*. Carbondale, IL: Southern Illinois University Press.
Horner, B., Donahue, C. and NeCamp, S. (2011) Toward a multilingual composition scholarship: From English only to a translingual norm. *College Composition and Communication* 63 (2), 269–300.
Jenkins, J. (2014) *English as a Lingua Franca in the International University: The Politics of Academic English Language Policy*. New York: Routledge.
Jones, D. (2001) Bertolt Brecht. In D. Jones (ed.) *Censorship: A World Encyclopedia* (pp. 290–293). New York: Routledge.
Jones, R.H. (2010) Creativity and discourse. *World Englishes* 29 (4), 467–480.
Keller, E.F. (1995) *Refiguring Life: Metaphors of Twentieth-Century Biology*. New York: Columbia University Press.
Lillis, T. and Curry, M.J. (2010) *Academic Writing in a Global Context: The Politics and Practices of Publishing in English*. London: Routledge.
Lu, M.Z. (1994) Professing multiculturalism: The politics of style in the contact zone. *College Composition and Communication* 54 (4), 442–458.
Lu, M.Z. and Horner, B. (2013) Translingual literacy, language difference, and matters of agency. *College English* 75 (6), 586–611.
Mayers, T. (2007) *(Re)Writing Craft: Composition, Creative Writing, and the Future of English Studies*. Pittsburgh, PA: University of Pittsburgh Press.
Novak, M.E. (1966) Defoe's *Shortest Way with the Dissenters*: Hoax, parody, paradox, fiction, irony, and satire. *Modern Language Quarterly* 27, 402–417.

Nowacek, R.S. (2011) *Agents of Integration: Understanding Transfer as a Rhetorical Act*. Carbondale, IL: Southern Illinois University Press.
Ohmann, R. (1979) Use definite, specific, concrete language. *College English* 41 (4), 390–97.
Ohmann, R. (1982) Reflections on class and language. *College English* 44 (1), 1–17.
Ohmann, R. (2003) *The Politics of Knowledge: The Commercialization of the University, the Professions, and Print Culture*. Middletown, CT: Wesleyan University Press.
Orwell, G. (1946) Politics and the English language. *Horizon* 13 (April), 252–265.
Pennycook, A. (2007) 'The rotation gets thick. The constraints get thin': Creativity, recontextualization, and difference. *Applied Linguistics* 28 (4), 579–596.
Pennycook, A. (2010) *Language as a Local Practice*. London: Routledge.
Petraglia, J. (ed.) (1995) *Reconceiving Writing, Rethinking Writing Instruction*. Mahwah, NJ: Erlbaum.
Pope, R. (2005) *Creativity: Theory, History, Practice*. New York: Routledge.
Rose, M. (1985) The language of exclusion: Writing instruction at the university. *College English* 47 (4), 341–359.
Schroeder, C., Fox, H. and Bizzell, P. (eds) (2002) *ALT/DIS: Alternative Discourses and the Academy*. Portsmouth, NH: Boynton/Cook.
Seitz, J. (1993) Eluding righteous discourse: A discreet politics for new writing curricula. *Writing Program Administration* 16 (3), 7–14.
Selfe, C.L. (2009) The movement of air, the breath of meaning: Aurality and multimodal composing. *College Composition and Communication* 60 (4), 616–663.
Severino, C. (1994) Inadvertently and intentionally poetic ESL writing. *Journal of Basic Writing* 13 (2), 18–32.
Silva, T., Leki, I. and Carson, J. (1997) Broadening the perspective of mainstream composition studies: Some thoughts from the disciplinary margins. *Written Communication* 14 (3), 398–428.
Slevin, J. (2001) *Introducing English: Essays in the Intellectual Work of Composition*. Pittsburgh, PA: University of Pittsburgh Press.
Smit, D.W. (2004) *The End of Composition Studies*. Carbondale, IL: Southern Illinois University Press.
Swann, J. and Maybin, J. (2007) Introduction: Language creativity in everyday contexts. *Applied Linguistics* 28 (4), 491–496.
Thebo, M. (2013) Hey babe, take a walk on the wild side – Creative writing in universities. In D. Donnelly and G. Harper (eds) *Key Issues in Creative Writing* (pp. 30–47). Bristol: Multilingual Matters.
Tompkins, J. (1989) Me and my shadow. In L. Kauffman (ed.) *Gender and Theory: Dialogues on Feminist Criticism* (pp. 121–139). Oxford: Blackwell. Reprinted from *New Literary History* 19 (1), 169–178.
Tompkins, J. (1990) Pedagogy of the distressed. *College English* 52 (6), 653–660.
Torgovnick, M. (1990) Experimental critical writing. *Profession* 90 (1), 25–27.
Trimbur, J. (2003) Changing the question: Should writing be studied? *Composition Studies* 31 (1), 15–24.
Wardle, E. (ed.) (2012) *Writing and Transfer*. Special issue of *Composition Forum* 26. Available at http://compositionforum.com/issue/26 (accessed 10 February 2016).
Williams, B. (2015) Digital technologies and creative writing. In A. Peary and T.C. Hunley (eds) *Creative Writing Pedagogies for the Twenty-First Century* (pp. 243–268). Carbondale, IL: Southern Illinois University Press.
Williams, R. (1977) *Marxism and Literature*. Oxford: Oxford University Press.

Willis, P., Jones, S., Canaan, J. and Hurd, G. (1990) *Common Culture: Symbolic Work at Play in the Everyday Cultures of the Young.* Buckingham: Open University Press.

Wysocki, A.F., Johnson-Eilola, J., Selfe, C.L. and Sirc, G. (2004) *Writing New Media: Theory and Applications for Expanding the Teaching of Composition.* Logan, UT: Utah State University Press.

Yancey, K.B. (2004) Made not only in words: Composition in a new key. *College Composition and Communication* 56 (2), 297–328.

Yancey, K.B., Robertson, L. and Taczak, K. (2014) *Writing Across Contexts: Transfer, Composition, and Sites of Writing.* Logan, UT: Utah State University Press.

Young, V.A. (2009) 'Nah, we straight': An argument against code switching. *JAC* 29 (1–2), 29–46.

Zawacki, T.M. (1992) Recomposing as a woman – An essay in different voices. *College Composition and Communication* 43 (1), 32–38.

8 Toward an Interdisciplinary Creative Writing

Joseph Rein

In considering how Creative Writing as a discipline might better adapt its practices for the 21st century, I have turned, as I often do, to my students. And the trend I've noticed most often – not a new trend, but a persistent and seemingly escalating one – is the question of viability post-graduation. Increasingly my students have visited me in my office, near to achieving their bachelor's degree in English, and their primary expression is fear: fear bred of uncertainty, like anyone soon to undergo a life change; fear of responsibility; but mostly, a fear – unfortunately warranted – of the increasingly challenging 'real world' into which they will soon graduate. They hear it from relatives, from friends in STEM fields, from their English counterparts in Teacher Education: *What kind of job do you hope to get with your degree?*

The question is both fair and unfair. University degrees such as English are necessarily flexible, and translate to many employment contexts. We do not strive to be a vocational school. When I answer this question, however, I find myself in an odd position between encouragement and hesitancy. Yes, nearly every employer values effective communication and creative expression, skills at which my students typically excel. After all, my majors have the unique distinction of being the only ones to bear the mark 'Creative' in their title. But outside of the realm of the specific genres – generally speaking, fiction, poetry and creative nonfiction – what exactly are we doing in our classes to prepare students for their futures?

Many of my students wish to enter graduate programs in creative writing, and perhaps these students receive the preparation they need to excel in that context. Likewise, others who pursue the aforementioned English Teacher Education degree undergo rigorous preparation and certification in order to enter their classrooms as educators. But what of the rest? How could I argue against Jen Webb (2008: 118) when she states that those students who are not 'exposed to ways of thinking and seeing that emerge from other creative traditions ... will be less capable of working productively in what the media call "the real world"'?

First published in 1996, D.G. Myers' seminal text on Creative Writing, *The Elephants Teach*, ended with the sentiment that 'Finally, creative writing had become a national staff of writers who teach writers who go on to teach, and to hope for tenure and promotion' (Myers, 1996: 168). In other words, creative writing programs exist to create and nourish more creative writing programs. In 2005, Paul Dawson lamented that our discipline 'hovers today between a vocational traineeship for the publishing industry and an artistic haven from the pressures of commercialism' (Dawson, 2005: 214). And though Creative Writing has done much in recent decades to defy these definitions, more and more it seems we haven't done enough to counter the growing challenges our students face. We haven't provided enough beyond the 'artistic haven' where our students bide time as writers, almost as a placeholder, before 'real life' begins. We haven't adequately provided an answer to the growing contingent of students with legitimate concerns over how a degree based primarily on both genre-specific writing and workshop skills might benefit them. These students align their course catalogues and objectives alongside the list of potential future vocations and oftentimes fail to see the overlap. How does learning the craft techniques of short fiction prepare them for anything other than a life of pursuing publication? It may seem to these students that their future goals must happen in spite of, not because of, their degree. In these situations, creative writing can become a sideshow, a hobby, instead of the integral asset a college degree should be. In other words, in the face of increasingly hostile worlds both inside and outside the university, we have not adequately served those students who simply want – and rightfully so – their undergraduate degree in Creative Writing to mean more. To do so, we need to adjust our curriculum to better suit all students, not just those on the graduate school or teaching tracks. And interdisciplinary work is the place to start.

Genre or Craft: Two Slices of the Same Pie

Like many institutions nationwide, mine divides the Creative Writing major between courses in Creative Writing, Literature and a scarce few in Composition. For creative writing, the mainstays are fiction, poetry and creative nonfiction; only recently have we added screenwriting. This course selection aligns, at least historically, with nearly every institution that offers Creative Writing as a major or emphasis, at the undergraduate and graduate levels. This format is familiar; it creates necessary continuity across our discipline; it is even, in most instances, what students who pursue creative writing wish to learn.

However, to offer these as the sole areas of study stagnates creative writing, and weakens the argument for our validity as a discipline. It also creates a culture of exclusion: by taking ownership over these particular genres, we essentially state that other forms of creativity – particularly ones more aligned to potential employment beyond the literary publishing world – exist outside our field. A creative writing major who then becomes employed as a copywriter will often see the former as 'creative' and the latter as 'professional', when in truth both forms of writing blend creative and professional skills all the time.

Genre-specific courses focus on a particular end product – the short story, the poem, the essay. However, like all writing, a process-based argument is often made for the validity of such courses. In other words, instructors will argue that skills acquired in a fiction or poetry or creative nonfiction class translate to other writing tasks because of an improvement in a writer's overall process – that character development or imagery or juxtaposition need to be learned within the genres so that they seep into writing without. I have entertained this argument from colleagues who wish to require their courses; I have presented the argument myself to students looking for practical application of their skills.

But this is not the only model; instructors have often sought a more fluid approach to process-based learning in creative writing. In his article 'Creative literacy pedagogy', Steve Healey discusses how he teaches to 'a broad range of skills used not only in literary works or genres but in many other creative practices as well' (Healey, 2015: 170). By focusing less on the genre of the product, but instead on the processes of creative expression themselves, Healey attempts to 'conceptualize the skills and awareness that creative writing students actually learn and use in their lives' (Healey, 2015: 192). Implied in this statement is that a product-based approach – teaching to write fiction, poetry or creative nonfiction – are things students *don't* 'actually learn and use in their lives', a point that, for those students who do not become professional writers, may be hard to argue against.

Popular texts like Janet Burroway's *Imaginative Writing* and Heather Sellers' *The Practice of Creative Writing* tackle this issue in a similar way: by encouraging creativity instead of employing convention. Arranging their chapters around craft issues such as voice, character and setting in the former, and tension, energy and pattern in the latter, they seek a similar aim of showing students, as Burroway (2003: xv) states, 'the extent to which *all* writing is imaginative ... and the fact that different genres share similar sources and build on similar skills'. In her Preface for Instructors,

Sellers (2008: vi) states that 'instead of separating the genres and learning their conventions, we bring to the forefront the strategies and techniques common to all good creative writing'.

I have taught using both these texts, and have noticed that the change in approach does, in many cases, create a livelier, more risk-promoting atmosphere. Students in an introductory multi-genre course, for example, can often see creative writing as a continuum when strong imagery appears in any genre. However, I ultimately feel that though impulse is good, the artifacts – the creative output and the skills necessary to produce such works – are ultimately the same. We may take a different road, but we arrive in the same destination. We change the *how*, but not the *what*. Like so many fast-food chains, we rearrange the ingredients, call it a different product and hope that the repackaging will trick our consumers into believing they have ingested something new.

Writing as a process has received so much cultural value that we have, perhaps, gone too far. We state that the process matters more than the product but, ultimately, students will not be evaluated – with grades, with performance reviews, with raises or promotions – based on their processes. Instead of devaluing the product, and thus causing our students to do the same, we might instead offer options in creative writing that diversify the potential products and thus create a richer, more varied possibility for both their processes and the resultant products. And these possibilities most commonly arrive from interdisciplinary work.

Toward an Interdisciplinary Creative Writing

In her book *Establishing Creative Writing Studies as an Academic Discipline*, Dianne Donnelly (2012: 139) forecasts the potential of our field, stating that a re-envisioned discipline may mean 'cross-fertilization possibilities such as merges with media studies – team-taught classes by composition specialists, poets, fictionists, technical communication specialists and media scholars'. Indeed, such collaborations have already begun in many institutions across the country, projects that expand beyond traditional creative writing and even beyond English departments themselves to generate new opportunities and possibilities.

In their essay 'Concentration, form, and ways of (digitally) seeing', Anna Leahy and Douglas Dechow detail their department's integration with Digital Humanities in order to offer their students a wider variety of skills. In addition to re-envisioning creative output to include such projects as blogging or what they term 'Prezi portfolios', Leahy and Dechow (2015: 40) detail an emerging curriculum that includes English courses with titles such as 'Online magazine production' and 'Advanced digital media workshop'. These courses are 'open to all arts and humanities students' and were built 'largely using existing resources' (Leahy & Dechow, 2015: 39). Such an ambitious program moves well beyond the general skills taught in creative writing courses; just from above, one can imagine an 'Online magazine production' course offering more than even one which builds a traditional print literary journal. Though graduate-run, national literary magazines are the norm, far less common is a literary magazine solicited, edited and produced by undergraduates;[1] even less common are those with a strong online presence, which is where our students do much of their reading. The interdisciplinary approach to literary magazine creation – marrying the skillsets of English majors with artists and with graphic designers, with musicians and with web developers – would expand the scope of such literary magazines, and would provide students with an avenue to work collaboratively with students experienced in a variety of creative venues. The journal itself would also give these students a viable, multimedia addition to their portfolio.

Similarly, an 'Advanced digital media workshop' would present students with the ability to discover, create and critique on numerous different platforms. And unlike interdisciplinary work which may be seen as obtrusive to a current curriculum, as Leahy says, 'I changed my creative writing course, not because this shift serves a DH [Digital Humanities] curriculum ... but because DH serves my course and my students' (Leahy & Dechow, 2015: 40). So often, interdisciplinarity is portrayed as an unbalanced relationship, where one field encumbers the other in order to gain. But as is evidenced here, the students themselves make whatever institutional or historic barriers we typically face irrelevant. As such, moves like the one to teach 'Writing for video games' came for Leahy because 'students expressed interest in game design and worked with the faculty to build a case' (Leahy & Dechow, 2015: 40).

In the field of gaming studies, Trent Hergenrader has done extensive work in intermingling disciplines. Among other articles, his 'Game spaces' details a collaborative world-building project that incorporates game design with technologies such as wikis in order to create a fully immersive composition experience. In these projects, the students enter 'a meta-possibility space' in which 'students and instructors explore the boundaries of what kind of work can be accomplished' (Hergenrader, 2015: 56). Concepts such as 'emergent gameplay' and 'environmental storytelling' enter the creation of a collaboratively built fictional space, one that, like great interdisciplinary work, merges the skills of multiple artists to create a specific but as yet unexplored product.

Such products, specifically newer, technology-driven ones, necessitate an interdisciplinary approach; in order for creative writers to compose in video game design, they often seek the expertise of those well versed in it. The term 'coding' is likely to be as frightening to many creative writers as composing a sonnet would be to a tech design major. But in working together, in finding the possibility beneath the strictures that seem to create specific forms – in other words, in being creative – these students inevitably discover hidden potential in their own works. It is these crossover talents with which an interdisciplinary creative writing can play.

Webb champions this sort of collaboration in her classrooms; she seeks for her students to 'acknowledge and value the sorts of work carried out by those in other disciplines, and learn the extent to which anyone practicing at a professional level is dependent upon other parts of the creative field' (Webb, 2008: 118). Like myself, Webb primarily engages in collaborative work in screenwriting and film departments; as such, she understands that most 'learning and assessment tend to focus on the individual student, while in fact it is rare to work purely as an individual in the world of creative production' (Webb, 2008: 119). In this sense, we mislead our students when we allow them primarily to work alone or control entire aspects of their creative output. In doing so, we perpetuate a larger myth that, for a vast majority of our students, will be undone almost immediately after graduation.

I sought to tackle this very issue in my own teaching. In 2014, I offered a screenwriting course for the first time. At the same time, I co-piloted a collaboration with two courses in our film department: a production course and an acting course. Working with the professors[2] of those courses, I designed a writing assignment tailored to the resources and enrollment of the collaborative project. The screenplay had such stipulations as: 8–12 pages (or minutes, as screenplays often follow a one-to-one ratio); at most four major characters, all with similar 'camera time'; sets in the immediate vicinity of campus and accessible to the production crew. My students wrote screenplays with these guidelines for their midterm assignment. Once collected, we three professors collaboratively chose five scripts based on quality and production capability. From there, during the second half of the semester, the acting students familiarized themselves with their characters while the production crew worked on pre-production. Eventually, collectively, each group filmed the script, some over a few weeks, some in a matter of a day. And finally, after post-production work, we presented these films at the end of the semester to an audience of students, family members, faculty and administration.

I find it hard to undersell the importance of this work to our creative writers. The class is split between creative writing and film students, which offers both perspectives into the writing process. The restrictions of the screenplay genre themselves create unique challenges which students typically grate against initially, but with which they ultimately experiment and explore. Previously, my students, like Webb's, 'were not explicitly provided with the literacies they would need to step outside the confines of their own practice, and hence to move from a good idea to an achievable product' (Webb, 2008: 118). Here, however, they participated in the creation of a product both more visual and more collaborative than any of their work in our traditional creative writing courses. And most importantly, for me, they experienced a new form of creative output for their efforts. Characters previously demarcated to their heads or their word processors now spoke to them through multiple creative interpretations: an acting student, a director, even a lighting crew member all placed a creative stamp on this character. And, in the end, when the credits rolled and their name appeared under 'Screenplay by…' they had another form of creativity they could claim as their own.

Just over a year later, in part because of the success of our initial collaboration, and in part because of the idea of another colleague,[3] our departments offered our first 'Web series' course. Though the collaboration worked similarly, this time all students enrolled in the same course, which we then co-taught. Writers, actors and production crew members all interacted and collaborated on a short fictional four-episode series, from the initial premise down to the final cuts. Many of my team of six writers acted and worked as script supervisors; one even directed an episode. With each new script and episode, the entire class offered feedback and suggestions on how to improve. The project was entirely collaborative, in nearly every aspect of the process.

Like the short-film collaboration, this project creates an artifact – a live web series open to the public[4] – for which each contributor can stake a claim. For each student, the benefits of such work will differ: the producer of the show may use the series as a marketing tool for her ability to organize and lead a large team; the actor may include clips on a professional reel; the writer may show an episode as proof of his ability to write collaboratively, under a deadline (often two weeks) and to specific conventions. For any student, unlike a traditional creative writing course or workshop, the work created in this course becomes something much larger, a possibility that she likely otherwise would not have without.

Finally, as an extension of these collaborations, I recently had a discussion with a colleague in our art department. He teaches primarily graphic design, and is interested in collaborating with creative writers in a course specifically tailored to producing advertising material. The idea is to collaborate with local businesses in order to create real-world experience in advertising and copy writing in or near the Twin Cities metropolitan area. In the past two years, six of my creative writing majors ended up in just such a business. I imagine how much more beneficial it might be to tell my students of a course that would give them such experience before graduation, that would place a tangible, collaborative project in the portfolio they bring to the job interview.

These are just some examples, from recently published articles and my own experience. They certainly are not exhaustive; this type of work is growing, and it seems as though it will only continue to rise. It is important to note that most of these courses proceed like a practicum: they favor production over study, play over control. In many cases they rely on student self-motivation. As such, they're primarily suited for upper-division courses. But if creative writing wishes to do more than simply hone and sharpen a student's craft at the big three genres – and if we want to move beyond the notion that doing so somehow implies creative ability in other contexts – these courses become crucial. Instead of assuming other contexts for which their creative skills will translate, these courses create them.

The link between all of the above projects is collaborative work outside of the confines of what we typically term 'English' or even 'Creative Writing'. It is not hard to imagine a course concurrently run with a history department which focuses on historically researched creative writing; or a concurrent psychology or sociology course that creates using both literature and case studies on specific phenomena; or even a biology course that intertwines basic scientific concepts with a creative output. When I look not just at the future of creative writing, but at the immediate present, I see excitement, opportunity and growth in the above areas. I see my students gaining more and more from nontraditional, interdisciplinary approaches that require more of us and of them, and which ultimately deliver more in return. I see a creative writing which must increase and diversify its creative output. Essentially, we need to embrace our inherent interdisciplinarity.

Departmental Territorialism

The largest challenge to such an interdisciplinary approach may very well come not from without, but from within. Understandably, departments fight among and within themselves for resources, for students. I acknowledge that many institutions already have such interdisciplinary principles in place: departments founded on 'Writing Studies' as distinguished from study of English literature; Arts and Design colleges, which necessarily favor creative production across disciplines; technical colleges which often do the same. I present the following, then, as a brief discussion on the challenges particular to those creative writing programs entrenched in English departments as a 'major' or 'emphasis' area, particular to the undergraduate level.

In his book *(Re)Writing Craft*, Tim Mayers discusses at length the place of Creative Writing. He notes:

> On one level, academic disciplines are territories: bounded spaces where rules and customs operate and where dwellers (or at least some of them) guard against incursions by those from other territories. This territorial aspect of academic disciplines is perhaps the greatest barrier to reform. (Mayers, 2005: 104)

In this seemingly pessimistic but often all-too-truthful view, interdisciplinary work can be seen as encroaching on previously established turf in order to establish dominance over it, an institutional colonialism of sorts. Therefore, the notion that creative writers must branch out of their own discipline fights against the idea that we must corral and hoard interested students in an attempt to 'keep our own'.

But putting aside the effect on other disciplines, English itself may stand to lose a lot by what I'm suggesting. The addition of interdisciplinary work alongside the traditional creative writing curriculum may necessarily call for a downsizing of other areas of English itself, primarily literature. This is in part due to 'What has been a mostly hegemonic English department in which literary studies has occupied the terrain, and thus the power' (Donnelly, 2012: 133). Since English departments have traditionally been founded on literature, various 'tracks' of undergraduate English – including Professional Writing, Composition, Education and Creative Writing – often require as much as half, if not more, of a literature-based curriculum: period-specific study on English, American or World literatures, both contemporary and classic. In comparison, creative writing classes overlap generally at the introductory level and nowhere else: in other words, roughly 4 credits as opposed to 24. As Mayers (2005: 105) notes, 'The scales in English studies have been tilted far too much toward textual interpretation [as opposed to] production', causing discrepancies in the workload of any English major.

Traditionally, the argument has been that creative writing cannot exist without literature; today, the opposite may be much closer to the truth. Donnelly (2012: 135) notes that 'The important new work in the field of *creative writing studies* combined with the noticeable decline of 20th century literature, may mean that the discipline of literary studies may have "no other place to go" than to creative writing'. As the one vine of English studies that continues to grow – as Myers (1996: 171) notes, 'If nothing else, student interest in the subject assured creative writing's future' – many creative writing programs find themselves in a position they have never occupied: that of the dominant force. To make room for more interdisciplinary courses that broaden a student's creative output, English departments may need to scale down on course requirements in other areas. For most, literature courses seem the most logical place to start trimming. And without creative writing majors occupying those seats, these courses – and the professors who teach them – may become less and less.

There is precedent for such an undertaking. As Mayers notes when describing his concept of 'craft criticism', the work of interpreting literature alters when one aims to produce. In truth, much textual analysis enters a given creative writing classroom when an instructor assigns a text like Burroway or Sellers, an anthologized collection, or a contemporary literary magazine. To assume that, in a creative writing course, one 'produces' work without critical or creative interpretation sells short the intellectual rigor of our field.

Thus, adding interdisciplinary work will inevitably come at the expense of some other established practice. Literature professors – still often those who hold power, as department chairs or otherwise, in an English department[5] – may resist the notion of reducing their requirements in order to push them outward to other disciplines. And in a sense, primarily financial, this makes sense for the health of English departments on the whole. Creative writers – myself included – will unlikely want to trim or eschew their courses on fiction, poetry or creative nonfiction as service to those students who wish to enter graduate studies, if not their own interests. And territorialism needn't be painted as wholly obtrusive: there is something to be said for establishing and holding ground that is uniquely ours. Students arrive to us because we offer something no other discipline does. But at our best, creative writers are artists, historians, humanists, designers, all at once. We meld interests every time we create. To focus inward is perhaps to succumb to institutional vanity, to solipsism: it is why Myers questions whether the institution of Creative Writing itself can effect the necessary changes. He states that 'A value system that transcends the subjective needs of individual expression may be necessary to produce good writers or even public intellectuals' (Myers, 1996: 179).

That value system, I would argue, becomes inherent when creative writers engage in interdisciplinary work. Such work expands possibilities for our institutions, our departments, ourselves as professors and, most importantly, our students.

Creative Interdisciplinarity (or, The Future)

Creative writing as a discipline would do well to acknowledge, as Webb (2008: 119) states, that 'in the long run, very few creative practitioners actually work alone'. If interdisciplinary work becomes its own form of institutional capital – if, as I have seen at our institution, the collaborative work between departments gains momentum as a recruiting strategy – then student numbers would rise on the whole, regardless of department. This holistic view of strengthening the university can and already has been championed. Therefore, those deemed 'Creative Writing majors' may in fact be nomads, samplers, who experience a major which allows for multiple interdisciplinary options. Given enough of these options, one may offer a 'traditional' track and a 'multidisciplinary' track, or even a 'multimedia' track, in service of the students who wish to compose this way. In this situation, when those students who don't want to attend graduate school and don't want to teach arrive at my door and ask me that dreaded question – *What kind of job can I get with my degree?* – I will feel armored, at the ready. I will feel, as I do more and more, that I can offer them possibilities.

Notes

(1) Our university runs an undergraduate literary magazine, *Prologue*, through a student organization group, which provides much more funding than our department could. The journal includes both written and visual art; I do bemoan, however, the fact that few students outside of creative writing work on the journal and that, as a result, an opportunity for expansion feels missed.
(2) Erik Johnson and James Zimmerman, both to whom I am forever grateful.
(3) Joe Blum, to whom I am also indebted for this work.
(4) The series, titled *Pass or Fail*, can be viewed on YouTube under the 'Falcon Web Series' channel.
(5) I would be remiss here not to mention that my current department chair is a literature professor, who has been wholly supportive of the collaborative work I have piloted. I do not take this for granted, as he may be the exception to the rule.

References

Burroway, J. (2003) *Imaginative Writing: The Elements of Craft*. New York: Penguin Academic.

Dawson, P. (2005) *Creative Writing and the New Humanities*. New York: Routledge.
Donnelly, D. (2012) *Establishing Creative Writing Studies as an Academic Discipline*. Bristol: Multilingual Matters.
Healey, S. (2015) Creative literacy pedagogy. In *Creative Writing Pedagogies for the Twenty-First Century*. Carbondale, IL: Southern Illinois University Press.
Hergenrader, T. (2015) Game spaces: Videogames as story-generating systems for creative writers. In M.D. Clark, T. Hergenrader and J. Rein (eds) *Creative Writing in the Digital Age* (pp. 45–60). New York: Bloomsbury Academic.
Leahy, A. and Dechow, D. (2015) Concentration, form, and ways of (digitally) seeing. In M.D. Clark, T. Hergenrader and J. Rein (eds) *Creative Writing in the Digital Age* (pp. 29–44). New York: Bloomsbury Academic.
Mayers, T. (2005) *(Re)Writing Craft: Composition, Creative Writing, and the Future of English Studies*. Pittsburgh, PA: Pittsburgh University Press.
Myers, D.G. (1996) *The Elephants Teach: Creative Writing Since 1880*. Chicago, IL: Chicago University Press.
Sellers, H. (2008) *The Practice of Creative Writing: A Guide for Students*. Boston, MA: Bedford/St Martin's.
Webb, J. (2008) Acting, interacting, and acting up: Teaching collaborative creative practice. In G. Harper and J. Kroll (eds) *Creative Writing Studies: Practice, Research and Pedagogy* (pp. 117–129). Clevedon: Multilingual Matters.

9 Creative Writing in First-Year Writing: Let's Remember, or Re-teach, the Value of Fiction

Kate Kostelnik

> [B]egin by rejecting the assumption of 'natural value' in what we do: in writing, literature, scholarship, art. Our first task is reassessment, as we proceed problematizing writing itself: What is it? Why do it? How? Where is the pleasure and value? In what ways may it continue in our lives?
> Katharine Haake, *What Our Speech Disrupts*

> Because we are less sure of what fiction is 'saying,' we are less pre-emptively defended against it or biased in its favor. We are inclined to let it past our fortifications. It's merely a court jester, there to amuse us. We let in the brazen liar and his hidden, difficult truths.
> Rivka Galchen, 'What's behind the notion that nonfiction is more "relevant" than fiction?'

In *What Our Speech Disrupts*, Katharine Haake uses critical theory in creative writing classes in order to make what is invisible visible. She calls for bricolage, 'some of this, and some of that. Nothing pure, but whatever is at hand and what will work. If you need a screw and you only have a wire, why wail?' (Haake, 2000: 26). She knows full well that both theorists and creative writers might take issue; likewise, I foresee compositionists, literary critics and creative writers objecting to the kinds of courses and moves toward sociological poetics that I posit in this chapter.

Although my greater project is to incorporate creative writing into first-year writing, I build on Haake's call to cross-disciplinary lines and use whatever we have to make our students stronger and more critically aware writers. As an instructor and writer who moves between creative writing, composition and literary studies to create classes that fuse all three strands, this essay draws on diverse texts from literary critics, compositionists, Creative Writing Studies[1] theorists and novelists. Nothing pure. In fact, I'm a creative writer who no longer teaches pure creative writing and I hope this chapter, like Haake's work, will 'raise such issues for our discipline so as to illuminate the questions that will guide us, without any guarantee, to wherever in the world we are going next' (Haake, 2000: 26).

Theorists have suggested where we might go in addition to our work in creative writing classrooms. Tim Mayers concludes 'Figuring the future: Lore and/in creative writing' by asking for the reconfiguration of writing programs and further consideration of how creative writing might fit into redesigned university writing curricula. He explains, creative writing instruction in numerous other kinds of writing 'promise[s] to help create more adaptable and rhetorically aware student writers, writers whose knowledge of different genres and contexts allows them to succeed at multiple writing tasks' (Mayers, 2007: 12). Alexandria Peary argues that imaginative writing can even be useful beyond writing curricula: '[t]hrough creative writing, students from any major can master course content as well as critically consider information in the disciplines' (Peary, 2015: 195). In 'The pedagogy of creative writing across the curriculum' she gives examples of how Sociology students write stories about their future selves on the job, Psychology students create dialogues between characters enacting research methodology and medical students write from the perspectives of cadavers (Peary, 2015: 194, 198). I'm not a historian of English Studies, but let me nonetheless say it's pretty remarkable that, while creative writing instructors were questioning workshop pedagogy, imaginative writing found its way into disciplines beyond English departments.

However, as exciting as this moment might be for Creative Writing Studies, common core guidelines, imposed in primary and secondary schools, will likely make entering freshmen less receptive to imaginative writing. I will explore why and how writing and reading fiction are valuable specifically in first-year writing/composition (FYC).[2] In Part III, I explain how I integrate writing processes, writing studies and multiple genres into my first-year writing courses. As contradictory as it may sound, the best place for me to discuss the significance of imaginative writing and fiction, in terms of its purposes and social contexts, is the first-year writing classroom, where students learn and compare multiple kinds of writing for various rhetorical purposes. Fiction instructors, in addition to their teaching in creative writing courses, have an opportunity to bring their talents and energy into first-year writing. As I explain in Part II, although common core's language arts guidelines might make entering freshmen rhetorically savvy in their ability to move between genres, this may come at the price of primary and secondary curricula that lack fictional literature.

Arguments over imaginative texts in the writing classroom[3] are certainly nothing new; compositionists valuing process-oriented writing classes have cautioned against the inclusion of revered (finished) literary texts beside newer student drafts. Rather than choosing a side, Wendy Bishop, in 'The literary text and the writing classroom', goes deeper, to 'locate the tensions of disciplinary turf, professional allegiances, and unexamined teaching practices that intersect in [a] first-year, writing with literature class' (1995: 436) at Florida State. From the perspective of a writing teacher educator, with training in literary studies, creative writing and rhetoric, she considers how conflicting ideologies within these three strands initiated the debate. Bishop acknowledges that the study of literature can overpower the study of writing (1995: 449) and calls for 'writing and reading instruction in *all* our English courses' as well communication across departmental divisions (1995: 451). Although I've never let imaginative texts eclipse my teaching of writing processes, I agree that all courses should include writing instruction and that professors in the separate strands of English Studies should talk to one another and possibly also collaborate – even if the latter is odder than creative writers happily accepting first-year writing assignments.

Creative writers may or may not follow my lead into composition courses, but they should consider where they might also be useful during these difficult times in English Studies. Although I see myself more as crossing boundaries than joining camps, I understand Elbow's explanation that '[w]hen [he] came to see himself as a composition person, [he] felt an enormous relief at finally feeling *useful* – as though [he] could make an actual difference for people' (2002: 536). To be clear, I'm certainly not claiming (and will later elaborate on in this chapter) that imaginative writing is useless. But I am saying that I feel useful working with students beyond English departments. New and wider audiences from across the disciplines have enriched my teaching.

In using creative writing in first-year-writing – in addition to composition pedagogy that supports argumentation, exposition, inquiry and description – I've begun to 'create more adaptable and rhetorically aware student writers, writers whose knowledge of different genres and contexts allows them to succeed at multiple writing tasks' (Mayers, 2007: 12). Being transparent to a generation of first-year students who generally don't value fiction – neither reading nor writing it – has enabled me to articulate the importance of imaginative writing. These kinds of discussions can enrich creative writing courses as well. In Part I, I begin by reframing fiction's purpose in 21st-century classrooms. Imaginative writing, specifically fictions that depict the clash of social forces, can help us incorporate discussions of social justice into our creative writing classes. If creative writing and English studies are to remain vital on our campuses we need to better articulate, in addition to doing the important work of teaching craft and revision, why we write, why fiction is important and what our work does.

Part I. Getting Beyond Art for Art's Sake

As creative writing instructors versed in teaching our students to do the generating,[4] drafting, receiving feedback, revising and so on, we rightfully de-emphasize the product that writing becomes after so much work. Rather than praising 'genius' or discussing book deals, I've focused my creative writing classes on teaching the processes of writing. However, we *shouldn't* forget what 'the product' can do. While processes are crucial, we can also consider how 'finished' fiction does more than art for art's sake. We can remind, or re-teach, our students that imaginative writing does something.

Compositionists who cross into Creative Writing Studies have investigated our discipline's New Critical foundations. Tim Mayers (2007: 4) explains:

> Another aspect of creative writing's conventional wisdom or lore is the tendency to think of fiction and poetry in artistic rather than rhetorical terms. The type of writing most creative writers aspire toward is not sullied by involvement with political, economic, or social concerns. It exists, first and foremost, for its own sake, and aims at timelessness, or transcendence of the concerns of everyday. The primary aim or purpose of composing, within this scheme, is to produce work itself, and not to have that work *do* anything such as persuade or inform an audience.

I understand the rationale that imaginative writing is its own good, just as 'any attempt to justify the existence of humanities education "confers value on an activity from a perspective outside its performance. An activity that cannot be justified is an activity that refuses to regard itself as instrumental to some larger good"' (Fish quoted in Cain, 2009: 232). Nonetheless, I'm suggesting that creative writing can be both art and a means of discussing social justice or, as I'll explain, injustice.

Much has been written about creative writing's social purposes,[5] but put simply: imaginative writing shows the clash of social forces. Imaginative writing can be both socially illustrative and artful.[6] In advocating the redesign of creative writing programs, David Radavich concludes 'Creative writing in the academy':

Courses that teach poetry, fiction, and drama writing can offer students valuable insights and experience on today's college campuses, but only if creative writing classes are brought into deeper and wider relation with other courses in the curriculum; only if such programs maintain a pedagogy not geared toward packaging for the marketplace but instead emphasizing reading skills, critical thinking, language awareness, and historical consciousness, qualities and abilities that will prove useful in many walks of life, and only if such programs can be made to foster more understanding of public concerns and social responsibility. In short, if creative writing is to have meaning in the academy of the future, it needs to partake of those very qualities and purposes best representative of true scholarship – namely, broad, informed, intensive reading, thinking, and writing and a commitment to the social betterment of a troubled world. (Radavich, 1999: 112)

I include so much of Radavich's argument – which famously (and, to some, infamously) states that creative writing programs' goals and purposes need to be revised and rationalized – because I agree that creative writing classes can and should include rigorous intellectual work. Moreover, I underline Radavich's move toward sociological poetics and claim that fiction depicts our 'troubled world' (Radavich, 1999: 112) as it really is. Literary fiction isn't about transcending everyday experiences; it's about stating human problems as clearly as possible through the lives and conflicts of characters. It's about showing how and why people act and think as they do. As a fiction teacher, I've asked my students 'What happens to a person?[7] What are their conflicts? With whom do they come in contact? What do they want that others do not want them to have?' Diversity in classrooms varies these responses in endless ways. But here is why the processes of writing and reading fiction are critical for our students. Our classrooms – where we attempt to create just spaces where diversity is respected – are unlike the world beyond them.

Although I may appear to veer away from the 'real world versus university' division, allow me to reference arguments for imaginative writing in freshman composition. I've tried to separate sections on how creative writing courses can move to sociological poetics, bringing disparate genres into conversation in creative writing classrooms, and why the multi-genre approach is particularly suited to first-year writing, but unbraiding these may prove more unnecessary than difficult. Just as sections overlap, arguments from theorists in literary studies, creative writing (like Radavich's) and composition speak to both imaginative writing *and* what students need in order to navigate the real world. Similarly, in response to the replacement of literature with rhetoric in freshman composition,

Gary Tate mourns the loss of 'the entire world of imaginative texts: the canonical texts, of course, but also the imaginative texts of students, young children, and amateurs' (Tate, 1993: 319). He fears that increasingly the modern university prepares students for their specific writing tasks in their disciplinary communities. Tate argues that there is 'another "community" that we should be preparing our students to join' (1993: 320). He doesn't just categorize students by their various majors but 'treat[s] them as people whose most important conversations will take place *outside the academy*, as they struggle to figure out how to live their lives – that is, how to vote and love and survive, how to respond to change and diversity and death and oppression and freedom' (1993: 320). I agree with the inclusion of imaginative texts, but, as I'll explain shortly, we can use equal parts rhetoric and literature in FYC.

I stress Tate's dividing line between the academy and the world outside it. As a fiction writer, I live in and write about the real world. As an educator, I acknowledge the real world exists, but expect dignity, dialogue and respect for diversity in my classrooms. Yes, I advocate for social justice, but I don't believe that writing that depicts reality should be kept from students or offset with trigger warnings. Imaginative writing, specifically fiction,[8] is important in that students can write it and read it in order to explore how social forces play out.

For example, in a 2013 section of an introductory creative writing course,[9] a student returning from Iraq, whom I'll call Jake, began writing unspecific patriotic poems that didn't acknowledge the real situations he'd witnessed and endured while serving. In class we talked about how imaginative writing should strive to depict the truth, even if fiction is 'made up'. Jake understood and began writing detailed fictional scenes showing how some young soldiers really behave – in one scene drunkenly berating an Iraqi citizen. Although Jake had had positive experiences with the Iraqi people, he'd witnessed plenty of altercations. His fiction writing allowed him to tell the truth about how some young soldiers behave during war. Jake's short story didn't directly denounce the war or the young soldiers' actions in it, but his depiction of it stated the problem(s) with horrific clarity.

This probably all sounds pretty dark: I advocate for social justice and tell my students to write about the opposite – how people behave as conflicts play out. I accept this tension between my dual roles as teacher and writer. The instructor is supportive, energized and faithful in her students' efforts and potential; she might be naïve, but her students improve, and some delightfully surprise her. No surprise for the writer; no surprise for the reader. That writer wrestles her novel drafts and follows characters into scenes both beautiful and horrible, mostly the latter. Lore asserts that dualities and consistent inconsistencies make rich characters. Stronger lore dictates that only conflict is interesting; it's trouble I gladly visit on my own character.

One might also say that students can get enough reality from the news, but reporting doesn't allow readers to spend extensive time with characters. Reporting doesn't necessarily explain how and why we act and react. Because writing is epistemic, a means of creating new knowledge – as well as a mode of learning in itself – we need to write into how and why things happen. Fiction brings readers and writers intimately into the lives of characters and complex historical contexts using scenes (in real time) with concrete detail.

For example, reading fiction alongside nonfiction from the 1960s can show how and why deep-seated racism persists despite legislation. Although I'm getting ahead of myself – in that this particular lesson takes place in first-year writing – I believe it is applicable to creative writing courses as well. In one unit, I begin with the classic, rhetorically rich, 'Letter from Birmingham Jail' (Martin Luther King, 1963). In addition to the text's incorporation of cogent argument, careful counter-argument and gripping emotion, King expresses his disappointment with the white moderate and religious leaders who claimed his protests untimely. In teaching this text to contemporary students, I've found that more than the passionate writing and masterful balance of ethos, pathos and logos, students are taken aback by the blatant racism of southern politicians and basic lack of sense from the white moderate.

Students can study nonfiction and informational texts to try to understand context, but a different kind of understanding comes from reading and discussing Flannery O'Connor's 'Everything that rises must converge' (1965), the fictional story of white generations colliding over polar responses to desegregation. Although the character Julian, in his performative attempts at progressive politics, is patronizing to the African American characters in the story, his mother's fierce attachment to antebellum values and segregation are both infuriating and, as I'll explain shortly, understandable to students. Student readers want the mother character to learn her 'lesson' (O'Connor, 1965: 287) as much as Julian does. Likewise, students feel Julian's conflict in loving his mother nonetheless. Students may have a hard time understanding what it was like to coexist with older generations during the time of the Civil Rights Movement, but they can relate to O'Connor's fiction when we discuss how we handle less than progressive statements from our own grandparents. Students realize Julian's conception of what would be the 'ultimate horror' of bringing home an African American fiancé (O'Connor, 1965: 288) is not so hyperbolic or dated when considering how some of their own family members might react to a partner of the 'wrong' race, sex or religious affiliation.

O'Connor writes a narrative with high stakes, strong characters and scenes that bring us into these conflicted times. In my opinion, the story is as rhetorically rich as MLK's 'Birmingham Jail' in that it illustrates complicated contexts and diverse points of view. Her fiction shows characters' behaviors, but rather than directly castigating them, she leaves that to the reader. Our anger at characters' racism is all the more tricky as we have a sense of how and why characters have come to think and act the way they do. I certainly don't mean to pit MLK's work against O'Connor's, to privilege the experiences of white characters or to justify unjust behaviors. I'm saying that fiction does important work in showing difficult and complicated realities. In speaking to the importance of teaching diverse authors and points of view, Junot Diaz states that our students need to '"look at this country and [they] look at this world and [they] need to understand it in complex ways"' (quoted in Moreno, 2015). I agree with the incorporation of diverse voices, but I stress that our students deserve and need fictional texts that facilitate their understanding of intricate social issues. Fiction, when read alongside nonfiction, offers theories and explanations for *how* and *why* injustice occurs, and it continues to occur despite designations of what is right and wrong.

Conflicts that can't easily be addressed, argued or explained are the heart of fiction. Writers, like Flannery O'Connor, write what they see – the predicaments and struggles that characterize human experience – not what they believe or their solutions to social problems. As our campuses' concerns about social justice increase, and many are (rightly or wrongly) accused of insensitivity, fiction writing – if it is responsible and fair to characters and situations – offers students a space to state problems and depict the world as it is, warts and all, without overt arguments or blatant accusations. Paraphrasing David Foster Wallace, Robert McLaughlin explains that fiction doesn't offer 'us a cure for the difficulties of being human; rather, it reminds us of these difficulties and joins us to others who resist the "don't-worry-be-happy" siren song of consumer culture' (McLaughlin, 2008: 110). The study of fiction, like fiction itself, is not an antidote to injustice, but it can be a valuable space for our students to consider human nature. We can fight and argue against injustice as vehemently as we can – and I believe that we should; however, this doesn't offer students understanding as to how and why injustices occur. We can acknowledge the need for social justice as easily as our students can 'like' something on Facebook, but liking and disliking pale in comparison to understanding. We can say 'everyone knows racism is wrong', but denouncing it doesn't do much in terms of helping us comprehend how it happens and why it persists.

Creative writing instructors who continue to teach from the New Critical stance that writing is useless and/or apolitical can or cannot consider imaginative writing's potential to discuss the social world. However, those of us who seek to create more cohesive, vital English Studies courses and want to help our students grow as both people and writers have a larger role in maintaining the importance of imaginative writing in our curricula. In addition to discussing the significance of fiction in our creative writing classrooms, we might also consider entering first-year writing classrooms, as I have. In fact, in light of common core legislation that prioritizes the teaching of informational over imaginative texts, our incoming freshmen will have written and read considerably less fiction than previous generations. This will potentially affect enrollments in creative writing as well as in all English classes.

Part II: Common Core's Influence

In order to clarify how and why common core potentially impacts creative writing and English Studies in the academy, I'll begin with what common core is and how it privileges informational texts. However, in light of mercurial state legislative responses, I can't assess how pervasive or powerful the common core guidelines will be.[10] Media coverage of the conservative and other activists' rallies against common core 'evok[e] the kind of anguish and horror once reserved for the so-called death panels' (Murphy, 2014: n.p.). A quick Google search turns up plenty of rancor as well as misinterpretation[11] from humanists in the academy and beyond.

In the wake of No Child Left Behind, common core is a set of educational benchmarks (not a curriculum per se) consistent across state lines. The guidelines were adopted quickly; states that did so could compete for $4.35 billion in funds from the Department of Education (Murphy, 2014: n.p.). The 'Key Design Consideration' of the standards themselves align with a 2008 study by the National Assessment of Education (see Table 9.1), which 'requires a high and increasing proportion of informational texts on its assessment as students advance through the grades' in order to 'meet the requirements of college and career readiness' (Common Core Standards Initiative, 2015: n.p.).

Amanda Christy Brown and Katherine Schulton explain:

Table 9.1 Distribution of literary and information passages by grade in the 2009 National Assessment of Educational Progress (NAEP) Reading Framework

Grade	Literary	Information
4	50%	50%
8	45%	55%
12	30%	70%

NAEP (2008) *Reading Framework for the 2009 National Assessment of Educational Progress.* Washington, DC: US Government Printing Office.

Because most of what students will read in college and in the workplace is not fiction, but texts that are 'informational in structure,' the standards say that by fourth grade, half of what students read should be informational texts, while by 12th grade, students should be reading nonfiction 70 percent of the time. (Brown & Schulton, 2012: n.p.)

While the guidelines won't completely remove literature from primary and secondary education, something will have to give in order to make room for these informational texts.

Instructors of Creative Nonfiction should also be wary. In a talk titled 'Bringing the common core to life', David Coleman, the architect of common core, explains the standards' emphasis on argumentative writing: '[I]n [grades] 6–12 there's a balancing at the core of literature and a new form, literary nonfiction' (Coleman, 2011: 39). He doesn't mean 'narrative literary nonfiction like biography or memoir' (2011: 39). The standards privilege 'well-wrought arguments and informational texts that are written to a broad audience' (2011: 39). As I said, I do feel that aspects of common core potentially threaten enrollments in English and creative writing courses, and I'm as uncomfortable as Coleman's most vehement critics with his position as President of the College Board.

However, as a teacher of first-year writing and courses that integrate literary studies, composition and creative writing, I agree with Coleman's inclusion of a wider range of texts in English classes (Coleman, 2011: 39). Call it another duality, or possibly a complex understanding and response to the problems of aligning educational guidelines nationwide and preparing students for college-level reading and writing. Yes, the standards potentially threaten English Studies courses that prioritize imaginative writing and literature, but the integration of multiple genres with imaginative writing might 'create more adaptable and rhetorically aware student writers, writers whose knowledge of different genres and contexts allows them to succeed at multiple writing tasks' (Mayers, 2007: 12) – even before they arrive on our campuses.

In first-year writing classes, I teach about half nonfiction (ranging from literary nonfiction, memoir, scholarship and journalism) and half imaginative (novels, short stories and poems). Students need to be availed of a broad range of genres and rhetorical options. However, common core's slighting of imaginative texts from primary and secondary education, compounded with students' increasingly vocational mindsets, will likely make them less receptive to the teaching, reading and writing of fiction. In addition to articulating the social value of fiction writing in their creative writing courses, creative writing teachers might also consider getting on the front lines, first-year writing, to give fiction back to our entering students.

Part III: More on Fiction in FYC

Discussing imaginative writing in first-year writing, as an important genre[12] that explores the clash of social forces, maintains the relevance of imaginative writing and reading. Argumentative writing, which clearly delineates meanings and messages, should be read alongside less direct fictional texts. As I state in Part I, students should read and write in a variety of genres as well as investigate different rhetorical situations and modes of writing. This approach would be similar to Wardle and Down's[13] move away from first-year composition to writing studies; however, in addition to using rhet/comp scholarship about writing – instructors, versed in creative writing studies, would incorporate their expertise and reaffirm imaginative writing's role in the depiction of the social world.

Students could learn to craft arguments as well as imaginative writing.[14] Instructors could teach students to 'read "as writers"' (Barden, quoted in Cain, 2009) in addition to how they are traditionally trained to read 'for information, unaware of the particularities of language, style, and form that are crucial to a writer's understanding of craft' (Cain, 2009: 235–236). In other words, students could interpret the social messages conveyed as well as consider how the writing has been crafted.[15] Instructors should offer:

> choices of genre from [students'] earliest experiences of composing within the university setting.... [C]onjoining the disciplines [composition and creative writing] in college students' earliest writing experiences helps students understand that writing has many functions beyond research and persuasion and that more than one genre can facilitate the teaching of such skills. (Berg & May, 2015: xx)

As a fiction writer in the first-year writing classroom, I design courses around various genres of texts that illustrate similar social issues. In some class sessions we focus on depictions of racism; in others we look at representations of a historical moment from multiple genres. For example, in the final unit of my first-year English and Writing course themed 'Fiction vs. Nonfiction', we examine representations of racial tensions in Haitian and Dominican literature, specifically those of the 1937 Parsley massacre. Texts include: Edwidge Dandicat's *Farming of Bones* (1998), Rita Dove's 'Parsley' (n.d.), Julia Alvarez's *A Wedding in Haiti* (2012), Junot Díaz's *The Brief and Wondrous Life of Oscar Wao* (2007), as well as witness accounts of Trujillo's regime in *The Dominican Reader* (Eyewitnesses, 1987). Students consider the benefits and drawbacks of each genre's depiction and complete exercises to mimic rhetorical and literary techniques. In considering effective writing in multiple genres, students understand the value of using different genres for various purposes.

For final projects, students can choose a cluster of texts and explore which genre they find most valuable. While many write convincingly of their revived understanding of fiction, a great many also write compelling discussions about their allegiance to nonfiction. Of course, I bring my own biases; I admit that I want them to see how fiction is successful in showing the intricacies of historical events through different points of view. Despite the title of the course and the assignment above, my goal as an instructor isn't for students to choose a dominant genre: more than anything I want students to see merits in different kinds of writing and to use genres appropriately for varying purposes. Comparing and contrasting genres enables students to consider and question what they are reading, how writing is made, what purposes and audiences different texts serve, and how different genres depict and address the social world.

Another option for the final project is for students to write a piece of fiction where they explore a historical moment through a character in scene(s). After they've drafted and revised their fictions, they step back and consider the literary and rhetorical choices they've made; they write an analytical paper that accompanies their creative work about what they are trying to do and for whom they are writing. This analytical component is part rhetorical analysis and part author's note. Critics may spur that the creative portion of the project is not academic or useful as crafting academic arguments. In 'The pedagogy of writing across the curriculum', Alexandria Peary discusses the validity of creative writing as an academic assignment and explains that the 'usual genres of college are a strange import' (2015: 202). Research papers, along with lab reports and lecture notes – which constitute most of contemporary college students' writing – come from the German university model implemented in the 19th century. Emphasis on 'academic' genres means that students are assigned texts that 'resemble the research journal article rather than the creative or workplace genres that college graduates might encounter such as a memo or client project proposal. Students have been forced to become "Mini-me"s – to replicate the genres of scholarly value produced by faculty' (Peary, 2015: 203). In other words, the scholarly genres that we privilege are not the kinds of texts most students will continue to produce in their lives and careers beyond the academy.

Of course, I value academic arguments and explain to my students that writing a paper for a course is an excellent way to learn and explore content – even if they won't continue as a professional in academe. However, scholarly argument is one of many valuable genres from which students can learn. Students should have opportunities to choose and explore the kinds of writing and inquiries that are pertinent to their academic goals as well as those that they can be passionate about. If English Studies and creative writing are to remain vital on our campuses we need to give students options for writing as well as exposure to genres that facilitate different kinds of learning in addition to argumentation. We've all heard accusations from outside (and sometimes inside) the academy that students 'can't write'. Everything from bad teaching, texting and Twitter gets blamed. What's most upsetting isn't the claim; it's that students hear it loud and clear. Some of our students believe they'll never grow as writers; even worse, others avoid writing at all costs. However absurd, these future leaders and professionals – who will absolutely need to join written conversations and posit innovations and questions through discourse – don't take writing and Humanities courses.

Now is not a moment to narrow conceptions of what constitutes practical writing and reading. It's time to bring the strands – composition, creative writing and literary studies – together and offer students more possibilities that keep them writing and learning. Technologists denounce the Humanities (Hipps, 2016: n.p.) and state legislatures 'promote STEM education and cut liberal arts funding' (Cohen, 2016: n.p.). Yes, there are algorithms that project earnings of Computer Science versus Humanities majors, and we've all read the arguments and think-pieces. Students should make informed decisions about their courses of study, but how we encourage them to continue these conversations and put forth their own writing and explorations of larger questions rests in our hands. We must foster flexibility and nimbleness in thinking and writing. Again, we've got to train them to '"look at this country and look at this world and … to understand it in complex ways"' (Díaz quoted in Moreno, 2015: n.p.). We've also got make sure that think-pieces and written conversations persist.

Conclusion

Creative writers on college campuses can give fiction back to entering freshmen who might not value the writing and reading of imaginative texts. This can happen in creative writing classrooms, but another place is on the forefront in first-year writing courses, where different genres of writing can be read, practiced and discussed in terms of how texts depict the clash of social forces. As creative writing instructors, we are equipped to reintroduce and/or reassert the importance of fiction to new generations of students. Of course, we also face the 'alarming shortage of academic jobs that allow for the teaching of creative writing only' (Mayers, 2007: 11). It's time to consider how we can reach students in addition to those enrolled in creative writing classes. Again, we can help in crafting what Mayers calls 'a more coherent and less fragmented version of English studies' (2007: 11). More cohesion can support students of English Studies as well as general populations of students. FYC may be the first, last and only course where some students read and write imaginatively.

Finally, some fiction. In 'Don't cry', Mary Gaitskill's story from the collection of the same name, a professor travels to Ethiopia with a friend who plans to adopt a child. The process is fraught with red tape, rejection, payoffs and images of extreme poverty; all the while, war erupts in the streets of an unnamed city. The character, Janice, owns her past and future in a place far away from campus. After she is robbed of wedding rings – one belonging to her deceased husband – she narrates how she pursues the offender: '[t]he boy was bright movement that I chased like an animal with a single instinct. I turned a corner, stumbled into a pothole full of warm brown water and nearly fell' (Gaitskill, 2009: 221). The author takes us further into this moment with action and concrete detail.

> Faces peered from the broken hole of a window. Skeleton dogs fierce and cringing, watched with starving eyes. My instinct felt them all as it felt itself: quick force in slow mammal bodies; soft brain in hard bone; a machine of thoughts; a machine of sex. The dark radiance of emotions; the personality; eyes, nose, mouth. *You, specifically.* A little boy with a large round head pointed at me and said words I couldn't understand. My instinct broke; everything that had been joined was now in pieces again. I put my face in my hands and cried like an animal. (Gaitskill, 2009: 221)

As machine gun fire sounds, a small crowd of teenagers in school uniforms follow Janice. She tells them that without her husband's ring she has nothing left. To this, a girl replies 'It will be alright', 'God will help you' (Gaitskill, 2009: 222). Then an elderly man appears, puts the rings in Janice's hand and tells her not to cry (2009: 223).

Years later, when telling this story at a university party, a woman chastises Janice, saying '[r]eally, you make too big a fuss of yourself. You should not go to Africa and then make such a fuss' (Gaitskill, 2009: 223). Janice accepts this; '[b]ecause in that room, she was right. I was a privileged and foolish woman running around bawling about rings while a whole city fell apart and were killed' (Gaitskill, 2009: 223). The character's retelling in the artificial university setting fails to show this complex, beautiful scene that took place in the human world. Nonetheless, the event resonates. She explains:

> But I didn't meet the old man in that room. I met him in a place of biblical times and modern times, where people walked back and forth between times, all times. In this place, I walked back and forth between the time of the living and the time of the dead. In the middle of my walking, war broke out, and the path between the living and the dead opened up and everything dear to me fell down the crack. I fell too, and I might've fallen forever – but the old man came and said, 'Stop.' And I stopped. (Gaitskill, 2009: 223)

Reading fiction is our pathway to experiences and learning far beyond us. Writers write stories, show scenes and discuss fiction in our classrooms. We connect however we can to our readers, our students and our world beyond the academy.

Notes

(1) Tim Mayers (2009: 218) explains: '*Creative Writing Studies* ... is a still-emerging enterprise that has been set in motion by some of the internal problems and contradictions of creative writing. Creative Writing Studies is a field of scholarly inquiry and research. It can be characterized, in the words of Katharine Haake, as scholarly work that 'seek[s] to move us beyond our preoccupation with the writer or the text to the role of Creative Writing as an academic discipline inside a profession that includes, but is not limited to the production and teaching of imaginative writing.'
(2) The predominant title for the course is First-Year Composition (FYC), which refers to the teaching of writing processes rather than literary analysis and interpretation. Generally, FYC courses support the drafting of expository/nonfiction/scholarly texts. However, many FYC courses do incorporate literature. With my multi-genre approach, I support and advocate this inclusion. I also prefer the term 'first-year writing', as it emphasizes the study of writing. At the University of Virginia, where I teach, composition courses are called ENWR: English and Writing.
(3) See Bishop (1995), Gamer (1995), Lindermann (1993), Roemer *et al.* (1999), Steinberg (1995) and Tate (1993).

(4) We say, or I've said, in creative writing classrooms:
- Follow your characters and your instincts in language, its own logic (Haake, 2000: 89), and don't write about ideas (Murray, 1989: 108).
- Character is destiny. Character is everything. Write as much as you can concretely and in scene. Readers will derive whatever meanings they want. Themes must be evoked from within (Gardner, quoted in Burroway, 2009: 15).

Some of us, trained prior to the influence of composition studies, may even say:
- 'Never worry about the reader' (Hugo, 1979: 5).

(5) For an overview of scholars who infuse critical theory and social concern into creative writing see my brief lit review on works by Patrick Bizzaro, Katharine Haake, Mary Ann Cain, Chris Green and George Kalamaris in 'Innovative frameworks and tested lore for teaching creative writing to undergraduates in the 21st century' (Kostelnik, 2014: 437–438), an essay that argues for the incorporation of theory and multi-culturalism in the creative writing classroom. Another important discussion appears in Paul Dawson's conclusion of *Creative Writing and the New Humanities*, in which he argues for 'shifting the pedagogical focus of workshop from narrowly formalist conceptions of craft to the social context of literature, but without diminishing the importance of craft as an intellectual skill, and without detracting from the purpose of improving students' writing. This means paying attention to the content of a literary work, as this is what connects it to the outside world, but without isolating content from form. What is required, then, is to demonstrate how content is realized in the formal construction of a text, and this means shifting from a formalist poetics to a sociological poetics' (Dawson, 2005: 208).

(6) To further clarify how art that 'does nothing' is unfairly exclusive, I refer to Bishop's 'Afterword – Colors of a different horse: On learning to like teaching creative writing'. Bishop quotes Tomkins' discussion of new criticism: 'Instead of moving audiences and bringing pleasure to bear on the world, the work is thought to present another separate and more perfect world…. The imputation that a poem might break out of its self-containment and perform a service would disqualify it immediately from consideration as a work of art. The first requirement of a work of art in twentieth century is that it should *do* nothing' (Tompkins quoted in Bishop, 1994: 281). 'Of course … the do nothing school of Art was a strategic move to keep insiders safe and outsiders safely out. The still hotly debated issue of art as political action illuminates the insider/outsider struggle' (Bishop, 1994: 281). Bishop goes on to assert, quoting Toni Cade Bambara and Trihn Minh-ha, that marginalized writers don't agree with 'do nothingness' and put imaginative writing in service of communities. It is perhaps writers from the margins who have helped us realize, or reminded us, that indeed writing 'does' something.

(7) Murray clarifies in his essay 'Unlearning to write' that students need to learn to write to explore. This begins when 'character meets character. There is action and reaction, push and pull, cause and effect. The scene in which characters act and react is the engine of the story, the energy produced from this dramatic interaction between characters drives the narrative forward – not meaning, idea, theme, or thesis; not literary style or voice; not background or setting; but character against character' (Murray, 1989: 108).

(8) I acknowledge that literary nonfiction can also show the social world, but in terms of writing – following a character, visiting trouble on her and understanding conflict – fiction allows students to explore why and how things happen without knowing how something ends. Writers explore the lives and changes of characters in real time, or

scenes. Fiction writing allows us to learn what happens as we write. Nonfiction does a fine job describing how and why things happen, but I believe that fiction allows more possibility and exploration.
(9) This course took place the University of Nebraska, Lincoln, where I served as a graduate teaching assistant.
(10) As of January 2017, not enough assessment data had been released, and states originally onboard had or had begun procedures to repeal. Forty-two of the 50 US states and the District of Columbia are members of the Common Core State Standards Initiative.
(11) One guideline is frequently misinterpreted to mean that 70% of the material in English classes will be informational; the 70% refers to texts in *all* subjects, including History, Science and English.
(12) See Anis S. Bawarshi and Mary Jo Reiff's *Genre: And Introduction to History, Theory, Research, and Pedagogy* (2010).
(13) Wardle and Down's argument in 'Teaching about writing, righting misconception: (Re)envisioning "First-year composition" as "Introduction to writing studies"' moves 'first-year composition from teaching "how to write in college" to teaching *about writing* – from acting as if writing is a basic, universal skill to acting as if writing studies is a discipline with content knowledge to which students should be introduced, thereby changing [students'] understanding about writing and thus changing the ways students write' (Wardle & Down, 2007: 553).
(14) I use chapters of Burroway's *Imaginative Writing* (2009) and Burroway *et al.*'s *Writing Fiction* (2009).
(15) For example, in my FYC course, we mimic third person limited POV in 'Everything That Rises Must Converge', cogent argumentation in 'Letter from Birmingham Jail', sensory detail in 'Battle Royal'; and story structure in 'Everyday Use'; students practice analyzing these skills as well as enacting them in their own writing.

References

Alvarez, J. (2012) *A Wedding in Haiti*. Chapel Hill, NC: Algonquin Books of Chapel Hill.
Bawarshi, A.S. and Reiff, M.J. (2010) *Genre: An Introduction to History, Theory, Research, and Pedagogy*. West Lafayette, IN: Parlor Press.
Berg, D. and May, L. (eds) (2015) *Creative Composition*. Bristol: Multilingual Matters.
Bishop, W. (1994) Afterword – Colors of a different horse: On learning to like teaching creative writing. In W. Bishop and H. Ostrum (eds) *Colors of a Different Horse* (pp. 280–295). Urbana, IL: NCTE.
Bishop, W. (1995) The literary text and the writing classroom. *JAC* 15 (3), 435–454.
Brown, A.C. and Schultan, K. (2012) Fiction or nonfiction? Considering the common core's emphasis on informational text. *New York Times*, 13 December. Available at http://nytimes.com (accessed 5 June 2015).
Burroway, J. (2009) *Imaginative Writing: The Elements of Craft*. Boston, MA: Pearson.
Burroway, J., Stuckey-French, E. and Stuckey-French, N. (2009) *Writing Fiction: A Guide to Narrative Craft*. Boston, MA: Longman.
Cain, M.A. (2009) 'To be lived': Theorizing influence in creative writing. *College English* 71(3), 229–241.
Cohen, P. (2016) A rising call to promote STEM education and cut liberal arts funding. *New York Times*, 21 February. Available at http://nytimes.com (accessed 23 May 2016).

Coleman, D. (2011) Bringing common core to life. Available at http://NYSED.gov (accessed 7 July 2015).
Common Core Standards Initiative (2015) Common Core Standards. In *Common Core Standards Initiative*. Available at htttp://commoncorestandards.org (accessed 7 July 2015).
Danticat, E. (1998) *The Farming of Bones: A Novel*. New York: Soho Press.
Dawson, P. (2005) *Creative Writing and the New Humanities*. London: Routledge.
Díaz, J. (2007) *The Brief Wondrous Life of Oscar Wao*. New York: Riverhead Books.
Dove, R. (n.d.) Parsley. Available at http.PoetryFoundation.org (accessed 9 September 2014).
Elbow, P. (2002) The cultures of literature and composition: What could each learn from the other? *College English* 64 (5), 533–546.
Eyewitnesses (1987) The Haitian massacre. In E.P. Roorda, L. Derby and R. Gonzalez (eds) *The Dominican Reader* (pp. 281–285). Durham, NC: Duke University Press.
Gaitskill, M. (2009) *Don't Cry: Stories*. New York: Pantheon Books.
Galchen, R. (2013) What's behind the notion that nonfiction is more 'relevant' than fiction? *New York Times*, 22 October. Available at http://nytimes.com (accessed 13 August 2014).
Gamer, M. (1995) Fictionalizing the disciplines: Literature and the boundaries of knowledge. *College English* 57 (3), 281–286.
Green, C. (2001) Materializing the sublime reader: Cultural studies, reader response, and community service in the creative writing workshop. *College English* 64 (2), 153–174.
Haake, K. (2000) *What Our Speech Disrupts: Feminism and Creative Writing Studies*. Urbana, IL: National Council of Teachers of English.
Hipps, J.B. (2016) To write better code, read Virginia Woolf. *New York Times*, 21 May. Available at http://nytimes.com (accessed 23 May 2016).
Hugo, R. (1979) *The Triggering Town: Lectures and Essays on Poetry and Writing*. New York: Norton.
Kalamaras, G. (1999) Interrogating the boundaries of discourse in a creative writing class: Politicizing the parameters of the permissible. *College Composition and Communication* 51 (1), 77–82.
King, M.L. (1963) Letter from Birmingham Jail. In S. Cohen (ed.) *50 Essays* (pp. 67–90). Boston, MA: Bedford.
Kostelnik, K. (2014) Innovative frameworks and tested lore for teaching creative writing to undergraduates in the twenty-first century. *Pedagogy* 14 (3), 435–454.
Lindermann, E. (1993) Freshman composition: No place for literature. *College English* 55 (3), 311–316.
Mayers, T. (2007) Figuring the future: Lore and/in creative writing. In K. Ritter and S. Vanderslice (eds) *Can It Be Taught? Resisting Lore in Creative Writing Pedagogy* (pp. 1–13). Portsmouth, NH: Heinemann.
Mayers, T. (2009) One simple word: From creative writing to creative writing studies. *College English* 71 (3), 217–228.
McLaughlin, R.L. (2008) Post-postmodern discontent: Contemporary fiction and the social world. In R.M. Berry and J.R. Dileo (eds) *Fiction's Present: Situating Contemporary Narrative Innovation* (pp. 101–118). New York: State University of New York Press.
Moreno, C. (2015) Junot Diaz on why it's so important to read author's who don't look like you. *Huffpost Latino Voices*. Available at http://www.huffingtonpost.com/entry/junot-diaz-breaks-down-the-importance-of-reading-authors-from-diverse-backgrounds_560edbbae4b0af3706e0c355 (accessed 17 January 2015).
Murphy, T. (2014) Inside the mammoth backlash to common core [electronic version]. *Mother Jones*, September/October.

Murray, D. (1989) Unlearning to write. In J. Moxley (ed.) *Creative Writing in America: Theory and Pedagogy*. Urbana, IL: NCTE.

O'Connor, F. (1965) Everything that rises must converge. In J. Burroway (ed.) *Writing Fiction* (8th edition) (pp. 282–292). Boston, MA: Pearson.

Peary, A. (2015) The pedagogy of writing across the curriculum. In T. Hunley and A. Peary (eds) *Creative Writing Pedagogies for the 21st Century* (pp. 194–220). Carbondale, IL: Southern Illinois University Press.

Radavich, D. (1999) Creative writing in the academy. In *Profession* (pp. 106–112). New York: MLA.

Roemer, M., Schultz, L. and Durst, R. (1999) Reframing the great debate on first-year writing. *CCC* 50 (3), 377–392.

Steinberg, E.R. (1995) Imaginative writing in composition classrooms? *College English* 57 (3), 266–280.

Tate, G. (1993) A place for literature in freshman composition. *College English* 55 (3), 317–321.

Wardle, E. and Downs, D. (2007) Teaching about writing, righting misconceptions: (Re)envisioning 'First-year composition' as 'Introduction to writing studies'. *CCC* 58 (4), 552–584.

Wardle, E. and Downs, D. (2010) *Writing About Writing*. New York: Bedford St Martin's.

10 Against Appropriation: Creative Writing in/and the Making of Knowledge

Patrick Bizzaro and Christine Bailey

> Content on growing on its own terms, creative writing in all but rare cases performs no service role, aspires to no 'across the curriculum' infiltration of chemistry or sociology, and worries little about assessment.
> Douglas Hesse, 'The place of creative writing in composition studies' (2010: 32)

> Creative writing thus tends to be positioned as an anti-academic field existing within academic institutions.
> Tim Mayers, *(Re)Writing Craft: Composition, Creative Writing, and the Future of English Studies* (2005: 21)

> Poetry ... is at once the centre and circumference of knowledge.
> Percy Shelley, 'A defence of poetry' (1840: 1084)

In the short passages that introduce this chapter, Douglas Hesse and Tim Mayers voice the standard narrative describing the 'place' of academic creative writing and creative writers in English departments. In the third, farther from Creative Writing Studies but nearer to the social perspective from which we have viewed creative writing and the making of knowledge in this essay, Percy Shelley connects poetry with all new knowledge in society in a way that merits examination precisely because Shelley's vantage point is *outside* academe. For Shelley, poetry and all knowledge are synonymous, but the real value we find in referring to Shelley's 'Defence' is that he has not limited his view to knowledge in English Studies. From his perspective, then, Shelley intimates that creative writing is different from – perhaps inclusive of – all other intellectual endeavors. Poetry is, indeed, privileged by Shelley. But his view offers a solution to the isolation of creative writing in English Studies that Hesse and Mayers identify.

While, admittedly, Hesse is primarily concerned with the relationship between creative writing and Composition Studies, Mayers has taken as his task a study of creative writing's place in English Studies as a whole, especially in his critique of the view that English Studies is comprised of but two parts, the rhetoric and the poetic, as James Berlin (1987) urged so influentially, echoing divisions associated most often with Aristotle. Hesse and Mayers study the *academic* status of creative writing. As an interesting contrast, Shelley examines the *social* function of poetry, reminding us that creative writing, especially the writing of poetry, long before it became a school subject housed in English departments, was connected to cultural knowledge as its 'centre and circumference'. Shelley's view stands in contrast with much contemporary thought, but its tenets may be at the heart of the efforts that we want to highlight in this essay in making and articulating new knowledge in this day and age. They also serve as the foundation for a research study we have undertaken and examine later in this chapter. We have chosen to briefly articulate Shelley's view because it serves so well as a reminder of the high ideals we should strive for as teachers of creative writing – and creative thinking – in all disciplines. Acting on this reminder is, indeed, difficult work. Nonetheless, Mayers provides a framework for understanding the kind of effort required.

By investigating 'discourse about where English studies came from, where it is now, and where it can or should go in the future', one goal of his book, Mayers (2005: 22) wisely urges us to go beyond the kind of thinking that accepts the status quo. We are also reminded that it is possible, even likely, that we can better understand the way things are now by going back in time – to Shelley, let's say. In either case, discourses that we use to bring about change in the boundaries between literature, composition and creative writing are what Mayers calls 'structural' as opposed to 'theoretical' discourses. 'By structural discourses', writes Mayers, 'I mean those that challenge, disrupt, and perhaps even break down the boundaries within English studies' (2005: 23). Structural discourses change the institution of English Studies that has been dominated for so long by the Aristotelian bipartite division Berlin popularized. Mayers is not alone in his view of English Studies as inherently limited by the notion that all things in it are either poetic or rhetoric, literature or composition, a view we have seen persist, especially at and because of meetings like the Conference on College Composition and Communication (CCCC) and of bodies such as the Modern Language Association (MLA).

In a sort of agreement with Mayers, D.G. Myers in *The Elephants Teach* contributes the notion that '[h]istorically, creative writing has beckoned a third way' (Myers, 1996: 8), the way Shelley writes about, which leads us to think that creative writing has an epistemological function that has come, in part, to characterize the modern English department. One might argue, as many scholars in the profession do when they employ what Mayers calls theoretical discourse, that we most easily place academic creative writing in the rhetoric or the poetic. After all, this placement is what has transpired, rightly or wrongly, for at least 120 years. So what's the fuss? And why bring up Shelley at all? By aligning creative writing as it has been aligned, creative writing rarely is studied *as* creative writing. Rather, we have tended to study it for its usefulness in the academy as though it has no function outside English departments. Recent history shows it alternatively as a partner in the teaching of literature or, more recently, as 'composition's helper', studied chiefly for its points of contact with instruction in composition (Bizzaro *et al.*, 2011). These characterizations of creative writing portray it as primarily a school subject. The reference to Shelley's social theory of poetry in 'A defence' reminds us that creative writing had a long history that shows it as complicit in the making of cultural knowledge. But historically, creative writing has also been placed in the poetic, the oft-referenced justification, by most creative writers anyway, for creative writing's entrance into the academy at all. It is easy to forget that creative writing has not always been a 'school subject' and that it held a place of esteem in culture as a whole apart from universities. While it might seem to poets and novelists *in the academy* that creative writing, as literature, is linked naturally to literary studies, shifting emphases in English departments over the past 30 years have contributed to the insistence among many that creative writing may be found not in literary studies but instead in rhetoric, connected thusly to composition. Courses in screenwriting, leisure software writing and lyric writing may, for a time, like creative nonfiction before them, be shared by invested departments (e.g. screenwriting cross-listed between creative writing and theater).

Myers complicates this issue further:

> Although creative writing leads to the production of texts, it is not rhetoric.... Although it is a form of literary study, it is not a form of literary scholarship. (Myers, 1996: 12)

Well, what is it then? Mayers and Myers seem to agree on this point: contemporary English departments have moved beyond the longstanding rivalry associated with the poetic and rhetoric in their various incarnations, more recently in the guises of literature and composition. Indeed, we agree that it might be time to think outside the academic box. English Studies has evolved in such a way that it has come to include a third 'idea', to use Mayers' useful conception of it, creative writing. And this has been a dynamic, if sometimes confusing, event, described variously in Mayers' book as 'a constantly shifting coexistence' and an arrangement of ideas, which occasionally 'overlap with one or more of the others' (2005: 21). Mayers might agree, at least when he wrote *(Re)Writing Craft*, that the burden of studying creative writing as creative writing has been complicated by ideological and economic considerations, which have variously placed creative writing in the poetic or in rhetoric, fields that value evidence irrelevant to creative writing as a discipline. More recently, creative writing has sought a place of its own, echoing the well worded call made by Bishop (1999) on behalf of those of us interested in both composition and creative writing who seek 'places to stand'.

We hope to complicate this perspective on English Studies even further by revisiting the Shelleyan notion that poetry – indeed, all creative thinking in society – is connected to knowledge in important ways and, thereby, has served scholars in departments other than English both as a form of knowledge and as a foundation of language from which knowledge is made. Until now, creative writing has indeed been characterized as isolated in English Studies. Isolated and misunderstood, writers who teach creative writing in universities live with what Mayers calls 'privileged marginality' in their home departments, 'insulated largely from the turmoil of English studies, not drawing much attention from outside their own coteries of students and like-minded colleagues' (2005: 21). This marginality has caused Mayers to describe academic creative writing as 'an anti-academic field' and creative writers as outsiders to the efforts to make and dispense knowledge. What's more, creative writing has not developed in its role as knowledge-maker, which includes becoming accepted as an 'academic field' with all that means in universities, including development of research methods and agendas. In this context, even Donald Hall has asserted his belief that academic creative writing is anti-intellectual: 'It is ... true that many would-be poets lack respect for learning' (1988: 6).

In our effort to understand creative writing in the academy as a discipline characterized inevitably, given its history, by epistemological differences from literature and composition, our perspective is shaped by our belief that creative writing is and should be an independent discipline in English Studies. We take this stand because creative writing has already served various disciplines, including sociology, communication and education, with efforts in those disciplines to make and describe new knowledge. We expand here on the assertion Bizzaro (2004) makes in the following passage:

> For a subject area to assert its independence as a discipline, it must assert its epistemological difference from other subjects. It must make clear,

through ongoing conversations in journals and at conferences and in departments, that what it construes as evidence differs from what other fields view as evidence. (Bizzaro, 2004: 308)

In this chapter, we demonstrate, on the basis of our examination of the relationship between knowledge making and creative writing, the epistemologies that comprise creative writing and demonstrate the ways in which they differ from the ways of knowing that characterize literary study and composition. Creative writing constitutes a third place in English Studies.[1] To make this argument, we build upon the work of Mayers and Myers by demonstrating ways in which creative writing functions epistemologically *in* and *as* knowledge. In doing so, we employ what Mayers has called 'structural discourse' in order to 'challenge, disrupt, and perhaps even break down the boundaries within English studies'. We argue that creative writing may be viewed as cultural knowledge, as it has historically, prior to its appropriation by English departments. And we argue that creative writing has been useful in making knowledge in other fields. We offer, thereafter, description of a research study that combines both of these elements, creative writing in the making of knowledge and creative writing as knowledge. Our goal is to argue that creative writing constitutes a third epistemology in English Studies, equal and related in critical ways to literature and composition but also independent of the two.

Creative Writing *and* the Making of Knowledge

Some scholars believe an independent creative writing has no necessary connection to composition or literature at all.[2] Given this view, which builds upon the fact that creative writing first existed outside the university and would likely have continued to have found a healthy role there, we better grasp the point of Hall's *Poetry and Ambition*, that creative writing's entrance into academe was a chance and possibly unnecessary event; literature had been created and had evolved just fine in culture without the intervention of the Master of Fine Arts (MFA) or even without the existence of English Studies. Hall seems to work from the belief that creative writing exists in the poetic. Certainly, once in English departments, creative writing has been lauded for its service to literature, as noted above, 'since 1880', as the subtitle to Myers' book states. But this view does not tell the whole story of academic creative writing's birth in education. Nonetheless, histories of creative writing make inevitable the narrative of creative writing as isolated in English departments and even in Composition Studies, given the dynamics of English departments and their ideologies. Creative writing was an outsider discipline, an add-on, 'positioned as an anti-academic field' from the start (Mayers, 2005: 26). But there has been dispute about when and where that beginning occurred, views that place creative writing's origins in two different camps, in writing studies and literary studies, as a technique of instruction in writing for children of all ages and as an aid in teaching the techniques and aesthetics of literature to university students. It certainly can be found in both places: as a means of teaching writing to school children in the Progressive Education movement and as an aid to teaching literature in a time of rebellion against philology.

In *The Program Era*, Mark McGurl (2009) sees the emphasis on 'autonomous self-creation', the 'abiding concern' of Progressive Education, as just as valid a starting point for discussions of academic creative writing as is literature's appropriation of the subject. The plan for Progressive Education was to work against the then prevalent emphases in schools on empirical methods of educating our youth: 'What could be further from the dictates of rote learning, or studying for a standardized test, than using one's imagination to invent a story or write a poem?' (McGurl, 2009: 3). Importantly, Progressive Education, with its emphasis on creative expression, predates the Iowa Writers' Workshop by nearly a decade: 'The Workshop was formally founded in 1936, with the gathering together of poets and fiction writers under the guidance of founding director Wilbur Schramm' according to the Writers' Workshop website (http://writersworkshop.uiowa.edu/about/about-workshop/history). Indeed, as early as 1927, Alice Bidwell Wesenberg in her *English Journal* essay 'The American public: Poet', advocated the teaching of creative writing in all writing courses. At roughly the same historical moment, the current-dominant narrative of creative writing's entry into academe was developed: creative writing as one way to study literature. And herein lie the two perspectives on our histories of creative writing. Is creative writing composition or literature? Can it be both without undermining the epistemologies of each?

Creative writing does indeed have an epistemological foundation different from that of either literature or composition, though it has been used as a way to supplement instruction in those subjects in the academy, subjects that are necessarily different from creative writing's social function because they are academic subjects. It may be self-evident that what literature and composition construe as evidence, the textual productions of students, differs from the way creative writing makes knowledge, a way that we argue for in this chapter. What's more, literary study continues to value the finished product whereas Composition Studies values social equity and, often simultaneously, the processes involved in writing. In the meantime, when creative writers are free to study creative writing and how it might be taught, they have tended to privilege writers' self-reports. But to make this argument, we must also defend the view that creative writing may be studied as a way of making knowledge in either of its places of origin in academe, in the writing of eighth graders or in the study of literature, as Myers has memorably described it, 'as if [literature] were a living thing, as if people intended to write more of it' (1996: 4). What's more, we forward the view that poems and stories have, historically, generated knowledge. This is not a new view – that is, the view that creative writing and knowledge-making coexist, as the reference to Shelley surely suggests. Creative writing is a certain kind of knowledge, to be sure. Indeed, Literary and Composition Studies could hardly prevent poetry and fiction from finding a place in other departments or from serving those disciplines in making knowledge because techniques employed in creative writing are similar to techniques of knowledge making and description of knowledge used in other disciplines that require the use of correspondences (see Seitz, 1999).

Monica Prendergast ably demonstrates this perspective on creative writing in her introduction to *Poetic Inquiry: Vibrant Voices in the Social Sciences*, when she writes, 'Poetic inquiry is an area of growing interest to arts-based qualitative researchers. This is a fairly recent phenomena [*sic*] in qualitative inquiry ... with only a few [studies] stretching back to the early 80s' (Prendergast, 2009: xxi). While this view has had immediate, if sparse, utility in research, its roots go at least as deep as Percy Shelley's 1840 'Defence'. Perhaps what makes this view a recent phenomenon is that we are so focused on creative writing as an academic enterprise that we have neglected the notion that it existed long before the MFA as a means of determining and reporting cultural knowledge.

It is important to go back to our social and cultural roots as writers and in doing so to study works we rarely acknowledge any more for their pertinence in providing perspective when we discuss the teaching of academic creative writing in contemporary English departments. One such work is Shelley's 'Defence', because in that work Shelley makes the claim that poetry has the capability Prendergast notes. Shelley's reasons are more idealistic than Prendergast's, of course, but shed some light on Prendergast's view that poetry is knowledge. Shelley attributes this belief to the fact 'language, gesture, and the imitative arts become at once the representation and the medium, the pencil and the picture, the chisel and the statue, the chord and the harmony' (1840: 1072). To a large extent, Shelley seems to refer to creative thinking as best represented, in his view, in poetry. Interestingly, we may count among poets, from this uniquely

Shelleyan perspective, all those who innovate creatively for the betterment of society: 'All the authors of revolutions in opinion are not only necessarily poets as they are inventors, nor even as their words unveil the permanent analogy of things by images which participate in the life of truth' (Shelley, 1840: 1074). And this is true because of the unique and special function of poetic language: 'A poem is the very image of life expressed in its eternal truth'. It 'is the creation of actions according to the unchangeable forms of human nature' (1840: 1075). The Shelleyan articulation of poetry as knowledge-maker is, perhaps, best stated by Shelley in the following, well known passage from which our epigraph comes:

> Poetry is indeed something divine. It is at once the centre and circumference of knowledge; it is that which comprehends all science, and that to which all science must be referred. It is at once the root and blossom of all other systems of thought. (Shelley, 1840: 1084)

Prendergast does the important work of bringing this Shelleyan view of knowledge into a conversation with other forward-thinkers in research in the 21st century. Interestingly, she advocates the use of poetry in her essay both as a way of reading poems already written and as a method for recording new-found data. In this sense, poets and fiction writers of our time are making records of important cultural events, as we argue briefly below with specific reference to poetry slams. Prendergast's reading of Muriel Rukeyser's 1938 long poem, *The Book of the Dead*, demonstrates excellently an adaptation of the Shelleyan principles briefly outlined above. Prendergast insightfully reads the poem as 'an Autoethnography [*sic*] of a West Virginia mining town where the miners were dying of lung disease due to unsafe working conditions' (Prendergast, 2009: xxiv). As a demonstration of the basis for Prendergast's view, here is an excerpt from Rukeyser's poem:

> these carrying light for safety on their foreheads
> descend deeper for richer faults of ore,
> drilling their death.
>
> There touching radium and the luminous poison,
> carried their death on their lips and with their warning
> glow in their graves.
>
> These weave and their eyes water and rust away,
> these stand at wheels until their brains corrode,
> these farm and starve,

> all these men cry their doom across the world,
> meeting avoidable death, fight against madness,
> find every war.

Prendergast's reading, in principle, brings to mind recent efforts that we want to briefly identify here as knowledge in the form of what we now call cultural criticism. We believe the impetus of cultural criticism has been exactly what we have in mind, as a demonstration of the way literary theory and inquiry into the social sciences have worked with creative writing to make meaning.

The foundation for a 'cultural criticism' approach to the understanding of creative writing as knowledge stems from the belief, voiced most influentially by Vincent Leitch, 'that cultural critics share interests and methods … with anthropologists, historians, media specialists, and sociologists' (Leitch, 1992: x). Thus, Leitch's encouragement that we view the potential usefulness of cultural criticism lends support to and justification for Prendergast's reading of Rukeyser. Leitch writes, 'Advocates of cultural studies are predisposed to intervene actively in issues of social struggle'. The phrase 'to intervene actively in social struggle' nicely describes Prendergast's work when she furthers her range by writing, 'the work of poets across time who have written about themes of social injustice, poverty, war, alienation, and so on, offer[s] strong inspiration to a social science scholar who wishes to explore poetic methods in his or her own work' (Prendergast, 2009: xxiv). Among efforts by contemporary writers who fit this description, we might point specifically to anthologies rendering the professions, such as *Primary Care*, a collection of poems about medical training (Belli & Coulehan, 2006), and an anthology like Fellner and Young's edited collection *Love Rise Up* (2012), which includes poems of social justice, protest and hope. We see poems by poets as diverse as Ai and William Heyen as efforts likewise to reflect knowledge in the particular way poetry can.[3] Their writing makes knowledge and records the thinking of a time and place. Our era is also filled with innovations in the writing of fiction that include twists on scientific findings in the stories of Fred Chappell and a strict adherence to accuracy by Robert Morgan in his historical fiction.[4]

From this perspective, we may see various under-examined cultural events as knowledge making. Among them, as one example, is the poetry slam, which by form and function gives voice to social issues rarely heard before by those living through them. Susan B.A. Somers-Willett underscores this point in her study *The Cultural Politics of Slam Poetry*:

> In addition to fostering a cultural atmosphere and disseminating poetry in unconventional venues, the slam has thrived through the exercise of certain democratic ideals meant to contrast with exclusive academic conventions. Slams are rowdy yet welcoming events on the whole. From its beginnings, the poetry slam has adopted an open-door policy: anyone can sign up to slam, and anyone in the audience is qualified to judge. (Somers-Willett, 2009: 5)

Anyone at a poetry slam may use the venue to voice the living conditions of those whose lives are often overlooked in traditional poetry readings. This approach admittedly affects the 'quality' of verse presented at slams. But it is important to note that the quality of the poetry used in knowledge generation has become a question theorists have addressed as well, a problem posed in Chapter 4 of Sandra Faulkner's *Poetry as Method*.

Faulkner notes that 'poet-researchers have raised ... concerns of truth, representation, aesthetics, researcher ethics, and voice' (2009: 42) in complicating the ways poetry might be used in generating knowledge.

> Some poets use dates and epigraphs from historical texts in the titles of poems (e.g., Smith 2000), include chronologies of facts and appendices with endnotes and source material (e.g., Cooley 2004), while others use prefaces with a description of the historical event and time frame, pictures, maps, quotations, and prose exposition about the sources between sections of poetry (e.g., Hudgins, 1988). Poet-researchers include footnotes and end notes; use a layered text with explicit context, theory, and methodological notes surrounding poems; and sometimes, just the poems (e.g., Faulkner, 2007). (Faulkner, 2009: 42)

In fact, Faulkner advocates for the quality of the poetry, its 'aesthetics', used in knowledge making and even in reporting findings as an important element and one that should be taught to students in every discipline where 'research poetry' might be usefully and effectively written.

It has not been an enormous leap, then, to move from autoethnographic writing to the writing of fiction in making and aiding in the making of knowledge. In *Revision: Autoethnographic Reflections on Life and Work* (2009), Carolyn Ellis, a Communication professor at the University of South Florida, uses 'personal stories' to reinforce the power of autoethnographic research. She notes:

> As an autoethnographer, I am both the author and focus of the story, the one who tells and the one who experiences, the observer and the observed, the creator and the created. I am the person at the intersection of the

personal and the cultural, thinking and observing as an ethnographer and writing and describing as a storyteller. (Ellis, 2009: 13)

The Ethnographic I, which Ellis wrote a few years earlier, is appropriately subtitled *A Methodological Novel About Autoethnography*, and focuses chiefly on the teaching of autoethnography in a fictional graduate course she instructs.

Interestingly, Patricia Leavy, in *Fiction as Research Practice*, writes directly to people we envision as readers of this chapter. Of her book, Leavy (2013) writes:

> I consider the book the ultimate blurring of my artist-researcher-teacher identities because it represents all I have learned over the years through those overlapping roles, as well as many life experiences that are inseparable from how I think about and act in the world. (Leavy, 2013: 10)

Her book offers short stories, novellas and novels that report knowledge and make knowledge, simultaneously.

Clearly, creative writing is not isolated in the academy. It plays an important role in the way scholars in various disciplines outside English envision knowledge. And this practice has roots deep in literary history. We conclude, then, that creative writing, mostly outside English departments, has been employed as a form of knowledge. Interestingly, the ways of thinking most intimately related to creative writing — analogy and metaphor, for instance — have clear connections to all fields that make knowledge, as they must in science, technology, engineering and mathematics (STEM) programs that are currently popular.

Creative Writing in the Making of Knowledge

When Professor Hesse, in the epigraph to this chapter, says 'creative writing ... aspires to no "across the curriculum" infiltration of chemistry or sociology', he is recording what he sees in his department, and that perception is repeated in our own departments. Clearly, creative writing nowadays seems divorced from 'across the curriculum' activities, except, as he says, 'in all but rare cases'. Those are the cases that interest us here. Hall's *Poetry and Ambition* reminds us that we should be very careful in generalizing about poetry, what it is and how it might be used. Creative writing has evolved in the university, but not everyone has been happy about that fact. Nonetheless, it has been adopted in various disciplines as a way to record and express various matters difficult to describe in any other way.

Writers have long represented new knowledge by using the skills most often associated with creative writing; they have done so with some serious misgivings, however. We are reminded of Edgar Allan Poe's warning in 'Sonnet: To science' in the question, 'Why preyest thou thus upon the poet's heart, / Vulture, whose wings are dull realities?' (ll. 3–4). Or, consider Walt Whitman's learned astronomer who leaves the lecture hall 'tired and sick' after looking at 'the proofs, the figures' of the stars, figures that reduce the dynamic of nature to static visual aids ('When I heard the learn'd astronomer', 1900, ll. 5, 3). In these passages, science is portrayed by poets as untrustworthy, a systematic means for reducing knowledge to charts and graphs, products of the head but not the heart, not the transient and spiritual significance of the natural world. Poe claims science 'alterest all things with thy peering eyes' (l. 2). We rightly accept these warnings, even in the 21st century. Because our best thinkers have given voice to the failure of language to capture these moments of insight, as John Locke did in *An Essay Concerning Human Understanding* (1690), science had turned away from the language poets might use in describing new knowledge and used instead the language of mathematics.

Not until James Britton and the Bullock Commission gave us insight into the different ways language might function did we have terms that helped us understand that 'the poetic function of language' need not include the poetry of a Dante, to use Hall's example. Rather, what Peter Elbow calls for in *Writing with Power*, when he asserts the belief that poetry is 'no big deal', is, we believe, what Britton was referring to as the poetic function of language and Hall called 'McPoems'. Elbow confesses:

> I write here as a non-poet, that is, someone who enjoyed trying to write profound poems as an adolescent, got over it when introduced to sophistication, and then restricted himself to writing a birthday poem to a loved one about every seven years.... (1998: 101)

This, the writing of poetry by 'non-poets', seems akin to the way poetic language, the poetic function of language, to use Britton's term for it, functions as an aid in the making of knowledge. But we also want to argue, as the rest of this section notes, that science makes use of skills usually associated with creative writing, especially, perhaps, in its use of metaphor and analogy.

Why is poetry a useful aid in the making of knowledge in all disciplines? Elliot Eisner says, when he writes about poetry and research:

> The open texture of the form increases the probability that multiple perspectives will emerge. Multiple perspectives make our engagement with

the phenomena more complex. Ironically, good research often complicates our lives. (Eisner, 1997: 8)

We might argue that, in a more succinct fashion, William Wordsworth says much the same thing in 'Tintern Abbey' when he writes, 'We see into the life of things' (l. 49). We hold that this assertion applies equally to the writing of fiction. So, let's examine this claim a bit before proceeding.

Rich Furman, a professor of social work at the University of Washington, Tacoma, and his colleagues extend this argument that poets have been making for hundreds of years by identifying poetry as a genre well suited to relaying 'the human experience'. Increasingly in the past 20 years, scholars have included the human consequences of their actions, including of their research. Why through poetry? As the authors state, taking a socio-cultural perspective on poetry, as Shelley had:

> As a document of social phenomena, poetry can be viewed as a vehicle through which to communicate powerful and multiple 'truths' about the human experience. While poetry may not commonly be thought of as a source of knowledge, poems are powerful documents that possess the capacity to capture the contextual and psychological worlds of both poetry and subject. (Furman *et al.*, 2007: 302)

A look at scientific and poetic language might be helpful here in understanding the connection between poetry and knowledge.

Physicists Stephen Hawking and George Ellis describe a black hole in the following excerpt from 'New theoretical approaches to black holes' as reported by Gourgoulhin and Jaramilo (2008):

> The standard mathematical definition of a *black hole* is ...
>
> $B: = M - J^-(I^+)$
>
> where M is a 4-dimensional manifold, endowed with a Lorentzian metric g such that $(M; g)$ is asymptotically flat, I^+ is the future null infinity, and $J^-(I^+)$ is the causal past of I^+ (cf. Fig. 1). In common language, this means that a black hole is the region of spacetime where light rays cannot escape to infinity. The event horizon, H, is then defined as the boundary of B. Provided that it is smooth, it is well-known that H is a null hypersurface (hence it appears as a line inclined at 45° in Fig. 1).

Here, for contrast, is a poetic rendering of a black hole offered by Coleman Barks (2008), as described in the following excerpt from 'The center', first poem in his new and selected poems, *Winter Sky* (ll.1–9):

> Praise to what we must give in to,
> the big laziness, spiracle blowhole,
> where matter comes breathing out,
> where matter gets sucked back in
> to be nothing, or changed to a lightshaft
> a trillion trillion lightyears tall
> pouring periodically from this whirlpool
> that has no bottom. Does some rhythm
> coming round ordain this making/unmaking?

This dramatic pairing of representations of knowledge, from physics and poetry, invites analysis. For starters, the pairing seems to suggest that the same event might be seen and recorded in at least two ways. The records are, indeed, subjective and provide what Eisner in the quote above describes as 'Multiple perspectives [which] make our engagement with the phenomena more complex'. We will argue that this use of language is not the least bit new. It has simply not been studied.

Famously, Plato uses much the same technique in arguing for the immortality of the soul by comparing it to a pair of winged horses and a charioteer. From this perspective, one might argue that the act of writing a poem about scientific discovery is not a frivolous waste of time. Nonetheless, we would not be shocked if a scientist were to claim that the Barks poem must be dismissed as a representation of black holes because the poem, by its very nature, is more subjective than the more technical report of Hawking and Ellis insofar as Barks relies on figurative language and makes a text that is, therefore, unreliable. Thus, the plight of the poor poem: its great strength, subjectivity and inclusiveness, may be turned against it as a grievous weakness.

Therefore, one might also argue that the great strength of the Barks report is that it is dynamic and suggestive of human responses that the Hawking and Ellis description tries to avoid. Barks' view is not fixed, as much scientific writing is. It is a content rather than a static, self-contained and replicable procedure. The kind of statement Hawking and Ellis make reflects the much-sought-after objectivity science has long valued, science's way of making knowledge. It fixes knowledge in absolute terms. After all, absolute, unchanging certainty is the disciplinary goal. But to be understood at all, even by other scientists, scientific researchers must employ the knowable to understand the recently known: 'The standard mathematical definition', 'a Lorentzian metric', 'asymptotically flat', a 'future null infinity', as well as 'the causal past'. This language is acceptably static but is inevitably referential, as all language must be to be language. Hawking and Ellis refer to known standards, Lorentz, an imageless future and a 'causal past'. But science, especially physics, is dynamic. Richard Feynman writes, 'What looks still to our crude eyes is a wild and dynamic dance' (1998: 12). We believe skills relegated to the creative writing classroom are pertinent and useful in describing new findings in all disciplines and suggest a way writing might evolve in the university to help researchers describe the 'wild and dynamic dance' that needs to be acknowledged in every discipline in efforts to describe knowledge at its cutting edges.

But these same skills characterize methods employed in gathering information. When Hawking and Ellis try to make the black hole more recognizable, they rely on 'common language' in asserting that 'light rays cannot escape to infinity'. The key terms in this short description – 'rays', 'escape' and 'infinity' – require the readers' subjective envisioning to be of any value as a kind of information – that is, they rely on metaphor and scientific correspondences. Figurative language in this example characterizes reports of fixed knowledge.

Challenging these kinds of reports opens up possibilities we hadn't thought of before. Katherine Haake might describe Barks' poem as 'an enriched experience of the various activities that we engage in' (2007: 15). This perception might lead to pedagogical changes. James E. Seitz, for instance, urges that 'we consider the possibilities offered by a *metaphoric*, rather than a literalist, curriculum' (1999: 200). Seitz asks 'that students in individual courses explore the resources of metaphorical discourse instead of simply attempting to ascertain their literal views of the subject matter or texts before them' (1999: 200). Increasingly, scholars are able to see the way the techniques of creative writing impact upon our abilities to reach understandings and posit knowledge. And there is good reason for that.

Recently, PBS televised a special on NASA's exploration of Saturn, the Cassini mission.[5] Findings of the mission thus far are tentative at best. The most compelling finding, the one that drives NASA's investigation of the deep universe, is the announcer's enthusiastic statement that 'Hydrocarbons have been detected on Titan!' Titan – Saturn's largest moon – is analogous to the early Earth, in large part because both have hydrocarbons in their makeup; as a result, study of the evolution of Titan may render correspondences with the evolution of Earth through similar stages. It might also show how much Creative Writing Studies has already influenced our ability to understand the outermost reaches of the universe.

In a sense, records scientists have made about their explorations make demands on language – that is, require proficiency of text and ambition of spirit – similar to the demands poets make in articulating deep imaginings. Plans for collecting data in the Cassini mission have made us come to see that belief in scientific and poetic data is an act of faith. Here is an example of Plato showing his faith in language in *Phaedrus*, straining ambitiously to describe the immortal soul: 'it is within human power to describe it briefly in a figure: let us therefore speak that way'. Plato goes on to 'liken the soul to the composite nature of a pair of winged horses and a charioteer' (see Bizzell & Herzberg, 2001: 149). Likewise, many hundreds of years later, Feynman points out that 'Trying to understand the way nature works involves a most terrible test of human reasoning ability. It involves subtle trickery, beautiful tightropes of logic on which one has to walk in order not to make a mistake in predicting what will happen' (Feynman, 1998: 15). This statement seems to be Feynman's description of faith: 'beautiful tightropes of logic'. Many would agree that Feynman is a poet as well as a physicist, much as they might agree that Plato's writings are often poetic because both see the necessity that new knowledge be described 'briefly in a figure'. Indeed, one must employ 'beautiful tightropes of logic' in order to follow Plato's 'winged horses'. One does not have to *intend* a poem to write (or even to speak) poetically, as Shelley might insist. This notion may change our view of creative writing as a kind of composition if we come to view creative writing as a production of a set of rhetorical skills and limit its impact in the university to Composition Studies or even to English departments. No doubt the skill at making correspondences should be taught in every department in the university, especially to graduate students who will be called upon to make new knowledge and to express it to others. Poetry does not always look like a poem on the page. We must have faith in the search for correspondences that render new insights. Such insights are 'poetic' in the largest sense of the term, Feynman's 'beautiful tightropes of logic'. Shelley, again, reminds us that, 'All the authors of revolutions in opinion are not only necessarily poets as they are inventors, nor even as their words unveil the permanent analogy of things by images which participate in the life of truth' (1840: 1074).

In his 'Defence', Shelley writes about poetic faith, another topic that should be addressed by young scholars in every university department (and, perhaps, in STEM programs). Shelley writes, 'Those in whom it exists in excess are poets' (1840: 1077). It might be fair to suggest, then, that the engineers who have worked on the Cassini project are poets, at least from Shelley's broad and inclusive perspective, as we argue below. Shelley has more to say about those who possess poetic faith: 'their language is vitally metaphorical' (1840: 1077). This insight helps us understand the relationship between two horses, a charioteer and the immortal soul, in one famous example, and, in a more recent example, the relationship between colors and descriptions of a distant planet. To obtain one, we must use our imaginations to probe the immortal soul; to obtain the other, we must send a spacecraft to Saturn.

We make this connection because all the data we have about Saturn are necessarily representative and in need of interpretation. Colors are important to NASA for gathering data on the Cassini mission. To scientists who designed the investigation of Saturn, colors correspond to things and quantities of things that these faithful scientists must believe in. They design their research so their data can be believed, so that our faith is not violated in seeing one thing in another, a thing we have never seen before in something we have seen, to paraphrase Feynman. In more poetic terms, the instrumentation used to collect data on the Cassini mission requires that we submit to 'a willing suspension of disbelief for the moment' (Coleridge, 'Biographia literaria'; see Perkins, 1967: 452). The data must be permitted to engage our imaginations, as we learn how to walk 'beautiful tightropes of logic'.

Consider the too-seldom-cited corollary to Coleridge's most important statement on imagination, which indicates that such a suspension of disbelief 'constitutes poetic faith'. One might argue that the faith of the poet, the scientist and the philosopher is a single category of thinking that works hand in hand in finding the correspondences between our data collection and the articulation of those data that we use to inform an audience. Reliance on correspondence, then, is relevant not only in the Cassini mission but also in probing the immortal soul. More specifically, we must have faith as scientists, poets and rhetoricians that different colors ('spectral measurements' they call them) define for us temperatures, chemical compositions, geological structures, heights, depths, weights – everything we think in our limited way that we want to know about a planet we currently cannot experience directly through our senses. The method of discovery used in the Cassini mission, like that used in *Phaedrus*, is more than analogy; it has much in common with our church experiences ... or our poetic ones. Through those experiences and the sense we make subsequently of our data, we introduce the deep universe to Creative Writing Studies. In any case, we might say that poetry, rhetoric and science have never been closer. The imagining required by metaphor is critical to making new discoveries known in every discipline we can think of; faith that metaphor will not deceive us spreads from creative writing to writing and thinking done across the campus.

We posit, then, that creative writing and various skills associated with it contribute to the making of knowledge. Let us enact both principles we have thus far argued for in the research study we describe next.

A Research Study: Genre as a Means of Knowledge Making

In the research study we briefly outline here, 'The role of aesthetic artifacts in creative writing research', we not only use creative writing to report data, but we also use creative writing *as* data (Bailey, 2014; Bailey & Bizzaro, 2017). Using this stratified approach, Christine Bailey (hereafter, Christine) responds to poems and creative expressions written by students in a first-year composition (FYC) classroom with her own creative writing, a novel. With the novel or metanarrative, a 'narrative about narratives of historical meaning, experience or knowledge, which offers a society legitimation' (Lyotard, 1984: 29), we argue for the use of creative writing to elicit a layered understanding of a particular phenomenon – to offer an aesthetic rendering in an attempt to make our and the reader's engagement with the phenomenon more complex (Eisner, 1997: 8). Further, by using an alternative form of data representation, we are able to present our findings in such a way that it allows a 'stylistic approach' to a set of data, thus inviting knowledge making through different genres.

In *Exercises in Style*, it's estimated that there are nearly 100 different ways to tell a simple narrative, 'each of which represents an alternative stylistic approach to the same set of characters and events' (Seitz, 1999: 155). Our metanarrative could have been told in any number of ways as well, with 100 different complications and conflicts, moods and dialogue exchanges. Key here are the many 'registers through which a story may be told and … the profound impact matters of style can have on even the most trivial of tales' (Seitz, 1999: 155). One of the goals with the novel is to illustrate that impact – to show how reporting data with a freedom for stylistic approach allows a researcher a creative outlet for expressing and sharing new knowledge. The novel enables us to 'synthesize and to adapt the student data into a larger work, one that captures and even honors the original works' (Bailey & Bizzaro, 2017). With regard to displays of stylistic flexibility, Seitz suggests that a 'separation of style from substance overlooks the ways in which substance is discovered *through* style, not apart from it or prior to it' (Seitz, 1999: 156). While we discuss here the significance of a researcher's stylistic flexibility in reporting data, we also suggest the same flexibility for student writers in creating data.

Our study asked student writers in the FYC classroom to use creative writing to tell their stories. The qualitative study began in an attempt to answer how creative writing – identity narratives written in aesthetic forms such as a poem – could serve as cultural data for a particular community: college freshmen at a mid-size private university in the southern United States; however, we were also curious to see what stylistic choices in writing could tell us about student writers in general. Seitz states: 'When we look to the teaching of writing, be it in composition or literature courses, style remains a minor concern, usually ignored until students are imagined to reach a more "advanced" proficiency as writers' (1999: 156). Fundamentals of writing are typically the focus in a writing classroom, with the idea that 'niceties of style' should come later, when a mastery of organization and invention are solidified (Seitz, 1999: 157). However, as Seitz acknowledges, a pedagogy that includes explorations of style, of writing under different guises, can result in students discovering 'some useful distance between themselves and their texts' (1999: 157). With this idea in mind, our study prompted an investigation into stylistic choice as a means to discover multiple ways of knowing and seeing from the perspective of both a researcher and a writer.

Our study asked students to consider metaphor, imagery, persona – to approach the personal narrative through a particular set of eyes or voice (Seitz, 1999). The writing assignment asked students to tell the story of *who they are* and to do so in a creative form such as a poem, a journal entry, an excerpt from a graphic novel or a scene from a script. Ten per cent of the freshman student body at that university participated in the study, yielding 57 aesthetic artifacts within one academic year. The research study looked to these artifacts, mostly poems, to see what the creative narratives revealed about student identities. The following research questions were asked. First, what language choices do students make when writing in creative forms? Second, what do the patterns or themes that emerge from the creative narratives reveal about each student's presented self or persona? In defining persona for the purpose of our research, we approached it as 'the writer's personal characteristics: beliefs, allegiances, prejudices, education, reading, experiences, emotional make-up, possibly even physical traits' (Miles *et al.*, 1991: 204). Further, a certain level of quality was not expected of the creative narratives; for example, we simply saw student poems as the poetic use of language, not as poetry itself.

Once the creative artifacts were collected from the FYC classroom, we analyzed the data in two ways. First, we asked reviewers to mine the pieces for clues as to who the students were, or claimed to be, and to note the 'cultural or social influences as well as local/micro concerns or place/time of the narratives' (Bailey, 2014: 99). Second, we asked reviewers to consider how the students used metaphor and other stylistic choices to author their stories. Reviewers coded the artifacts for language choice, including but not limited to syntactical structure, metaphors, verbs, adjectives and descriptive phrases. To illustrate this process, the following poem, collected from a FYC International section, shows one reviewer's initial notes about how the speaker uses a clown metaphor to illustrate his role in making others laugh. The reviewer described the speaker as 'someone who finds self-worth and happiness by making others smile; yet, the persona in the poem is also lonely and only playing the part of the funny/happy guy'. In the second stanza, the reviewer marked a shift in tone occurring from jovial and light to a darker image of uncertainty:

Hidden smile

A <u>clown</u> without a mask	*metaphor*
A costume I have worn	*costume and mask – hiding*
To fill my <u>lonely</u> task	*lonely persona putting up a front*
To find thy <u>smile adorn</u>	*smile and adorn – both positive images*
I'll <u>journey through the dark</u>	*tone is dark, uncertain*
I'll be a laughing stock	
Just bring thy <u>frown</u> to mark	
Just leash that <u>hardened</u> lock	
Although my <u>heart may rot</u>	*rotting heart – dark image*
At least your <u>sorrows</u> shot	

After reviewers marked and commented on all 57 pieces as in the example above, they were then asked to provide tags for each poem. Tags for 'Hidden smile' included the following: 'Speakers taking on various pursuits for finding happiness; masked insecurity; vulnerable; lonely'. The tags were then keyed into a spreadsheet and organized into groups by similar themes/threads. After examining these common threads, along with the results of a demographic survey given to student participants, we formed six final groups/characters, which we reported in two ways: in a traditional form and in an aesthetic one, the novel. As noted in the complete study (Bailey & Bizzaro, 2017), 'One major consideration at this stage was moving from a standard analysis of student writing, i.e. mining for words and phrases that reveal student identity, to synthesizing the data into characters'. While there were risks in reporting our data in an aesthetic form, we considered the novel as a means of further understanding the data and as an example of how creative writing contributes to the making of knowledge.

From Student Poems as Data to Reporting Data in the Novel

As previously noted, we provide here only a brief report of our research with a small sampling of data. One sample, the above poem, 'Hidden smile', was categorized along with three other works: two additional poems and a play script. While this grouping, identified as 'Descriptor #6', yielded only four creative narratives to build a character, the content of the student texts was more than sufficient to create a dynamic character. The student artifacts along with the demographic surveys were collected from 'INT-ENG': a first-year composition course for international students. All four of the creative pieces in this grouping 'revealed speakers who had taken on various pursuits for finding happiness within new cultural settings, pursuits such as religion, athletics, performance (dancing and singing), or friendships'; some of the speakers were also marked as 'vulnerable with masked (and sometimes overt) insecurities' (Bailey, 2014: 119). From the data, 'Harish' was developed as a student whose first language was not English and one who had lived in different countries. In the novel, Harish or 'Harry' offers that he grew up in New York, though his birthplace was New Delhi. We did not replicate the actual location of any of the participants (China, Korea and Portugal) as revealed in the demographic surveys but instead offered a representation.

The characterization of Harry as happy, kind, yet insecure began to develop after thoughtful analysis of the creative narratives. The following scene from the novel illustrates how 'little narratives' such as 'Hidden smile' helped inform the character of Harry in the metanarrative (Bailey, 2015: 72–74):

> 'These are my friends,' Lucas said. One by one, he pointed and called off their names. He stopped at the lead singer. 'And this is Harish. We're roommates. He goes to Alton, too.'
> Harish nodded and mumbled, 'Call me Harry.' He raked his fingers through his dark, wavy hair and smiled.
> I could have sworn he blushed, but it was hard to tell with only one streetlight beaming up the entire block. What a change from the front man who had just rocked the stage like a super star....
> A slight accent clung to his words, one I hadn't picked up on before.
> 'You're not from Mississippi, are you?' I asked him.
> 'Nope,' he laughed. 'I grew up in New York, but I was born in New Delhi. We moved to the States when I was three.'
> 'Bet it was hard to leave New York.'
> 'Yeah. But we've been here for about seven years now. My dad teaches Physics at Alton.'
> 'Cool.' I leaned back in my seat as we wound through back roads, listening to the radio. I couldn't place the band playing, and just as I was about to ask the name, Harry mentioned the show earlier.
> 'I knew I messed up on that last run of the chorus. Sorry, man,' Harry said to Lucas.

> 'Why are you sorry?' I asked.
> 'It's Lucas' song.'
> I twisted around in my seat and looked from Harry to Lucas and then back to Harry. 'What?'
> 'It's Lucas' band. He was the lead singer until he ditched us a couple weeks ago. It's his music we played tonight.'
> 'Are you serious?'
> 'Yes, I'm serious,' Harry said.
> 'Why did you quit?'
> 'Don't have time to work full-time, play and rehearse in a band, and be a pre-med major. Something had to give.'
> 'Pre-med, huh?' I asked. 'I have no idea what I want to do.'
> 'Don't feel bad,' Harry said. 'It helps that his mom is a doctor and so is his granddad. It's kind of like his life is mapped out for him. I have no idea what I want to do either.'

The above excerpt also introduces Lucas and the first-person narrator, named Liz Walker, both of whom were also born out of the data sets. As revealed in the scene above, Lucas is presented as someone who has everything mapped out for him; however, he later questions this path. The character of Lucas (Descriptor/Character #3) was developed from poems tagged as having 'conflicted speakers; those uncertain of identity, desiring change, and/or struggling with past and future; child of divorce/abuse' (Bailey, 2014: 112). From the creative data set, 11 poems were categorized as 'Uncertain of Identity'. Of those poems, one titled 'Complexity of simple' greatly impacted the development of Lucas' character. Through its use of metaphor, the poem portrays an intricately detailed persona, one who is tightly wound and constantly moving – the speaker's mind is mechanical, a piece of machinery. The speaker says: 'The constant turn of wheels and gears/No room for grey [sic] as my mind reflects/No room for rational fears' (Bailey, 2014: 108). From these lines, we see the 'mechanical logic' of the speaker and the inner workings of a complex mind. The poem captures someone in constant motion, never slowing to contemplate the 'grey' areas. From there, the character of Lucas developed on the page into someone hiding his true and richly complicated feelings behind a simple exterior (Bailey, 2014: 108–109), as noted in the following scene (Bailey, 2015: 83):

> Lucas answered his phone. 'Hey, Mom. I was going to call you later.' He stayed silent as she dominated the conversation on the other end. After a minute or two, he started jotting down some notes, saying 'uh-huh' a lot. Midway through the call, Lucas threw his pencil on the ground and

scooted to the edge of the couch. With one hand, he cradled the phone to his ear and with the other he swept his fingers through his hair. 'Whatever, Mom.' He stood up, paced a few times, and then moved inside the building.

I picked up the pencil, which had landed near my feet, and rolled it between my fingers. I inhaled the earthy, wood scent that took me back to the playgrounds, Play-Doh, and politics of grade school. It didn't feel like much had changed: Moms could still push our buttons or save the day; boys and girls still played games, and the world was still way too huge to grasp.

'Sorry about that,' Lucas said, stepping back out onto the balcony a few minutes later.

'Everything okay?'

'Yeah, it's fine. She just puts a lot of pressure on me. Grades and stuff.'

'Here's your pencil.' I handed it back to him.

'Thanks. I think I'm going to head home and blow some steam on my X-Box.'

Like Lucas, even the setting of the novel, Alton University, was built from the creative narratives written by FYC students. Since the prompt asked students to 'tell how they got to this place in their lives', some students answered literally in their creative works, mentioning details such as the city, the university, coffee houses and dormitories. However, most poems offered more of a feeling of dis*place*ment rather than of literal place. With this in mind, we sought to capture that uneasiness, as evidenced here (Bailey, 2015: 21–23):

Under the tent in the middle of the grassy quad, mammoth fans swirled the Mississippi heat over our bodies. I wiped the sweat from my forehead and then brushed my hand dry on the thin fabric of my black shorts. I felt woozy, even a bit nauseated, from the suffocating heat and the chorus of voices around me. More and more people poured in by the second, and the sweat continued to drip.

'I didn't see you at the dinner last night,' Emmy said.

'I was there. I came in late,' I lied. I'm not sure why I did, since my absence or presence probably made no difference at all to her – or *anyone* for that matter. Truth was, Mom and I had gotten into town late because I had stalled our trip at least a dozen times with fake stomach aches and trips to the bathroom, plus a convenient, last-minute visit from Piper, who was upset about her latest boyfriend.

I surveyed the crowd of freshmen and transfer students with nametags. Emmy, my new roommate, pleated the hem of her flowery sundress, and then bunched the fabric in a fist on top of her boney knee. She was naturally pretty with her bright and golden complexion and thick lashes. The smidge of mascara on them wasn't even needed. I figured she had been the it-girl at her high school – maybe a cheerleader, homecoming queen, class president? Like me – or more like I *had been* before everything changed, before I disintegrated into a thousand shards.

'So where are you from?' she asked.

'Michigan. Man, this sucks.' I looked down at my pale white thighs splayed out and sticking to the gray foldout chair. Sweat began to pool underneath them. I pulled a loose string from my shorts and coiled it tightly around my forefinger. Within a few seconds, it began to turn red and pulse.

'Why did you choose Alton?' she asked.

I let go of the string and shrugged. 'How long do you think we have to stay out here? This heat is killing me.'

'No idea.'

An awkward silence swelled between us, and everyone around us seemed to get louder. 'Look, I'm going to take off and maybe go look for a café or something. But, it was nice meeting you. I'll see later, when we move in.' I stood up slowly, unpeeling my legs from the metal chair and headed for some place with AC and fewer people. I felt like I had wet my pants as I crossed the quad to the student union building in my sweat-drenched shorts. I glanced back for a second and saw her still sitting there, alone. She seemed nice enough and for a milli-second, I regretted not staying and talking to her. But I was still trying to process being forced to go to a religious university in northern Mississippi so my mother could save me, or so Jesus could. I wasn't feeling social, like making new friends.

While the setting of Alton University was influenced by student artifacts, other considerations to place included field notes and observations from the campus coffee house, chapel services and university events, such as movies in the quad and public lectures. The following two paragraphs were crafted primarily using researcher notes:

Excerpt 1
I yanked open a glass door and welcomed the punch of cold air against my body. I pushed my sunglasses up on my head and blinked at the bright lights in the hallway. Immediately, the smell of roasted coffee beans lured me over to a darkened room to my right, lit only by soft white Christmas lights and a few windows at the back. I liked the coziness of the room and how it felt vacant and wide open at the same time. A strew of brown leather couches and mismatched tables and chairs were arranged around a large stage – the centerpiece of the room. Off in the back corner, where a screeching espresso machine beckoned me, stood a tall coffee bar lined with paper cups and pastries. Above it hung a huge chalkboard with prices and specials marked in white. (Bailey, 2015: 23–24)

Excerpt 2
I headed out of the library into the main hallway, where people strolled shoulder-to-shoulder for a mile stretch. I fell in step with the crowd, contemplating the idea of church at school. It confused me – all of the praying and singing mixed in with biology, physics, and poetry. The only religion I had ever witnessed was my mom's short stint with Buddhism and the kind on 20/20 episodes where big-haired preachers scammed money from old ladies and played with their snakes. So far I hadn't seen any snake handling, but it was still early. (Bailey, 2015: 63)

As illustrated above in Excerpt 2, the setting of the novel is a religious university, which replicates the actual study site. While the demographic survey revealed that most of the student participants claimed to be religious, not all were. In response to the survey results, we began questioning the following: 'How do students at a religiously affiliated university negotiate their identities for the particular assignments given to them? How much influence does social context and/or audience factor into their construction/choice of identity?' (Bailey, 2014: 121). Based on the data, the creative narratives and surveys, we determined that these factors did indeed influence the student texts; thus, we kept this aspect in mind when building the characters for the novel. We determined that 'ultimately, the relation found between religion and identity, for many of the speakers in the poems, was that no separation existed. However, whether these identities were falsely presented is yet another question' (Bailey, 2014: 121). Further, as noted in the study results, this idea points to an avenue of 'further investigation and application of these strategies that is outside the scope of the study, but promises to yield fruitful insights into the problem of how the self is infused into all writing, both fiction and academic work' (Bailey, 2014: 121).

The infusion of the self in these creative narratives offered rich, complex data for our research project. And using a creative form to present the 'little narratives' allowed us to bring our findings to life in a visual narrative – much like Eisner (1997: 6) argues researchers do with films or documentaries. Ultimately, the project revealed narrative impact in two ways: the first being the student stories themselves, revealing time, place and experiences within a particular community; and the second a metanarrative, which recaptured and re-envisioned those original texts. The novel honors those creative texts while offering an aesthetic composite; the work is a space in which 'students' stories exist within the subsequent creative work, reappearing in the author's reimagined space' (Bailey & Bizzaro, 2017). As Eisner writes of the alternative form of data representation, 'What we are dealing with is a conception of how meaning is made and what shall count as knowledge or, to use a more felicitous phrase, how understanding is enlarged' (Eisner, 1997: 7). We hope that our research, in some meaningful way, has accomplished this feat of enlarging understanding.

Conclusion(s)

Reporting data in creative forms

By reporting data in a creative form, we argue for the freedom of stylistic approach in research efforts; we argue for the equality and relation in critical ways to literature and composition; and we argue for the ways in which creative writing functions epistemologically *in* and *as* knowledge. Kroll and Harper (2013) ask of creative writing research: what do we already know and what do we want to find out? And, what methods can we use in order to make discoveries? Donnelly and Harper note the disparities among governing bodies and assert that the main argument rests with the need for global visibility of how creative writing research can contribute to 'human knowledge, understanding and critical engagement with the world around us' (2013: xviii–xix). They contend the significance of gaining attention and understanding from these bodies, to include universities, so that the research and work being done in creative writing is not overlooked or regarded as inferior in comparison to other, more income-producing research areas (Donnelly & Harper, 2013:

Reruns and other second chances
for Resa

As much reincarnation
as déjà vu,
knowledge returns to us
for reconsideration and a second
   chance
at understanding
like a television rerun,
not changed much
by any thinking we might have
   done
since we last saw it,
an echo
of itself echoing,
a wedding anniversary,
a birthday.

We resent that the mirror
gets all our attention, even invited
to the big dance,
while we stay home
staring at the blank wall.

If nothing else
comes of it right away,
knowledge
in a poem or painting
or movie, the representation
of ourselves in mirrors
even the endless repetitions
of love promises

xix). The producing of noteworthy creative research is needed, especially when such a dim forecast for creative writing looms in the academy (xxi). As such, there is more work to be done, and it is our hope that our research contributes to and perhaps even initiates other discoveries in creative writing research.

and commitments for life
do not disappear.
Instead, we are taught by the
   repetitions
we make of them
to worship
most loyally
knowledge
that transcends
what it represents
from the bride, let's say,
to the wife,
our baby son
to a young man.
My life into yours.
Reruns are acts of understanding.

Even if we want to resist the
   knowledge
reruns bring us,
understandings that fold
around us
in the fatal process of being
'without any possible
transcendent meaning,'
we know reruns do not trick us
   much
and promise repetitions that
shape our lives
and will not change much
   tomorrow.

Unformed data doesn't offer much.
So, we need to look at them
again and again, certain
the rerun will mean more
each time.

So, then, reruns
flourish each day in our house,
in our lives,

except Thursdays, the holy day
when new shows appear. Of
   course,
we do not understand them
at first. But they make us
look forward to
reruns
that remind us of what we already
   know,
images that repeat
with such ever-increasing perfec-
   tion
they seem to be familiar
and maybe, at long last,
 we truly understand them.

Reruns mean what they mean.
They mean more to us
each time we see them.
I'm alright
with that. Like the rest of us,
repetitions are eternally and only
themselves. So, okay.
What bothers me, then?
My laughter, Friday
through Wednesday,
at the same predictable jokes
or tired-out pratfalls
I enjoy publicly
as if I really do understand them
and understand them better
each time.

Patrick Bizzaro

Notes

(1) Screenwriting is undergoing the same stresses that advanced comp/creative nonfiction did about 20 years ago.
(2) See Bizzaro (2014) and Hall (1988).
(3) See also Heyen (1996) and Ai (1999).
(4) See for instance Fred Chappell (1980); and Robert Morgan (1999).
(5) For a description of the Cassini mission to Saturn, see https://www.nasa.gov/mission_pages/cassini/main/index.html (accessed June 2017).

References

Ai (1999) *Vice: New and Selected Poems*. New York: W.W. Norton.
Bailey, C. (2014) The role of aesthetic artifacts in creative writing research: Casting student identity narratives as cultural data. Doctoral dissertation. Available from ProQuest Dissertations and Theses database (UMI No. 3617064).
Bailey, C. (2015) *Waking Under Water*. Ladson, SC: Vinspire Publishing.
Bailey, C. and Bizzaro, P. (2017) Research in creative writing: Theory into practice. *Research in the Teaching of English*.
Barks, C. (2008) The center. In *Winter Sky: New and Selected Poems, 1968–2008*. Athens, GA: University of Georgia Press.
Belli, A. and Coulehan, J. (eds) (2006) *Primary Care: More Poems by Physicians*. Iowa City, IA: University of Iowa Press.
Berlin, J.A. (1987) *Rhetoric and Reality: Writing Instruction in American Colleges, 1900–1985*. Carbondale, IL: Southern Illinois University Press.
Bishop, W. (1999) Places to stand: The reflective writer-teacher-writer in composition. *College Composition and Communication* 51 (1), 9–31.
Bizzaro, P. (2004) Research and reflection in English studies: The special case of creative writing. *College English* 66 (3), 294–309.
Bizzaro, P., Cook, D. and Culhane, A. (eds) (2011) *Composing Ourselves as Writer-Teacher-Writers*. New York: Hampton Press.
Bizzell, P. and Herzberg, B. (eds) *The Rhetorical Tradition* (2nd edn). New York: Macmillan.
Britton, J., *et al.* (1975) *The Development of Writing Abilities (11–18)*. London: Macmillan Education.
Chappell, F. (1980) *Moments of Light (Stories)*. Los Angeles, CA: New South.
Donnelly, D. and Harper, G. (2013). Introduction. In D. Donnelly and G. Harper (eds) *Key Issues in Creative Writing* (pp. xiii–xxvi). Bristol: Multilingual Matters.
Eisner, E.W. (1997) The promise and perils of alternative forms of data representation. *Educational Researcher* 26 (6), 4–10.
Elbow, P. (1998) *Writing with Power*. New York: Oxford University Press.
Ellis, C. (2004) *The Ethnographic I: A Methodological Novel About Autoethnography*. Walnut Creek, CA: AltaMira Press.
Ellis, C. (2009) *Revision: Autoethnographic Reflections on Life and Work*. Walnut Creek, CA: Left Coast Press.
Faulkner, S.L. (2009) *Poetry as Method: Reporting Research Through Verse*. Walnut Creek, CA: Left Coast Press.
Fellner, S. and Young, P.E. (eds) (2012) *Love Rise Up: Poems of Social Justice, Protest and Hope*. Publisher: Benu Press.

Feynman, R.P. (1998) *The Meaning of It All: Thoughts of a Citizen-Scientist*. Reading, MA: Perseus Books.

Furman, R., Langer, C.L., Davis, C.S., Gallardo, H.P. and Kulkarni, S. (2007) Expressive, research and reflective poetry as qualitative inquiry: A study of adolescent identity. *Qualitative Research* 7 (3), 301–315.

Gourgoulhon, E. and Jaramillo, J.L. (2008) New theoretical approaches to black holes. *New Astronomy Reviews* 51, 791–798.

Haake, K. (2007) Against reading. In K. Ritter and S. Vanderslice (eds) *Can It Really Be Taught? Resisting Lore in Creative Writing Pedagogy*. Portsmouth, NH: Boynton/Cook Heinemann.

Hall, D. (1988) *Poetry and Ambition: Essays 1982–88*. Ann Arbor, MI: University of Michigan Press.

Hesse, D. (2010) The place of creative writing in composition studies. *College Composition and Communication* 62 (1), 31–52.

Heyen, W. (1996) *Crazy Horse in Stillness*. Rochester, NY: BOA Editions.

Kroll, J. and Harper, G. (2013) Introduction. In J. Kroll and G. Harper (eds) *Research Methods in Creative Writing* (pp. 1–13). New York: Palgrave-Macmillan.

Leavy, P. (2013) *Fiction as Research Practice: Short Stories, Novellas, and Novels*. Walnut Creek, CA: Left Coast Press.

Leitch, V.B. (1992) *Cultural Criticism, Literary Theory, Poststructuralism*. New York: Columbia University Press.

Lyotard, J.F. (1984) *The Postmodern Condition: A Report on Knowledge*. Minneapolis, MN: University of Minnesota Press.

Mayers, T. (2005) *(Re)Writing Craft: Composition, Creative Writing, and the Future of English Studies*. Pittsburgh, PA: University of Pittsburgh Press.

McGurl, M. (2009) *The Program Era: Postwar Fiction and the Rise of Creative Writing*. Cambridge, MA: Harvard University Press.

Miles, R., Bertonasco, M. and Karns, W. (1991) *Prose Style: A Contemporary Guide* (2nd edn). Upper Saddle River, NJ: Prentice Hall.

Morgan, R. (1999) *Gap Creek*. Chapel Hill, NC: Algonquin Books.

Myers, D.G. (1996) *The Elephants Teach: Creative Writing Since 1880*. Englewood Cliffs, NJ: Prentice-Hall.

Prendergast, M. (2009) Introduction: The phenomena of poetry in research 'Poetry is what?' Poetic inquiry in qualitative social science research. In M. Prendergast, C. Leggo and P. Sameshima (eds) *Poetic Inquiry: Vibrant Voices in the Social Sciences* (pp. xix–xlii). Boston, MA: Sense Publishers.

Rukeyser, M. (1938) *The Book of the Dead*. The Academy of American Poets. At https://www.poets.org/poetsorg/book/us-1-featuring-book-dead (accessed 2 February 2016).

Seitz, J.E. (1999) *Motives for Metaphor: Literacy, Curriculum Reform, and the Teaching of English*. Pittsburgh, PA: University of Pittsburgh Press.

Shelley, P.B. (1840) A defence of poetry. In D. Perkins (ed.) *English Romantic Writers* (1st edn). New York: Harcourt Brace Jovanovich (1967).

Somers-Willett, S.B.A. (2009) *The Cultural Politics of Slam Poetry: Race, Identity, and the Performance of Popular Verse in America*. Ann Arbor, MI: University of Michigan Press.

Wesenberg, A.B. (1927) The American public: Poet. *English Journal* 16, 212–218.

Contributors

Christine Bailey, Associate Professor of English and Director of composition at Union University, holds the MFA in fiction and a PhD in composition and has authored multiple young adult novels as well as academic texts on the cross-fertilization of creative writing and composition studies.

Patrick Bizzaro, Professor Emeritus of English at East Carolina University and retired Professor in Composition and TESOL at Indiana University of Pennsylvania, is the author of 11 books and chapbooks of poetry, two critical studies of Fred Chappell's poetry and fiction, a book on the pedagogy of academic creative writing, four textbooks and over 300 poems, reviews and review essays in literary magazines.

Dianne Donnelly, is Assistant Dean of Research for the College of Arts & Sciences at the University of South Florida, editor of *Does the Writing Workshop Still Work?*, author of *The Emergence of Creative Writing Studies as an Academic Discipline*, co-editor of *Key Issues in Creative Writing* and author of many articles on the subject of creative writing.

Angela Ferraiolo, is a writer, programmer, artist and filmmaker who has worked professionally at RKO, Electronic Arts, Westwood Studios and Hansen Literary as a journalist, playwright, game designer, storywriter, screen writer, filmmaker and installation artist. She has taught game design at CUNY Hunter College, and screenwriting at Brown University, and is the founding faculty member for the program in New Genres at Sarah Lawrence College.

Katharine Haake's new novel is *The Time of Quarantine* (forthcoming, What Books Press). She is the author of three collections of short stories, *The Origin of Stars* (What Books, 2009), *The Height and Depth of Everything* (University of Nevada, 2001) and *No Reason on Earth* (Dragon Gate Press, 1986), and of a hybrid novel, *That Water, Those Rocks* (Nevada,

2003). Her short fiction has appeared widely. A regular contributor to scholarship in the theory and pedagogy of creative writing, she is also the author of *What Our Speech Disrupts: Feminism and Creative Writing Studies* (NCTE, 2000), and, with Hans Ostrom and the late Wendy Bishop, of *Metro: Journeys in Writing Creatively* (Longmans, 2000). She teaches at California State University, Northridge.

Graeme Harper is a Professor of Creative Writing and Dean of The Honors College at Oakland University in Michigan, USA. An award-winning fiction writer, and former Commonwealth scholar in Creative Writing, he has published widely on Creative Writing and its development as an academic discipline. He is Editor of the journal *New Writing: The International Journal for the Practice and Theory of Creative Writing* and is Editor-In-Chief of the book series New Writing Viewpoints. His latest work of fiction is *The Japanese Cook* (Parlor, 2017). In 2015 he edited *Creative Writing and Education* (Multilingual Matters).

Bruce Horner is Endowed Chair in Rhetoric and Composition at the University of Louisville, where he teaches courses in composition, composition theory and pedagogy, and literacy studies. His recent publications include *Rewriting Composition: Terms of Exchange* (Southern Illinois, 2016), *Crossing Divides: Exploring Translingual Writing Pedagogies and Programs*, co-edited with Laura Tetrault (Utah State, 2017), *Economies of Writing: Revaluations in Rhetoric and Composition*, co-edited with Brice Nordquist and Susan Ryan (Utah State, 2017) and the digital monograph *Translinguality, Transmodality, and Difference: Exploring Dispositions and Change in Language and Learning*, co-authored with Cynthia L. Selfe and Tim Lockridge (Enculturation/Intermezzo, 2015).

Kate Kostelnik's short fiction, which won her a 2007 NJ State Arts Council Grant, has been published by *Hayden's Ferry*, *42 Opus*, *Fifth Wednesday*, *The Superstition Review* and *New Writing*. Her scholarship has appeared in *Creative Writing: Teaching Theory & Practice*, *Pedagogy* and *Creative Writing Pedagogies for the 21st Century*. She holds an MFA from the University of Montana and a PhD at the University of Nebraska, Lincoln. She teaches writing at the University of Virginia.

Tim Mayers writes fiction, poetry and scholarly prose. He is Associate Professor at Millersville University of Pennsylvania, where he teaches courses in composition, creative writing, writing studies, and the disciplinary and institutional histories of English departments.

Joe Moxley's edited work, *Creative Writing in America: Theory and Pedagogy* (1989) was recently the subject of a celebratory Conference on College Composition and Communication (CCCC, 2015) conference panel, where it was described as one of the most important books in the consideration of creative writing teaching and learning in America published over the past quarter of a century. Professor Moxley teaches graduate courses on pedagogy, research methods, scholarly publishing, and rhetoric and technology at the University of South Florida. Joe Moxley's most recent book is *Agency in the Age of Peer Production* (coauthored NCTE 2012). Presently, he serves as the Publisher of *Writing Commons*, a peer-reviewed, open-education resource for college-level writers. Joe Moxley also serves as founder of *My Reviewers*, which seek to improve students' writing, critical thinking, and collaborative competencies. His *College Writing Online* received the 2004 Computers and Composition Distinguished Book Award. The FYC Program at USF was awarded the Writing Program Certificate of Excellence Award by the CCCC. Joe Moxley has received three undergraduate awards for excellence in undergraduate teaching and the USF President's Award for faculty excellence.

Alexandria Peary is the author of four books, including *Control Bird Alt Delete* (2013 Iowa Poetry Prize) and with Tom C. Hunley *Creative Writing Pedagogies for the Twenty-First Century* (Southern Illinois University Press.) She maintains a dual career in creative writing and composition, and her work has appeared in the *Yale Review, Gettysburg Review, North American Review, New American Writing, College Composition and Communication, Rhetoric Review,* and *Pedagogy*. She is currently writing a book on mindful composition pedagogy for Southern Illinois University Press. At Salem State University, she is First-Year Writing Coordinator and a professor in the English Department.

Joseph Rein is Associate Professor of Creative Writing at the University of Wisconsin, River Falls, USA. He is the co-editor of *Creative Writing Innovations* (Bloomsbury, 2016), *Creative Writing in the Digital Age* (Bloomsbury, 2014) and *Dispatches from the Classroom* (Bloomsbury, 2011) and his fiction, poetry and essays have appeared in such publications as *The Pinch Literary Magazine, Iron Horse Literary Review* and *Ruminate Magazine*. He is also an award-winning short-film screenwriter.

Stephanie Vanderslice's most recent books are *The Geek's Guide to the Writing Life* (Bloomsbury, December 2017) and *Can Creative Writing*

Really Be Taught? (10th Anniversary edition, with Rebecca Manery). She publishes fiction, non-fiction and creative criticism and her work is represented by Pen and Ink Literary. She is Professor of Creative Writing and Director of the Arkansas Writer's MFA Workshop at the University of Central Arkansas. Her column 'The Geek's Guide to the Writing Life' appears regularly in the *Huffington Post*.

Index

Association of Writers and Writing Programs (AWP) 2, 10, 11, 13, 20, 21, 24, 36, 37, 53, 58, 77

Canon 37, 56, 70, 86, 149
Composition vii, viii, ix, 11, 17, 20, 22–23, 24, 27, 29, 30, 31–32, 54, 56, 58, 59–68, 69, 70, 73, 74, 76, 77, 79, 112–117, 119, 121, 127–131, 136, 144, 146, 148, 153, 154, 158, 160–162, 163, 165, 167, 168, 180
Craft 17, 32, 37, 38, 41, 42, 51, 69, 71, 72, 75, 96, 105, 113, 114, 125, 133, 134, 139, 141, 147, 154, 159, 160
Creative Writing and the New Humanities 21, 28, 133, 159
Creative Writing Studies 13, 14, 15, 17–21, 23, 24, 25, 26, 30, 31, 32, 51, 75, 76, 78, 141, 143, 144, 145, 147, 154, 158, 163, 177, 179
Creative Writing Studies Organization (CWSO) 13, 14
Creativity 23, 29, 72, 73, 95, 96, 97, 98, 101–104, 109–113, 117–119, 121–124, 128, 130, 134, 138

Dawson, Paul *see Creative Writing and the New Humanities*
Digital technologies 9, 21, 27, 55, 57, 72, 83, 92, 115, 117, 135, 136
Diversity 12, 77, 87, 9, 148, 149
Donnelly, Dianne 15, 17–18, 20, 23, 77, 128, 129, 135, 140, 141, 188

Experiment 81, 87, 127, 138

Fiction 42, 51, 57, 58, 71, 82, 84, 85, 86, 87, 88, 94, 109, 117, 133, 134, 145–162, 169, 171, 172, 173, 175, 187, 192; *also see* Short Story

Haake, Katharine (Kate) *see What Our Speech Disrupts: Feminism and Creative Writing Studies*
Habitat viii, ix, 2, 7, 8, 9–16
Harper, Graeme vii, viii, ix, 21, 26–27, 75, 128, 129, 188

Imagination 8, 23, 29, 94, 96, 97, 98, 168, 179

Journals 24, 57, 61, 78, 125, 136, 142, 156, 167

Leahy, Anna 19, 75, 135–136
Literary Studies 18, 22, 140, 141, 144, 146, 148, 153, 156, 165, 168
Low Residency Programs 14, 26, 37, 44

Mayers, Tim 18, 20, 22, 32, 158; *also see (Re)Writing Craft: Composition, Creative Writing, and the Future of English Studies*
McGurl, Mark *see The Program Era: Postwar Fiction and the Rise of Creative Writing*

Myers, D.G. *see The Elephants Teach: Creative Writing Since 1880*

Painting 45, 91, 97, 99, 188
Pedagogy 18, 19, 20, 21, 22, 23, 31, 32, 36, 37, 40, 42, 57, 58, 59, 61, 62, 66, 70, 71–72, 73, 74, 78, 92, 93, 95, 102, 107, 108, 115, 134, 145, 146, 148, 155, 159, 177, 181
Playwrights 87, 88
Poetry 29, 42, 52, 107, 110, 114, 117, 118, 119, 134, 161, 163–165, 169–172, 173, 174–176, 177, 178, 179, 181, 191, 192

Research 11, 17, 18, 19, 20, 21, 22, 23, 24, 25, 26, 27, 28, 29, 20, 31, 62, 63, 64, 65, 67, 68, 69, 70, 72, 73, 78, 95, 96, 98, 102, 108, 109, 110, 139, 145, 155–156, 158, 164, 166, 167, 169, 170, 172, 173, 174, 175, 176, 177, 179, 180–192; *also see* Scholarship
(Re)Writing Craft: Composition, Creative Writing, and the Future of English Studies 17, 18, 22, 43, 113, 140, 141, 145, 146, 147, 153, 157, 158, 163, 164–167, 168
Rhetoric 20, 23, 24, 25, 29, 30, 31, 32, 33, 56, 58, 64, 115, 116, 123, 127, 145, 148, 149, 155, 164, 165, 166, 179, 191

Scholarship 23, 30, 36, 61, 64, 65, 66, 67, 70, 95, 129, 148, 154, 165; *also see* Research
Screenwriting 80, 83, 87, 133, 137, 165, 191
Sellers, Heather *see The Practice of Creative Writing*
Short Story 4, 23, 80, 149

Storytelling viii, 82, 84, 85, 87, 88, 89, 90, 92, 93, 94, 136, 173
Students 17, 20, 21, 37, 38–39, 40–43, 53, 56, 57, 61–64, 67, 72, 73–74, 76, 77, 80, 84, 86, 87, 91, 96, 97, 104, 112, 114, 117, 120, 127, 132–138, 141, 142, 144, 145, 146, 147, 148–160, 181, 185, 187

Teaching 1, 9, 10, 11, 12, 13, 14, 15, 17, 20, 21, 38, 47, 50, 53, 54, 56, 59, 62, 65, 72, 74, 76, 77, 83, 85, 92, 94, 96, 112, 114, 115, 119, 120, 121, 134, 137, 145, 146, 147, 150, 151, 152, 154, 157, 158, 159, 160, 165, 168, 169, 173, 181; *also see* Low Residency Programs; Pedagogy; Students; Workshop
The Elephants Teach: Creative Writing Since 1880 16, 23, 28, 58–59, 133, 141, 164, 165, 167, 169
The Practice of Creative Writing 70, 72, 134
The Program Era: Postwar Fiction and the Rise of Creative Writing 11, 16, 168
Theory 17, 20, 21, 22, 31, 36, 43, 48, 49, 56, 58, 59, 63, 64, 65, 69–78, 98, 100, 144, 159, 165, 171; *also see* Research; Scholarship
Thomas, Mason (fictional) vii, 3–9, 16

Vanderslice, Stephanie 21, 42, 32, 33

What Our Speech Disrupts: Feminism and Creative Writing Studies 13, 14, 144
Workshop 10, 13, 18, 20, 28, 38, 41, 52, 56, 57, 66, 71, 79, 80, 86, 88, 90, 92, 120, 125, 126, 136, 145, 168

For Product Safety Concerns and Information please contact our EU Authorised Representative:

Easy Access System Europe

Mustamäe tee 50

10621 Tallinn

Estonia

gpsr.requests@easproject.com